AFTER DOUBT

How to Question Your Faith without Losing It

A. J. SWOBODA

BrazosPress

a division of Baker Publishing Group
Grand Rapids, Michigan

© 2021 by A. J. Swoboda

Published by Brazos Press
a division of Baker Publishing Group
PO Box 6287, Grand Rapids, MI 49516-6287
www.brazospress.com

Printed in the United States of America

Library of Congress Cataloging-in-Publication Data
Names: Swoboda, A. J., 1981– author.
Title: After doubt : how to question your faith without losing it / A. J. Swoboda.
Description: Grand Rapids, Michigan : Brazos Press, a division of Baker Publishing
    Group, [2021] | Includes bibliographical references.
Identifiers: LCCN 2020037129 | ISBN 9781587434518 (paperback) | ISBN 9781587435362
    (casebound)
Subjects: LCSH: Faith.
Classification: LCC BV4637 .S955 2021 | DDC 234/.23—dc23
LC record available at https://lccn.loc.gov/2020037129

22   23   24   25   26   27   7   6   5   4   3

"If you have ever experienced doubts about God (and who hasn't?), *After Doubt* will both comfort and challenge you. Speaking from two decades of experience ministering in the Pacific Northwest, Swoboda provides biblically sound direction for the doubting among us, filled with practical wisdom on how we can question our faith without losing it!"

—**Matthew Sleeth**, MD, executive director of Blessed Earth
and author of *Hope Always*

"Doubt often draws us into a spiral of isolation and mental exertion, which themselves can be our undoing. With pastoral insight, Swoboda brings doubt into the open, removing the shame and inviting us into practices that draw us back into our bodies, communities, and tradition. *After Doubt* builds our capacity and courage for the normal, lifelong process of being formed in the wrestling."

—**Mandy Smith**, pastor and author of *Unfettered: Imagining Childlike Faith beyond the Baggage of Western Culture* and *The Vulnerable Pastor*

"For many, deconstruction is viewed as a Christian's unraveling, a dead end to what was once a living faith. A. J. Swoboda makes a beautiful and compelling case for how the journey through doubt can actually lead to a stronger faith in Jesus. Deconstruction does not have to result in deconversion. This exceptional work is required reading for anyone who has ever wondered if it is possible to ask hard questions of our faith and come to deeper and more satisfying conclusions."

—**Terry M. Crist**, lead pastor, Hillsong Church

"The church is facing a crisis of faith in our post-Christian world, and the options before us seem grim: to either demonize doubt or wear it as a badge of honor. A. J. Swoboda invites us to go deeper, to join him on the messy but ultimately healing journey to find God on the far side of our brokenness. Warm and confessional, bold and prophetic, heart-stirring and intellectually deep, *After Doubt* is a book 'for such a time as this.'"

—**Richard Beck**, author of *Hunting Magic Eels: Recovering an Enchanted Faith in a Skeptical Age*

"Many pastors, leaders, and parents wonder what to do as multitudes of younger Christians deconstruct their faith, often losing it in the process. A. J. Swoboda offers a blueprint for the spiritual journey of all those facing real doubt. He weaves faith and hard questions together in a delicate dance while sharing a profoundly personal account of his own journey. The result is an intimate and practical book that's sorely needed. If you care about the epidemic deconstruction of Christian faith among young people, I recommend you read this book."

—**Randy Remington**, president, U.S. Foursquare Church

"'Not all those who wander are lost'—that was written by Tolkien a couple of generations ago. Swoboda reframes this: Not all those who doubt are faithless. Our questions and doubts can lead to a deeper and richer walk with Jesus. Swoboda brings hope to the cynics, the disillusioned, and even the 'dones.' So many disenchanted Christians have been yearning for a book to help point them back to Jesus. *After Doubt* is that book."

—**Nijay K. Gupta**, Northern Seminary

"A. J. has given a guide to one of the most necessary and scary processes Jesus asks his followers to walk through. Thoughtful and honest without pulling punches, A. J. leads you through this critical process like a good friend and a wise counselor. Every person who feels like they no longer fit comfortably inside their faith needs to read this book."

—**Rick McKinley**, lead pastor, Imago Dei Community, Portland, Oregon

"*After Doubt* is a timely book—an exploration of doubt and deconstruction, written winsomely by one within the faith and from the perspective of spiritual formation. As a campus pastor, a church planter, and now a professor, A. J. has helped people navigate the hardest issues of the faith. Yet what makes this book so valuable and unique is the attention it gives to *how* we are shaped by these experiences. *After Doubt* shows there's a way to reconstruct the faith and return to our 'first love' that forms us into more faithful disciples of Jesus."

—**Keas Keasler**, Friends University

"Swoboda has quickly become one of the most thoughtful, interesting, and engaging Christian writers of our day. I really could have used this book fifteen years ago."

—**Preston Sprinkle**, president of The Center for
Faith, Sexuality & Gender

"Swoboda claims that the community of faith has copious resources for the journey from doubt to faith—but far too few for the journey from faith to doubt and *back to* faith. I completely concur. Here Swoboda tells his twenty-year tale of 'walking with people along the paths of doubt and deconstruction' and offers himself as a companion along the way."

—**Sandra Richter**, Robert H. Gundry Chair of
Biblical Studies, Westmont College

"In this elegant and profound book, A. J. Swoboda has taken on the monumental task of addressing the dark side of doubt and disillusionment. It addresses these problems not by solving them but by *unmasking* them. In the spirit and style of G. K. Chesterton, A. J. reveals how doubt is actually an act of faith, that doubt is based on a firm belief that there is something truer and better and more beautiful than what one has perceived Christianity, or the church, to be."

—**James Bryan Smith**, author of *The Good and Beautiful God*

For my students

Contents

Foreword

John Mark Comer

"To struggle with one's faith is often the surest sign we actually have one."

When I read A. J.'s haunting line, I instantly felt a deep, tuning fork–like resonance in my spirit. It rang true to my felt experience of life as a disciple of Jesus in a secular age.

If he's right—and I believe he is—I have *a lot* of faith.

Regardless of your personality type (my Myers-Briggs type is "most likely to be an atheist"), doubt is the ambient air we breathe in the West. Learning to walk *through* doubt and deconstruction and out the other side into the *reconstruction* of an honest, humble, yet deep and robust faith that can flourish with both serenity and power in a chaotic and hostile world—*that* is no easy jaunt. It's more like a long, slow spiritual journey through what Eugene Peterson called "the badlands" of spiritual life—seasons of dryness and aridity, as personified by the desert stories of Scripture. A. J.'s newest (and I think best) book, *After Doubt*, isn't a flimsy self-help formula or an easy-to-read map with a shortcut around the badlands; it's more like the literary avatar for his presence and wisdom as a guide *through* the desert.

For ten years A. J. and I pastored alongside each other in Portland, Oregon, one of the most secular, post-Christian cities in the world. A. J. was more than a friend, he was a partner. His concept of "the New Oregon Trail" that you're about to read about put language to my experience as a pastor in our city.

But A. J. and I share more in common than the challenge of pastoring in a hypersecular city. We are both, in his language, politically "in exile," stuck in the crossfire of opposing ideologies that are *both* at odds with Jesus's vision of human flourishing. We are both disciples of Jesus of the orthodox, historic variety—an increasingly endangered species in a city like Portland. We both feel the weight of our cultural moment in our soul and just how much is at stake—the future of the American church itself hangs in the balance. Will this generation embrace a courageous fidelity to orthodoxy? Or bow to the idols of our time? Idols that promise life but all too often deliver death? But lest I sound like a harbinger of doom, A. J. and I also share a real and growing hope that in our time, despite secularism's militant march toward dominance, a remnant will arise to seed renewal across the church. That a small yet fiercely loving and loyal group of resilient, compelling Christians will stand firm in the way and truth and life of Jesus.

This book is searingly honest about doubt and the gravitational pull of deconstruction; but it's even more "joyful in hope" (Rom. 12:12) about what comes *after* doubt.

Preface

On February 24, 1791, Christian revivalist and pastor John Wesley penned a letter to encourage a Christian walking through some faith challenges:

> Unless the divine power has raised you up . . . I see not how you can go through your glorious enterprise in opposing that execrable villainy [the slave trade], which is the scandal of religion, of England, and of human nature. Unless God has raised you up for this very thing, you will be worn out by the opposition of men and devils. But if God be for you, who can be against you? Are all of them together stronger than God? O be not weary of well-doing! Go on, in the name of God and in the power of His might.[1]

The gravity of Wesley's letter that day comes into focus only as the letter's broader context is realized. Wesley was writing to a young Christian named William Wilberforce whose efforts would eventually end the slave trade in Britain. All the more, the letter would be Wesley's last. Wesley wrote it on his deathbed.

What may seem an insignificant little letter may have been the very encouragement Wilberforce needed. Who knows? After reading Wesley's letter, it becomes clear that the power of writing is often not the writing itself but the person reading it. As I write, I know that on the other side of this book are people, book clubs, small groups, faculties, and audiences who may (like Wilberforce) find themselves struggling with the task of following Jesus with integrity in our age of doubt and deconstruction. You are my Wilberforce. And to you I channel my inner Wesley: "Go on, in the name of God and in the power of His might." Keep going! Don't give up. Persevere. There's endless hope.

This book raises a question: Is it possible to question one's faith without losing it? Some time ago, I read N. T. Wright's *After You Believe*—an invaluable guide for those new to the Christian narrative.[2] Afterward, an epiphany struck me. While there exist countless resources specifically crafted to help those who are crossing the chasm from doubt to faith, far more sparse are resources that aim to help people whose faith has meandered back toward doubt. This book's title captures the other side of following Jesus: *After Doubt.* Doubt and deconstruction, I will show, play important roles in our journey of following Jesus. They can be exhilarating experiences. But also oppressive and hopeless. Though both have their dark sides, I will show that they can play a vital role in how we follow Jesus. This book is largely the result of countless requests from pastors, friends, and colleagues who've personally lamented the lack of resources on the topic. How do we follow Jesus *after doubt* takes hold?

Doubt—as a topic—has been given ample attention. As publications on the topic have proliferated, so have approaches to walking through it. Some valorize doubt. Others demonize it. The proposed solutions are almost always far too simplistic. Some point to progressive Christianity as a utopian community of freedom and liberation. Others warn that the only option is to retreat behind the safe walls of conservativism. This book forges an alternative path. The core conviction of this book is that Christ's invitation is not to the right or to the left. Rather, Christ's call is to go *deeper* into himself. There is an abundance of books on the philosophy, history, and theology of deconstruction; books on how to approach doubt using self-help; how to understand doubt and deconstruction from a purely academic and theological perspective; how to minister to those in doubt; how to parent the doubting child; how to love the doubting parent; and even how to lead churches in this cultural moment filled with doubt. This is not those. In short, what I'm trying to do here is help my reader think through the *how* of doubt and deconstruction—the spiritual formation side of these experiences. This book, as such, is less about deconstruction and doubt as it is about *how* we walk through these experiences faithfully with and toward Jesus.

The book is structured in two parts. Part 1 is primarily descriptive, providing critical language around the doubt and deconstruction experiences. Chapter 1 introduces us to doubt and deconstruction, and chapter 2 locates them in what I call the "theological journey." Chapter 3 explores how Western culture has shaped the way we doubt and deconstruct Christian beliefs. My reader will no doubt note a discernible shift in part 2, which turns toward vital disciplines and practices for those who are actually following Jesus in our age of deconstruction. These chapters explore and commend eight such practices, all rooted in ancient Christian practice and tradition.

I feel arrogant admitting it—but I'm disproportionately qualified to write this book. Walking with people along the paths of doubt and deconstruction has been my world for twenty years. For one decade, I served the spiritual needs of college students at the University of Oregon. For another decade, my wife and I founded and pastored a church in the heart of post-Christian Portland, serving young families and urban professionals. Now I serve the intellectual, theological, and spiritual needs of undergraduates, graduates, and doctoral students as a full-time theologian and lecturer in Bible. In sum, my entire adult life has been given to supporting the faith development of people who are going through the very things addressed in this book. I've seen doubt and deconstruction in all of its forms. Despite my advantages in writing this book, I am not immune to great error or folly. "Writing," preaching legend Haddon Robinson once quipped, "scrapes the fungus off our thoughts."[3] Similarly, the process of writing this book has helped me clarify what I've thought and taught for years on this topic. That's become quite a problem: the more writing I do, the more fungus I find.

My reader may be interested in the orienting convictions behind this book. Given the sensitive nature of what follows, I fear that any ambiguity in this matter could only alienate any reader who is walking through a faith crisis. The following are core convictions of mine:

- I worship the Triune God. And I believe Jesus is the only pathway to eternal life. No other way exists—although this has not kept people from looking. This core conviction means that Jesus is the only way to God—*I am not*.
- I love and believe in the church. With that, I'm convinced that loving God means loving God's people. If you're looking for a rationale to leave the church, this book will consistently frustrate you. It is unabashedly central to me that each and every reader take seriously God's invitation to serve, love, and care for God's people. I want the church to first love Jesus, mostly because Jesus first loved the church.
- I believe part of loving the church is naming the ways she's gone off-track or forgotten her true self. In short, part of love is naming sin in a context of abundant grace and love.
- I love the Bible and I believe it is inspired by God—entirely trustworthy in all it communicates. I also believe the Bible is wildly misunderstood. Therefore, I believe that everyone— theologians, pastors, academics, podcasters—must submit themselves before the scrutinizing light of Scripture in hopes of discerning truth and falsehood.
- Lastly, I believe all of our political and theological systems cannot contain the kingdom of God. Politically, I'm a man in exile. And so, I take great liberty in my attempts at subverting the "system" of what we have come to call the "right," "left," and "middle." While all three may reflect something of God's kingdom, neither can claim a monopoly on it.

Two final notes. First, language—my reader will note that I use the terms *doubt* and *deconstruction* interchangeably. There are indeed nuances in these terms. But, for our purposes here, they are used interchangeably. Second, endnotes. Endnotes are the Narnian closet of a writer's thinking. Entering that closet, the reader will find a whole magical world from which the writer has drawn inspiration. As you enter the closet of my endnotes, you'll notice something peculiar. The sources, thinkers, and theologians represent a broad diversity of thinkers from the theological right and left. In a church where everyone's guilty by association, I've opted to draw from a diverse range of the body of Christ so that I might be found a little guilty in everyone's eyes. Don't assume that my use of an author implies my unanimous agreement with their approach or outlook. From some I borrow once. From others I borrow a lot. It's said that when a theologian is confused, they go to C. S. Lewis. As you'll soon tell, I'm confused a great deal.

That leads us to our question: Is it possible to question one's faith without losing it?

PART 1

DECONSTRUCTION AND DOUBT

Gandalf: I am looking for someone to share in an adventure that I am arranging, and it's very difficult to find anyone.

Bilbo: I should think so—in these parts! We are plain, quiet folk and have no use for adventures. Nasty, disturbing, uncomfortable things! Make you late for dinner! I can't think what anybody sees in them. . . .

Gandalf: You'll have a tale or two to tell of your own when you come back.

Bilbo: Can you promise that I will come back?

Gandalf: No. And if you do, you will not be the same.

—From the film *The Hobbit: An Unexpected Journey* (2012)

One

Deconstruction and Doubt

Phil

When we first met, Phil had recently moved to the Pacific Northwest. Like so many, his journey had brought him from a small, rural, mid-American town for a promising software job at one of the city's prominent firms. He'd been hired on the spot after a phone interview. Before leaving home, Phil's youth pastor admonished him to find a "Bible-teaching, Jesus-worshiping, missional church" in Portland. Entering these exact descriptors into Google, the magical demigods of the internet providentially provided the name and contact info for the church I pastored. The subject line read: "Looking to plug in at your church."

We met at my office. Phil's story was like many stories of those who'd sat in my office before. The conservative evangelical home in which he had been raised had nurtured within Phil a deep piety for Jesus, a love of Scripture, and a commitment to church. Back home, Phil had been an integral part of his youth group and the sound guy for "big church" on Sunday mornings. Now in Portland, he expressed a desire to make Christian friends, build community, and serve in the church. His passion was palpable and authentic. Naturally, I shared in his excitement—nodding along with every swell of youthful zeal. As our appointment drew to a close, we discussed ways he might connect, find community, and intentionally follow Christ in his new environment.

He found himself again in my office just one year later. This time, Phil confessed he no longer believed he was a Christian. "A lot has happened in the last year," Phil began. "I've . . . evolved." After our first meeting, Phil came to church a few times. But his attendance soon grew sparse. He had found churchgoing challenging—if not altogether excruciating. By his own admission, he wasn't good at intentionally making new friends. In fact, he'd never *had* to make new friends. Back home, Phil was known by everyone. Coming to a new church triggered endless waves of sadness, homesickness, and isolation.

At the same time, work was thriving. He'd gotten a promotion within two short months and seemed to be on the fast track to software success. His coworkers soon became his best friends. One such coworker became Phil's new roommate. Enter Charles. Charles had grown up in a strong Mormon family. Existential questions during Charles's teenage years forged a chasm between his lived experience and the beliefs of his upbringing—to say nothing of the growing chasm in his relationship with his parents. In his freshman philosophy course, Charles found himself drawn to the quiet magnetism of his philosophy professor, whose lectures validated the questions within. Charles found resonance in those philosophical questions, never having dealt with the deep wounds of shame he felt placed on him for not embarking on a two-year mission after high school. After years of questioning, Charles left his Mormon faith and became an atheist.

Charles openly discussed his deconversion story with Phil. Their nightly talks became the norm. Phil soon found himself cautiously resonating with Charles's critiques of religion. What stood out to him was Charles's extensive Bible knowledge. He knew Scripture, and he knew it well. And everything apparently *wrong* with it. Phil found himself drawn to the honest, liberating, and authentic tone of his "freethinking" roommate. Never had Phil found such thoughtful, honest, and penetrating questioners in his hometown. Devouring Charles's recommendations of books, podcasts, and YouTube videos, Phil immersed himself in a world of doubt and deconstruction he never knew existed. New questions emerged by the day: *Why didn't his youth pastor talk about these "contradictions" in the Bible? Were they hiding these from him? And what to make of Charles's confidence?*

This all converged alongside Phil's dwindling connection to church and family back home. Most of what connected him to that community was a steady stream of Facebook posts about how good God was, why Donald Trump was apparently God's anointed leader for a Christian nation, and how "blessed" they always seemed to be. Less and less seemed to connect Phil's past with his present. With few trusted voices to dialogue with, Phil took his questions to the internet. There he discovered a virtual cottage industry of like-minded people who gave voice to these existential questions. They also offered him new questions he'd never considered. Life became one big podcast binge. At work, on the weekends, during his nightly jogs, Phil devoured everything he could get his hands on. Phil's existential crisis was being fed a steady diet of content—all at 2x speed.

The onslaught of questions and doubts became a cocktail Phil found intoxicating, painful, and liberating all at the same time. Phil felt alive in his freedom to ask fresh questions. But these questions also brought shame. He felt like he was turning his back on his childhood faith. At our second meeting, Phil let it all out. He began with the Bible. What about all the "contradictions" that Charles brought up? What was he supposed to do with those? Phil expressed resentment that nobody back home had taught on the real Bible and how complex it really was. Then he turned to how the Bible had been used to hurt people. "I mean," he passionately confessed, "how can I believe in a book that was used to silence the slaves?" Not to mention how it had emotionally hurt so many people today. Phil talked angrily about one gay coworker who'd been deeply wounded by Christians. This led to a general rage over politics. Watching his hometown family and friends gloat over Donald Trump's victory on Facebook created deep resentment. Even hatred. *I was raised by these people! This just isn't right! I can't be a part of this!* Eventually this led to a rant about how he saw evangelicalism as a campaign wing of the Republican Party. *What does that have to do with Jesus?* On top of all this, he'd started smoking weed to cope with the anxiety of his new job and his faith crisis.

Phil was in full doubt and deconstruction mode. And he was just scratching the surface—I could discern an aquifer of questions lying unseen. But he didn't continue. He stopped. And almost collapsed in defeat. Drawing in a deep breath, Phil dropped his shoulders and said, "Pastor, I *want* to believe. I *want* to pray. I *want* to know God. I *want* to be a Christian. I do. I just need answers. I have all of these questions—nobody to talk to. What am I supposed to do? You're the pastor. What do you say about all of this? I'm not a Christian anymore, right? Am I still a Christian? Can I still be a Christian?"

Tears cascaded down the contours of his youthful cheeks. Here he was, another young man in my office bearing his soul, his doubt, putting himself out there like never before. Sitting before me—bare, naked of spirit, showing every card—was a young man who seemed at the end of himself. Nothing in my pastoral training had prepared me to answer crises of faith like this. I just looked at him. No words. No answers. No quick fix. No platitudes. All I could give him was my full, undivided attention.

Welcome to the age of deconstruction.

Naming Deconstruction

We all must cross what theologian Kenneth Archer calls "the desert of skeptical criticism."[1] What Phil faced wasn't unique to him. Nor to Christians throughout history. Many have crossed this desert before. And many try to cross it today. Still, Phil's crisis raises many questions: How does one endure "skeptical criticism" faithfully and Christianly? Can one cross that desert of criticism into deeper faith, hope, and trust in Christ? Is there a way to question our faith without losing it?

Phil's story didn't end there. Phil eventually accepted his valley of skepticism, realizing he couldn't feel, think, or pray his way out of it. Underneath this emerged a hunger for Jesus that was unmatched by any desire for comfort, convenience, or cliché. Phil's perseverance eventually led him back to the God who'd been with him the whole time. Still, reality couldn't be altered by denying it. He had to cross his desert of skeptical criticism. Otherwise, he would die in it. Phil discovered he wasn't alone. He found a church community he could walk with. And not only a living church—he also discovered the "communion of saints" who had been traversing this desert for two thousand years. The living and the dead church became his companions. Phil's deconstruction crisis was nothing new. Today Phil follows Jesus. But there were no paths *around* the desert. The path forward was the ancient path—that holy precedent—which led along the ancient footsteps trodden long before *through* the desert. When he embraced this, he discovered something: when it rains, valleys have a habit of filling first. There is a way to walk across the desert of doubt and deconstruction toward the oasis of life: Jesus Christ!

What *is* deconstruction? Roughly speaking, deconstruction is the dismantling of anything that's been constructed. In architecture, it's a building demolished to make room for the new. In baking, it's the cookie torn apart for a pie crust creation. In child's play, it's an eight-year-old dismantling his LEGO invention. Deconstruction describes many aspects of everyday life. But since the 1960s, it has meant so much more. Deconstruction is now more broadly applied to literature and philosophy representing the dismantling of traditional cultural values, norms, and ideologies—most notably through the French philosopher Jacques Derrida.[2] This led to what's been called *postmodernism*. Theological deconstruction, as such, is the process of dismantling one's accepted beliefs.[3] It is Phil's painful journey of questioning, critiquing, and reevaluating previous faith commitments upon which he used to rely. And, in Phil's case, a reorientation to them—what we would call *reconstruction*. Back to that later.

Deconstruction is the new norm. Nearly 60 percent of people raised in Christian churches deconstruct their faith following high school.[4] These numbers have faces. Faith deconstruction isn't a one-size-fits-all experience. Nor does it always entail walking *away* from one's faith. Let me introduce you to three friends who reflect a variety of deconstruction experiences. John was raised a mainline Episcopalian with a passion

7

for social justice, a heart for the poor, and a belief that Christians were responsible for dismantling systems perpetuating injustice. John's father was a well-known environmentalist whose activism often took him away from the dinner table to neighborhood assemblies, board meetings, and watershed cleanups. At a campus ministry during his college freshman year, John heard the gospel in a way he'd never heard before. Raised in progressive Christianity, he'd heard of the Jesus of justice but not the divine Christ whose blood conquered sin and death. John's world was transformed. John's immersion into conservative Christianity led to a fissure between him and his father, who expressed embarrassment that his son had "become one of those damned evangelicals." John, in turn, expressed resentment that his father had cleaned up more watersheds than attended John's soccer games.

Sarah was raised in a conservative Christian home. In high school, she confessed to her parents about having unwanted sexual desires. Listening sympathetically, they believed their best recourse was counseling, Bible study, and weekly prayer. Sarah's desires never disappeared. In college, she encountered a Lutheran campus ministry that embraced nontraditional expressions of sexual identity. Sarah's desires were affirmed. And they suggested that her upbringing had caused her deep emotional and spiritual trauma. As Sarah's childhood theology disintegrated, so did her relationship with her parents. Thanksgiving and Christmas soon were their only visits—times increasingly marked by quiet distrust and subtle resentment neither knew how to overcome.

Carlos was raised in an atheist home. After a heart attack at forty-five, Carlos found himself relegated to a hospital bed facing his surprisingly early mortality. His mind naturally pondered the afterlife. Death had a surprising way of opening Carlos's eyes to spiritual questions. After a visit from the chaplain, Carlos's "God-awakening" left him entirely transformed and hungry to know God. His upbringing hadn't equipped him to face the suffering he faced in that hospital bed.

Each of these stories represents a face of deconstruction—John questioning his childhood faith; Sarah deconstructing her understanding of sexuality; Carlos learning why people rarely convert to atheism on their deathbed. Deconstruction can happen to atheists, Christians, conservatives, progressives, traditionalists, complementarians, egalitarians, even doubters. No one is safe.

Honoring and Leaving

The challenge each of these faced in their deconstruction—and what we may face—is walking the tightrope between becoming our own person and honoring our past. In *The Homeless Mind*, sociologist Peter Berger explores how traditional cultures in the past connected social value with "honor."[5] One's place in a society directly related to how one fulfilled their given role as a member of society—fathers, mothers, people in authority, or guardians of tradition. Honor was extended to those who dutifully fulfilled these roles. In contrast to traditional cultures, Western culture underscores individuality and breaking with the past by giving social privilege to those who "earn" it. Achievement, work, wealth accumulation, popularity, and education—these are how we find honor now. This slow shift from an honor society to an achievement society has greatly affected people, families, and communities. Value is no longer given to *who* one *is*. It is given to *what* one *does*. Philosopher Byung-Chul Han contends that while honor societies emphasize discipline and doing what should be done, the present achievement culture is obsessed with what we *can* do.[6] That obsession has driven us to epistemic anxiety and fatigue.

The shift from honor to achievement radically changes the way many in the West relate to the "old" beliefs of Christianity. Whereas honor cultures guard, protect, and pass along deeply held beliefs, achievement cultures privilege and prioritize breaking from past dogmas that are dogmatically dismissed as sheer naivete. New ideas, it's implied, are more likely to be true. Being an "evolved" person means breaking with these past superstitions. Being post-*anything* is now a sign of arrival and maturity—postmodern, post-Christian, post-Enlightenment, post-liberal, post-conservative, and post-political. Being post-something is powerful and intoxicating. We've been there. We've left. We've transcended, enjoying the "objective" and "neutral" view from the top. We caress our own ego by calling this "being on the right side of history."

Still, the journey of leaving should not be vilified. Part of biblical faith is about leaving. Consider Jesus's cousin John the Baptist. John ministered in the desert. Why might that be noteworthy? John's father was Zechariah—the high priest who was ministering in the temple when an angel of the Lord commanded him to prepare for a coming son. John's dad was the high priest. That places John in an elite spiritual lineage that could have led to John's working in the temple. But he doesn't. John breaks from his father. Rather than serving in the temple, John prepares the way of Jesus in the desert. Read through the lens of honor culture, this break, while unimportant to the modern reader, is significant. The Bible intentionally highlights many such moments of the faithful breaking from family, community, and the past to follow God's call. Ironically, John's work of preparing the way of Jesus was temple work. It's just that this new temple wasn't a building. The temple was his cousin. That raises an important biblical perspective: we sometimes leave not as a means to get away from God but as a means to actually encounter God.

Counselors call this *differentiation*: the journey of learning how we are different from those around us, our upbringing, or our social context. Differentiation is good and it's part of life. We all do it in varying degrees. I'm in a denomination. But I've learned many ways I'm different from my denomination. My wife and I are differentiated. We are "one," sure, but we couldn't think more differently on what to name our dog or what color the house should be painted. Jesus differentiated. Watch his relationship with his mother Mary as he consistently made it clear that his purposes were higher than being merely her son.[7] Even the Trinity models differentiation. The Trinity is three distinct persons in the Father, Son, and Spirit, who eternally remain in a union of love. Still, they remain three distinct persons with three distinct personalities. Every early church heresy pertaining to the Trinity, in fact, either conflated the Trinity into one person or saw them as three different gods. The Trinity is three persons, one being. God's nature is as differentiated persons.

Part of the reason so many young people deconstruct their faith so radically after leaving home is that they were never given a chance to differentiate in their earlier years. This deconstruction age is as much a reflection of our longing for boundaries as anything else. We react (even overreact) against the faith of our communities or families of origin because we were often never given agency as people in our younger years. One young woman in the throes of deconstruction described to me her Christian mother. There were no boundaries. Her mother, at every whim, would barge into her room—even into her late teenage years—without knocking. As the young woman began reexploring the faith she left during college, she read afresh the New Testament. One image of Jesus in Revelation struck her. Jesus will "stand at the door and *knock*" (Rev. 3:20). She was overwhelmed—even liberated—by this image. Jesus doesn't barge in. Jesus knocks. The idea that Jesus honored boundaries helped create the trust she needed to return to her faith.[8]

Differentiation is important and even healing. But it is nonetheless extraordinarily painful—especially for parents. I'm a father. It's terrifying being a Christian parent in an age of deconstruction, where every cultural impulse celebrates rejecting the Christian past in the name of liberation. I'm raising my son in a world that scoffs at tradition and upbringing and beliefs of the past. Sadly, this is leading to a Christian culture where the faith is not being passed along to the young—largely out of fear. Any Christian parent who's watched their child deconstruct the faith they were handed will tell you it is excruciating. To protect against the pain, many in my generation would rather withhold instructing children in the ways of the Lord in the name of letting them "find their own path." But even this is a mirage. Handing a child an absence of faith is still handing them a faith tradition—a hollow one indeed.

Trembling with fear, even I am being taught by our age of deconstruction. I'm learning to go toe-to-toe with my greatest fear: being rejected by my son. *Am I merely handing my boy something he'll ultimately reject?* In the raging storm of these fears, God is teaching me that his love for my son is greater than my own. And that I am invited to lovingly and faithfully instill a faith into my son that very well may be undone. I pray it isn't. I want my son to love Jesus. I want my son to be part of God's church. I want my son to live a right and good life. But I can't force him to believe. I can't force *anyone* to believe. I have to hand faith on to my son as a very act of faith, not an act of control, lest I forget that self-control—and not control—is a fruit of the Spirit. My new goal is handing my son a story of Jesus so beautiful and compelling that no philosophy professor during his first year of college could rip it out of his heart.

I've had to learn from Zechariah—John the Baptist's dad. One gift a parent can give their child is a rich story of faith and an opportunity to follow it for themselves. In our helicopter parenting culture—where parents clamor over their child's every move, ensuring safety and success—it is the children who are worshiped. In achievement societies, they're forced into being miniature deities who must master three sports, get all the scholarships, and never slip up in order to be approved of. It's no better in Eastern cultures where ancestors of the past are worshiped. Same problem. The only hope is Christ. Christ *must* be worshiped, or else we'll worship the future or the past. When Jesus is King, we no longer worship the fathers—we worship the "God of our fathers." When Jesus is King, the only child we worship is the one in the manger. Good news for Mary, who remains the only person in human history who could worship her child and not be an idolater.

We are called, like Abraham, to leave a homeland, family, and place of comfort to pursue God. Jesus's call was (and is) the same. "Follow me" meant for each disciple the leaving of business, family, or loved ones for God's kingdom. Part of discipleship is *leaving*—and becoming the person God has called us to be in this world.

But leaving must not be unhitched from honoring. Throughout the Mosaic code—enshrined in the Ten Commandments—we see God inviting us to respect and honor, with dignity and care, those who brought us into the world. "Honor your father and your mother," the Decalogue commands (Exod. 20:12). Malachi further states that the Messiah would come and "turn the hearts of the parents to their children, and the hearts of the children to their parents" (Mal. 4:6). That is what Jesus came to do. Jesus calls us to leave everything to follow him. And also to "honor" where we came from.

I wonder if we even see Jesus wrestling with the tension of leaving and honoring. In John 2, Jesus attends a wedding. Soon enough, Mary discovers there's no more wine. She tells her son. Alerted to the social faux pas, Jesus immediately responds to his mom, "My hour has not yet come" (v. 4). Seemingly ignoring his comment, Mary instructs the attendants to "do whatever he tells you" (v. 5). John describes something fascinating: Jesus listens to his mother and turns the water into wine despite it not being his time. If Jesus's time has not yet come, why does he obey his mom? Here I believe we see Jesus being a real human struggling with the real challenge of being faithful to God his Father *and* Mary his mother. In the end, Jesus responds to her faith and miraculously produces gallons of wine. "Jesus," writes New Testament scholar Raymond Brown, "can never refuse or resist faith."[9] Jesus Christ—God who became man—had to himself learn to live in the tension of being both the Son of God and the son of Mary.

Cultures, it seems, are always tempted to reject this tension and emphasize *either* honoring *or* leaving. The biblical world was an honor world. The Western world is a leaving world. In the honor society of Jesus's time, culture and religion preserved and protected the past at all costs. Honoring family and tradition was prioritized over everything. This is why Jesus comments, "A prophet is not without honor except in his own town" (Mark 6:4). When it came down to it, tradition and honor were held above even the prophet's message. The default structure of society was to protect, honor, and preserve the past. Western culture has swung to the opposite extreme. The contemporary Western world—framed by the Enlightenment—is a leaving culture that considers it liberating to set aside the past and tradition. Things are now backward. A hometown in the time of Jesus gave no honor to the prophet. In our time, a prophet gives no honor to their hometown. This is the framework of our deconstruction age. We've become a world of prophets armed with truth in one hand and disdain toward our hometown in the other.[10]

Jesus found a creative way through these tensions. So can we. Without holding to both leaving *and* honoring, we career toward the extremes of either burning down the past or forsaking the present and future.

Shipwrecked by the Extremes

For those walking through doubt or deconstruction, that tension of leaving and honoring is critical. In Paul's first letter to Timothy, he writes of two men named Hymenaeus and Alexander who have "suffered shipwreck with regard to the faith" (1 Tim. 1:19)—visceral language opted for by an apostle who'd *actually* been shipwrecked during his own seafaring. Paul knew the difference between a storm and a shipwreck. And Paul knew he was writing to churches that found themselves in storms as they faced division on the inside and persecution from the outside. Every New Testament letter assumes the churches harbored big questions about the Christian faith. They didn't have all the answers they needed. Storms were raging. But storms were—for Paul—very different from having a shipwrecked faith.

Thinking back on my second meeting with Phil, what still strikes me is how he assumed he probably wasn't a Christian simply because he had questions and doubts. Phil equated a storm with a shipwreck. Where did this idea come from? We too often assume that doubts and questions and critiques of one's own faith are the same as losing it. But this deception betrays the ways Christians have been following Jesus for two thousand years. Even the New Testament recognizes the difference between a Judas Iscariot and a Peter—both of whom turned their back on Jesus. The difference? One came back. The other gave up. There's a fundamental difference between doubt and unbelief in Scripture. Peter's doubt wasn't the end of his faith. Why should it be ours? Peter's crisis of faith eventually matured into an even deeper longing and love for Christ. Here is the mystery: to struggle with one's faith is often the surest sign we actually have one. "Doubt is not always a sign that a man is wrong," Oswald Chambers once wrote. "It may be a sign that he is thinking."[11] Phil loved Jesus enough to ask him his actual, real questions. The biblical witness has a word for this: confession. There's often no greater act of faith and fidelity to God than baring one's deepest held beliefs to divine criticism so that God might be loved more. To put it more simply: kicking the tires doesn't mean you hate the car.

A shipwrecked faith is a possibility. And, clearly, walking through doubt and deconstruction in our time is complicated by how popular it has become to question, challenge, pull apart, and reject one's deeply held beliefs. Deconstruction is "cool" now. Honor is now given to those who entirely leave their faith. This is further amplified by a form of hyperpartisan tribalism that utilizes soft power, wordplay, and emotional coercion through the liturgies of social media to manipulate people to one extreme or the other. For those in deconstruction, this culture calls out like Sirens in the dark whose songs beckon us toward the extreme rocks of the theological right and the theological left. One extreme—reflective of conservative Christianity—wants us to believe that doubt and deconstruction are inherently bad, a pathway inevitably leading to the cliffs of apostasy and faith abandonment. This extreme denies that deconstruction can be a legitimate place to encounter the living God. Here, deconstruction is caricatured as an all-out assault from the forces of darkness on truth, church, Christian culture, and ultimately the gospel. "If we really had faith in Jesus," they would say, "we wouldn't have doubts or questions about it." This is blissful nostalgia. Not to mention that it's the very black-and-white approach to faith that created the deconstruction environment we find ourselves in, where the young opt to leave church because their difficulties aren't allowed within. We can all thank God that doubting Thomas didn't have his doubt crisis in a fundamentalist conservative church.[12] They would have told him he didn't believe anymore—that he was doomed to destruction.

Still, the extreme of the theological left is as destructive. The ideology and spirit of a good deal of progressive Christianity almost requires us to undo traditional Christianity as a kind of compulsory experience. This is the sign that we're "evolved" and "liberated." Emerging from this seems to be a kind of laissez-faire approach to historic Christianity that rejects Jesus as the only way to God while seeming to suggest that doubt and deconstruction are (ironically) the only way to God. Here the Enneagram has more weight than the words of Scripture. Podcasts trump one's service to the bride of Christ. And theology is acceptable so long as it's sanitized of anything that might offend a Sunday afternoon audience on NPR. This has led to a kind of gnostic clique of naysayers who rest their pride on finding every last vestige of dirt on the church and the Bible with a pretense of arrogance that's nauseating. Go to the internet. Descend into the angsty, hopeless cesspool of Christian nihilism readily available online and you'll know what we're talking about.

Both sides miss the boat.

What's one to do? Conservative Christianity critiques the new questions. Progressive Christianity scoffs at old answers. This rips apart people like Phil, Sarah, John, and Carlos. One demonizes doubt, the other demands it. The goal, of course, isn't to run away from deconstruction, nor to run toward it. The goal is Jesus Christ and nothing less. It is Christ's kingdom—God's rule and reign in all things. It is the fruit of the Spirit: love, joy, peace, patience, kindness, goodness, faithfulness, gentleness, and self-control. The goal is a life of deep passion for what God has said and an actual commitment to the ways of justice and loving-kindness it demands of us. The goal is the rule and reign of God made manifest for those with questions and those without, a place where doubting Thomas can touch the scars of a living God and go transform an entire nation. For this to happen, balance is needed. As G. K. Chesterton writes, "An inch is everything when you are balancing."[13] Phil learned to walk that balance through deconstruction, wisely closing his ears to the deadly Sirens on both sides of the boat. In due time, we all need to begin to see the duplicity of our own deconstruction and the power of Christ despite our questions. We must learn that in persevering long enough, one comes full circle—eventually deconstructing our deconstruction, critiquing our critiques, doubting our doubts, and refusing to rest our anxious minds on the presumed inerrancy of our experience.

That's what Jesus seeks: a generation of followers who have learned to follow through the desert of deconstruction and doubt toward God's kingdom here and now. A people whose love and faith remain *after doubt*.

Is there a way to walk through this deconstruction with Jesus into a deeper faith? Is it possible to come out on the other side *more* in love with the living God? Is there a way to navigate deconstruction and have a deeper love for the church afterward? Can deconstruction make us more compassionate and gracious toward others with whom we disagree? Can it forge in us the character of God? Can we enter this deconstruction experience without it ultimately destroying our faith, causing us to eventually leave the church and resent Christians forever?

The answer is *yes!* Not every storm becomes a shipwreck.

Presence

Nestled in the heart of the Old Testament is the book of Job—that holy tale of a famed Eastern man facing unimaginable suffering. He has lost his children, land, and fortune. In the midst of Job's pain, he does what any sensible person might do: he gives voice to a litany of questions for the Divine. *Why has all this injustice happened to me? Is the world broken if this is what I get out of it? Does Yahweh even love me given that all this has happened?* Job demands answers. *Why has my moral life been met with so much loss? How could a just God let this happen?*

Job's questions are not unreasonable. How *is* one to understand a good and just God in the midst of life's chaos and complexity? Eventually Job's chance arrives to lay his existential questions before God. In one of the most penetrating chapters in the Hebrew Scriptures, Job 38 records God's responses to Job. The conversation, however, goes differently than one might expect. The questions aren't *for* God. The questions are *from* God. Laden with poetic wit and a flare for heavenly sarcasm, God lets Job hear his questions: *Was Job there when God made the foundations of the earth? Was Job there when God made Leviathan? Was Job there to watch the first sunrise?* Job just stands there—silent.

Remarkably, the text does not record God answering the questions that Job has brought. Not one answer. This perplexing turn of events reveals that the book offers little response to the "problem" of suffering. There are no answers to suffering in Job. Instead, God gives his presence. Job wasn't there when God invented the world. Job didn't see the first sunrise. And what in the world is a Leviathan anyway? The turn of events leads to an important vista. What begins as a man full of questions and empty on trust fizzles away before our very eyes—there are no longer questions but only hope, love, and trust. All that's left is the deafening silence of Yahweh's presence.[14]

I've watched as young people have moved to Portland and become overwhelmed by its culture and lulled by the Sirens of flesh and frivolity. I've argued, cried, and wept reminding the young of God's endless love for them in the midst of their questions and challenges. The tears on that office floor could never be counted. There are simply too many. I've endured sleepless nights watching what feels like a whole generation walk away from the church because its evils are more clearly exposed than ever. I've experienced heartburn, acute anxiety, and panic attacks while pastoring in a culture that rejects all external authority—especially the authority of the words of Jesus. In my darker days, I called it the New Oregon Trail. A century ago on their way out West, pilgrims died of dysentery. Now they spiritually die of deconstruction. I've felt sorry for myself, alone. I've wondered if I'm crazy. I've wondered if I was the only Christian left. Giving up became an appealing option.

Then Job would come to my mind. Most modern readers assume that Job is the story of *other* people who suffer greatly. Jonathan Edwards—the revivalist and eighteenth-century preacher—argues that reading Job in that way is unfaithful to the spirit of the story. Edwards believes Job isn't about a few unfortunate people who lose everything. Rather, Job is about each of us. Everyone loses everything—the very precious existence we love will at some point be taken from us. It may come during our life; it may come at its end. But we are all Job. All that I have that I think is mine will eventually be given to someone else and will make it back to God himself. There are no pockets in the resurrection clothes. In due time, we all will give it all away. The story of Job is about the fact that we're all generous—eventually.

It has become clear that Phil—from the beginning of this chapter—was having a Job-*like* experience. It wasn't exactly the same as Job's. Phil hadn't lost his family, his children, his respect, or even the clothes off his back. Phil hadn't lost people, stuff, or place. Phil was losing trust—particularly trust in God and his people, something that is perhaps harder to lose than life itself. How could he trust God anymore? How could he trust the Bible? How could he trust the church? What does one do when trust is lost?

Phil eventually learned Job's lesson—namely, that for some things there are no answers. And that the goal never was about getting all the answers. "Getting answers to my questions," once wrote Henri Nouwen, "is not the goal of the spiritual life. Living in the presence of God is the greater call."[15] The ancients learned this lesson. They whisper it to us. Phil learned to place his trust in God's presence—a place where his questions and doubts took on a less central place. Trust is not only an act of the mind but an orientation of the whole self in love toward someone. The questions still mattered, just not as much. What Phil needed, more than anything, was not answers to his existential crisis. The answers were important, and it is good to ask questions. But his itch was of the heart, not the mind. He didn't need answers; he needed his pain to be seen. Once Phil was seen by God, he could continue. Like Job, he did not come out the other side with the answers he wanted. But he did come out of it with a restored trust in the God who made him and knew him from his mother's womb.

Phil learned that answers are an inadequate substitute for the presence of an Almighty God.

Two

The Theological Journey

The Work of Belief

This chapter sketches the process by which we form beliefs about God. The process of forming beliefs takes a lifetime, often navigating terrain of pain, frustration, and breakthrough. Paul writes that faith is a "gift of God" (Eph. 2:8). Trust in God is a gift. But trusting in Jesus and having beliefs about Jesus are not always the same thing. Faith is a gift; beliefs are not. Forming beliefs takes time and often hard work.[1] The significance of belief formation is reflected in a three-year initiation process in the early church called *catechesis* wherein a person would convert to Christianity. During this season, the *catechumen* would memorize Scripture, learn apostolic teachings, fast, and receive prayer and exorcism. On the Sunday of their third Easter, they descended into the baptismal waters. Faith was a gift—a gift that could be received even instantaneously. But forming right beliefs required time and was a process. Beliefs take work.

Distinguishing faith from beliefs is critical. In the New Testament, the first witnesses to Jesus's messiahship weren't the disciples. They were the demons! The demons' accurate (we might say orthodox) declarations about Jesus reveal that they held many true beliefs about Jesus. Jesus *is* the Son of God. Jesus *does* have power. Jesus *is* from God. The demons were surprisingly orthodox. This explains James's warning against making right beliefs the whole picture: "Even the demons believe [there is one God]—and *shudder*" (James 2:19). The demons had good theology. Yet, though they held accurate beliefs about Jesus, they lacked faith in Jesus as Lord and King of the world. Having right beliefs but no faith was a very real possibility. And it still is.

Christian spirituality isn't *solely* about one's capacity to restate right, true, and accurate beliefs.[2] Christian faith is total trust, submission, and faith in Jesus reflected in a whole-person pursuit to know the One being trusted. True faith leads us to *want* true beliefs. If we trust God, we'll want to know who God is and what God says. Belief and trust are not mutually exclusive. Christian faith is about both—trusting and rightly believing. This is why Paul says we are saved by grace *through* faith (Eph. 2:8). None are saved by grace *through* right beliefs. Good works or good beliefs don't save. But they do reveal and reflect our trust.

As the thief crucified next to Jesus would affirm, one can be heaven-bound and have none of their theology ironed out. Does this mean beliefs don't matter? Of course not. Right beliefs matter exceedingly! If I wrongly believed my wife were having an affair—though she wasn't—I wouldn't trust her. Likewise, if I believed God to be a tyrannical oppressor whose lust for praise was a front for an even darker divine narcissism, then God couldn't be trusted. What we believe *about* God directly determines whether we can place our trust in God. Beliefs matter—greatly. Will one go to hell for not having all their beliefs ironed out? No! But we will likely go through it. If we willingly believe falsehoods about God, we'll never be able to fully trust him. Who could trust a divine oppressor?

Writing about marriage, Madeleine L'Engle suggests, "It takes a lifetime to learn a person."[3] How much more with God. The story of Nicodemus found in John's Gospel illustrates this lifelong learning process. Cowering in fear, the religious leader visits Jesus at night in an effort to sidestep the ire of his fellow Pharisees who'd likely condemn him for even visiting Jesus. We call him "Nic at Night." In John 3, Nicodemus packs in a laundry list of religious questions for Jesus. As with Job, Nicodemus's questions never seem to hit their target. Just as Nicodemus offers a question, Jesus raises a whole new path of discussion about the spiritual life. The ultimate questions are not *from* Nicodemus, they are *for* Nicodemus. "The dialogue," says Raymond Brown, "has become a monologue."[4]

Nicodemus's story does not end there. After Jesus's crucifixion, Nicodemus appears again. This time he bears no questions. Rather, he bears seventy pounds of myrrh to bury Jesus. The transformation between the two Nicodemuses is breathtaking. The man who first came to bury Christ with tricky and evasive questions now comes to bury Christ at his death in passionate love. His quiet journey from disbelief to belief no doubt exemplifies John's hope that his reader "may believe that Jesus is the Messiah" (John 20:31). Jesus doesn't just turn over tables. He also turns over unbelief. Christian discipleship is the Nicodemus path—the wholesale bending of heart, body, and mind to the person and work of Jesus, our stories forged around his.

Nicodemus's story reflects what I call the "theological journey." This theological journey is our lifetime process of refining and ironing out our beliefs about God. Why? Because even our thinking demands sanctification. None of us comes fully equipped with a perfectly developed, nuanced, articulated vision of God. The process of forming right beliefs takes time; it's messy, often embarrassing, and demands humility, passion, and perseverance. I love the story of Karl Barth—the prolific theologian of the twentieth century famous for writing *Church Dogmatics*, which totals about twelve million words. It's reported that he said he himself hadn't even read it all. Despite the vastness of his writings, Barth believed he'd find all heaven's angels laughing at him. "In heaven," Barth reflects, "we shall know all that is necessary, and we shall not have to write on paper or read more. . . . Indeed, I shall be able to dump even the *Church Dogmatics*, over the growth of which the angels have long been amazed, on some heavenly floor as a pile of waste paper."[5]

Nobody—not even the greatest of theologians—can provide a finished theological product. There are always "loose ends," to borrow from Eugene Peterson.[6] Before heaven, every belief is preliminary. Nobody is permitted the whole picture beforehand.[7] All earthly theology is essentially preparing for embarrassment. Heaven, as such, will be that eternal deconstruction where God undoes all the half-baked notions and half-truths and replaces them all with himself. Until then, "we see only a reflection as in a mirror; then we shall see face to face" (1 Cor. 13:12). Still—despite the fact that we never fully arrive during *this* life—Christians are to give themselves to the never-ending pursuit of learning, growing, and being intellectually sanctified through the Holy Spirit. A central task, then, is the cultivation and pursuit of right belief alongside faith. This is what Paul meant when he wrote that we would "reach unity in the faith and in the knowledge of the Son of God" (Eph. 4:13).

Right beliefs require will, intentionality, and discipline. In *Mere Christianity*, C. S. Lewis discusses the intentionality needed to believe rightly: "One must train the habit of Faith [by making] sure that . . . some of its main doctrines shall be deliberately held before your mind for some time every day. That is why daily prayers and religious reading and church-going are necessary parts of the Christian life. We have to be continually reminded of what we believe. Neither this belief nor any other will automatically remain alive in the mind. It must be fed."[8] This is later echoed in his *Christian Reflections* as he describes "the practice of faith that leads to the habit of faith."[9] For Lewis, beliefs aren't happenstance. They don't *just* happen. They're intentionally formed.

Three Stages

How are theological beliefs intentionally formed? There are many ways to think about the theological journey. Some look at it developmentally—such as the case of theologian and psychologist James Fowler in his *Stages of Faith* published in 1981.[10] Fowler identified seven stages of faith one goes through: (1) primal-undifferentiated faith, (2) intuitive-projective faith, (3) mythic-literal faith, (4) synthetic-conventional faith, (5) individuative-reflective faith, (6) conjunctive faith, (7) and universalizing faith. Others have looked at it through a more theological, biblical, and pastoral lens. Eugene Peterson, for instance, sees the first five books of the Bible as a framework for belief formation—Genesis serves as the "prenatal word of God," Exodus as the "birth and infancy," Leviticus as "childhood," Numbers as "adolescence," and Deuteronomy as "adult-hood."[11] As Israel walked through these stages, so do followers of Jesus.

As stated, there are many ways to think about the theological journey. For our purposes here—and based on my experience in spiritual forma-tion, in pastoring, and as a theologian—I would like to propose three fundamental stages in the theological journey: theological construction, *de*construction, and *re*construction.

What do these three stages entail? First, construction—those pre-liminary steps one takes in the faith journey. During construction, the basic structures of belief are accepted and established, usually in the context of a family of origin, church upbringing, or community where one becomes a Christian. Wherever construction occurs, one of its distin-guishing marks is the acceptance of beliefs *precritically*. That is, beliefs are accepted "as is." This is not all too different from a baby learning a language. A child will first use the language they hear their parents use. A toddler does not need years of critical reflection before using certain words. They simply assume those words. They trust them. They are the words they were first handed.[12]

A similar phenomenon takes place in Christian belief. We believe what we were first handed—thinking critically of it only later. By way of il-lustration, when I was given my first car, I depended on my stepfather's leading to know what car might be trustworthy. I knew nothing. In child-like naivete, I trusted uncritically what my stepfather suggested. Thank God I did. Similarly, in the early years of faith formation we receive from somebody a set of beliefs about God. Contrary to what some might pre-sume, this vulnerable trust is not a bad thing. We need someone to hold out their hands so we can take our first steps in Christ. In my early years of faith, I believed in the Trinity but not because someone offered me a perfect explanation. I received it "on faith" and as is. Nor did I accept the belief that the Bible is inspired by God based on a thorough reading of it. I trusted those around me who said that the Bible was trustworthy—and I could lean on it. I did not receive the belief that I was loved uncondi-tionally by the God of the universe because I did a philosophical study on the topic—I simply received it by faith, uncritically.

The beauty of construction is the trusting vulnerability one displays toward God and God's people as a person receives true and trustworthy Christian beliefs. But construction can simultaneously be disastrous. As we later discover in life, the uncritical reception of good beliefs can also make space for the uncritical reception of bad beliefs. That's always the problem with good soil: it has the capacity to grow both vegetables *and* weeds. We accept the gospel as is, and we can accept other stuff as is too. During this stage, we often pick up cultural, environmental, and theological additives alongside the gospel that slip in unawares. I often joke that you can tell exactly which church it was in my city where someone converted to Christianity. They literally start *sounding* like that church's pastor. This reveals something: we receive not only the gospel as is but also the opinions, attitudes, and postures of our new community. Even inflections of our new leader's voice! This is not necessarily bad, but it can be. We accept beliefs about God that are good, but because we are humans led by humans, we often receive beliefs that can betray who God actually is.

It is impossible to receive the good news of Jesus and our preliminary beliefs about God from a perfect community.[13] We will unquestionably receive some element of real, broken reality along with faith. This is part of following Jesus in a broken world. Consider an image: When someone goes to the hospital, they seek healing. And healing hopefully happens! But any visit to a hospital puts a patient at risk, for there are countless individuals with diseases, illnesses, and contractable sicknesses at the hospital. These illnesses are contracted when (ironically) one goes to the hospital to get better. The category for this in the medical community is *iatrogenic diseases.* That is always how the gospel works. While we may receive the life-changing story of Jesus, a love for the Bible, a commitment to mission, and a heart for justice from a community, we will likely pick up some iatrogenic beliefs from that community as well that we'll have to heal from later on.

After my conversion, I first worshiped in a phenomenal conservative evangelical church. God's hand of love was upon me. I needed that church! It was there I was handed a fierce love of Scripture, a passionate

pursuit of holiness, an evangelistic heart, and an unflinching commitment to Christian doctrine. These haven't left me. At the same time, I uncritically inherited some extraordinarily unhealthy perspectives toward
women that eventually needed deconstructing. Marriage, mistakes, and
a deeper reading of Scripture later revealed that my theology was way
off-kilter. My theological perspective on women has changed greatly
while my passion for the Bible, holiness, evangelism, and the centrality
of Christ have not. In one fell swoop, I received as is some marvelous
beliefs about following Jesus—and as is some *not*-marvelous things.
Distinguishing the two takes a lifetime of the Spirit's sanctification.
Turns out my grandmother's advice counts for theology too: it's good to
eat the meat and spit out the bones.

The second stage of the theological journey one may go through is
called deconstruction. Our theology often exists in our life the way our
pipes exist in our home. We give little thought to them, but we rely on
them unthinkingly. Too little attention is given to them. That is, until
grey water begins pooling in our bathtub or a pipe bursts, flooding our
kitchen. We usually begin rethinking our theology when it no longer
seems to work. Later in life, many come to reevaluate those earlier, uncritically received beliefs. This happens because no church, religious
environment, or denomination is immune to iatrogenic diseases. Though
we have been saved by the healing message of Jesus, we realize that part
of our belief structure may go against that message.

Deconstruction is a double-edged sword. It can edify our faith by helping us critically rethink wrong beliefs. But it can also go too far and bring
our faith to nothing. Any belief we uncritically received at some point that
remains hostile or opposed to the biblical message of Jesus Christ *needs* to
be deconstructed. But the minute deconstruction undermines the gospel,
our faith, or the Bible, we've deconstructed too much. There's a world of
difference between deconstructing wrong beliefs and deconstructing the
faith, just as there's a difference between remodeling a room in our home
and tearing down the house. Distinguishing between the two is essential:
one is intellectual repentance and the other faith abandonment. One is
healthy deconstruction; the other is faith destruction. In fact, a true and

living faith will often require us to undertake some type of deconstruction of our beliefs.

Forgetting this difference can destroy faith—a reality played out far too often. You know the story: someone raised in the church enters adulthood and a new environment and "wakes up" to how certain beliefs they've held either were wrong, did great harm to others, or were based solely on childhood emotion. Sadly, what often begins as a humble desire to believe rightly ferments into an all-out resentment (even hatred) of the family of origin, church community, or Christian identity that nurtured those beliefs. The hatred slowly turns inward. Resentment for others becomes hatred of self for having ever accepted said beliefs. As a kind of penance for having been wrong—and to signal one's remorse to others—their beliefs (and beliefs of others) are thrown to the curb. Self-hatred becomes a substitutionary atonement for a guilty conscience. I call it theological suicide. Because we committed the supposedly "unforgivable sin" of having been a Christian who was wrong about something, we crucify Jesus all over again.

Looming soon after is the cold chill of nihilism that pervades much of the post-Christian world—the rejection of *all* belief as a poor solution to bad belief. Soon we come to prefer no belief over the risk of a belief that might be found imperfect.[14] To protect ourselves from the pain or embarrassment of wrong beliefs, we cease risking belief at all. We follow Judas by jumping off the theological cliff, forgetting, sadly, the ancient path of Peter whose return to Jesus was met with grace and mercy. Being theologically wrong is not an unforgivable sin. God has grace for our bad theology just as he does for our sin. If he joyfully forgives our sins at the cross, surely he forgives our silly thoughts. Theologian Helmut Thielicke's words of wisdom are timely: "I don't believe that God is a fussy faultfinder in dealing with theological ideas. He who provides forgiveness for a sinful life will also surely be a generous judge of theological reflections. Even an orthodox theologian can be spiritually dead, while perhaps the heretic crawls on forbidden bypaths to the source of life."[15] In fact, one of the signs we're actually following Jesus is that the Spirit reveals our wrongness. Name one other religion where one's open confession of being wrong is the sign they're on the right track. Grace abounds!

The final—and often most exciting—stage is reconstruction. Having asked, challenged, and prodded, we return a second time to the same faith we were handed. We return to our "first love" (Rev. 2:4). It is here that we return to the simple faith we were handed after doing the complex and exhausting work of putting it through the fire. Sadly, as experience bears out, making it through the deconstruction stage to reconstruction does not always happen. There are many reasons why. But it bears stating that unless we do deconstruction well, we will likely not make it to reconstruction.

It is possible to be in multiple stages at once. The New Testament witnesses to the words of a man who had asked Jesus to heal his son: "I do believe; help me overcome my unbelief!" (Mark 9:24). This man clearly finds himself representing a few of the stages we've discussed. At any given time in our walk, we may find that we are in different stages at different moments.

What is the goal of the theological journey? If we don't know where we're going, any direction will do. If our goal in deconstruction is getting back at our parents, we will get what we seek. If our goal is to deconstruct because we want to sleep with whomever we want, we'll get what we want. If our goal is deconstructing because we want attention on social media, we'll get what we want. God is generous. We usually get what we want. Jesus would often ask people, "What do you want?" Why? Their goals mattered. I once heard of an Australian aboriginal tribe who greet each other around one's trajectory and direction. Rather than saying, "Hello, how are you?" the aboriginal asks, "Which way are you heading?"[16] When Jesus asks, "What do you want?" he wants to know our goals. If our goal is Jesus Christ at all costs, we'll get Jesus Christ. Put simply, anyone can deconstruct wrong beliefs. But it takes courage and intentionality to hold to a belief we believe in our bones to be right. That's the difference between a surgeon and a coroner. Both know how to cut apart. Only one knows how to put back together and bring life.

Experience, Crisis, Transition

It's been observed that some species of birds—to provoke their chicks to flight—will pick up small rocks below and slowly fill the nest. Eventually, the discomfort of the nest forces the young to fly.[17] Even God's creation builds in obstacles to help the process of maturity. The same is true in faith. Sometimes the rocks in our nest are simply God's way of getting us to walk on water.

In their book *Critical Journey*, Janet Hagberg and Robert Guelich describe seven stages of faith. The first and last three stages relate correspondingly to construction and reconstruction. But the binding between these two is a middle stage they call "the wall." The wall is marked by a sense that "things aren't working anymore. . . . There's got to be more."[18] Many Christians, at some point, hit some wall that leads to deconstruction. While there are unquestionably more, we will identify three walls here that play disproportionate roles in causing us to doubt or deconstruct our faith: experience, crisis, and transition.

Experience plays a role in our theological journey. In Isaiah 6, Isaiah sees the Lord with the train of his robe filling the temple. Isaiah observes seraphim encircling the Lord, praising their maker. They cry out in unison, "Holy, holy, holy is the Lord Almighty; the whole earth is full of his glory" (Isa. 6:3). The temple gates and thresholds shake at their song. Smoke fills the temple. Isaiah's response? "Woe to me," he cries. "I am ruined! For I am a man of unclean lips, and I live among a people of unclean lips, and my eyes have seen the King, the Lord Almighty" (v. 5). Isaiah is shattered, broken, humbled. His experience shakes him to the core. The experience becomes Isaiah's realization that he was called as a prophet to Israel.

There's no reason to believe that Isaiah did not believe in God before this experience. He held beliefs about the Lord. Still, he had yet to experience the one he believed in. Isaiah's cognitive belief became experiential reality in one fell swoop. No longer was God an intellectual belief; God was a being Isaiah had seen. Experiences like Isaiah's change one's perception of God. To be sure, there are many kinds of experience. There are what we might call *elevation* experiences and *valley* experiences. An elevation experience is one like Isaiah's—moments of revelation, epiphany, elation that awaken us to a deeper understanding of who God is. One could call these "mountaintop experiences." On the other hand, a valley experience occurs when we walk through darkness, brokenness, pain, loss, discomfort, and uncertainty. When we look carefully, Isaiah's experience appears to have elements of both. Not only was Isaiah's vision of God enlarged, his view of himself seems to have been annihilated.

The valley is the desire for marriage met by perpetual singleness. The valley contains prayers for healing that *don't* work. Valleys occur when hope and trust in God are put to the test. These valley experiences can push us to the edge of our faith. They make us ask, why did God let this happen? Where is God? How can he still be good? In pastoral and personal experience, I've observed that valley experiences leverage disproportional impact in leading one toward doubt or deconstruction. This is not to suggest that elevation experiences cannot lead to deconstruction. They certainly can. Seeing a friend healed of cancer can leave one appreciative of God's sovereignty. But being confused why there are still people dying of hunger in Africa can lead to doubt.

Here's my hunch: contemporary, conservative Christianity (of which I am a part) has a theological framework for understanding elevation experiences. We are great at serving people in their success, spiritual growth, and victory. But contemporary evangelicalism has less of a framework for valley experiences. We are elevation churches. We have communities where blessing, happiness, and joy are part and parcel of following Jesus. Which can be great. But we can only remain part of those communities as long as that remains the trajectory of our lives. The minute we enter a valley, being around all the happy-clappy rejoicing can get really difficult.

Here's my other hunch: contemporary, progressive, mainline Christianity in places like Portland has a framework for those walking through valley experiences. As a result, young people are opting for progressive mainline churches that do lament and grief and uncertainty. This is why so many modern Episcopalians grew up in evangelical churches. We are basically now at a point where there are churches for those who rejoice with those who rejoice and other churches for people who weep with those who weep.

But this sidesteps God's ultimate desires. What we don't need is one church for people who are rejoicing and another church for people who are weeping. Our souls need a space where people can weep and celebrate together. We need churches that follow Paul's command: "Rejoice with those who rejoice; mourn with those who mourn" (Rom. 12:15). We don't need to sacrifice good theology in order to be with those in pain. Nor do we need to allow human suffering and pain to keep us from seeking good and beautiful experiences with God. There is nothing wrong with mountaintops. The Bible is chock-full of them. What is wrong are those on the mountaintop who never come down below to be with those in the valley and those in the valley who spend their time judging those on the mountain.

Eugene Peterson eloquently suggests that while every person deep within their being desires God, it is often an experience that awakens that need:

> All men and women hunger for God. The hunger is masked and misinterpreted in many ways, but it is always there. Everyone is on the verge of crying out "My Lord and my God!" but the cry is drowned out by doubts or defiance, muffled by the dull ache of their routines, masked by their cozy accommodations with mediocrity. Then something happens—a word, an event, a dream—and there is a push toward awareness of an incredible Grace, a dazzling Desire, a defiant Hope, a courageous Faithfulness.[19]

If experience can do this, so can crises. They can be societal crises. For example, in the years following World War II, a radical Christian renewal captured the minds of the likes of T. S. Eliot, Evelyn Waugh, W. H. Auden, and Graham Greene. C. S. Lewis himself discussed how the horrors of trench warfare in the First World War had woken up his need for God. This is why churches were full in the aftermath of 9/11. Crises awaken our need for something we can trust in. These crises can be personal too: a lost spouse, death, a divorce, a child coming out of the closet, loss, broken trust, being hurt by the church.

One crisis I endured was realizing how broken my theological heroes are. Karl Barth is widely believed to have had an inappropriate (perhaps even sexual) relationship with his secretary who dictated his *Church Dogmatics*. Aimee Semple McPherson, the founder of my denomination, got divorced two times and died of a sleeping-pill overdose. Martin Luther, the father of Protestantism, finished his illustrious theological career with an anti-Semitic rant entitled *On the Jews and Their Lies*. John Howard Yoder—whose theology of peace changed the trajectory of my life—was posthumously discovered to be a womanizer. Even the most important theological dictionary to date—used by theologians, biblical scholars, and pastors alike—entitled *The Theological Dictionary of the New Testament* and edited by Gerhard Kittel and Gerhard Friedrich, added to my crisis. Notice their names are German? It is sobering to realize that one of the most important theological works in Christian history was commissioned by Hitler and the Third Reich during World War II. My favorite theological dictionary, it turns out, was funded by the Nazis. These led to a crisis of faith. How do I deal with the fact that all my heroes are so broken? That crisis taught me that God's merciful hand can be extended to the world even through the lives of greatly broken people.

Transitions also affect our theological journey. Major life shifts bring about a new onslaught of previously unasked questions. There are painful transitions: divorce, death, job loss, economic downturn, midlife crises, and lost hopes all beckon a renewed angst about the nature and meaning of life. But even good transitions can change one's belief structure.

Change is one of life's constants. Change is even built into creation. Weather and climate change. Over a lifetime, the human sheds all of their skin some seven times. Even lobsters lose their shells some twenty-five times before the age of five. Transitions in human history have provided generative space for creativity and ingenuity. Arnold Toynbee, the British historian, points out a pattern of "withdrawal and return" in the lives of St. Paul, St. Benedict, Gregory the Great, Buddha, Muhammad, Machiavelli, and Dante, giving them space for their most creative work.[20] Billy Graham's brother-in-law Leighton Ford once said, "The most important time is between the dreams, not the dreams themselves."[21] Change is a part of life whether we want it or not.

Back in Portland, it became vividly clear that even geographical moves from conservative, small-town environments to large, progressive, urban environments contributed disproportionately to one's faith deconstruction. Patricia Killen, a sociologist at Gonzaga University, spent years examining spiritual environments like Portland and how physical moves to such places greatly affect one's beliefs. How? First, Killen points out, there grows a general disconnect from the past for those who move. If someone moves to Portland, it's for a reason, sometimes to get away from one's past. Second, there is a high cultural density— meaning people are forced into more confined spaces. In that context, people are more likely to have ongoing contact with people who think differently from them. And they become part of a world where they aren't as known as they were before. Portland has become a great place to remain anonymous, isolated, and obscure. Last, there is the reality of physical and social mobility. People come from *elsewhere*. And when someone relocates to Portland, they move around more than anyone else. Adventurers have long loved the great expanse of the Pacific Northwest.

"Moving," Killen suggests, "disconnects people from social pressures to conform." Transitions provide new freedoms of exploration without the watchful eye of the family of origin or church back home. This also brings isolation. Killen writes, "Few people come to the Far West seeking what they left behind. Most hold dreams of a better life. Physical mobility and psychological mobility reinforce each other. When people move West, they must choose to reconnect to social institutions, to be part of communities. Having left one community, they find it easier to leave another and harder to reconnect."[22] When people move, her research suggests, they find new environments where it is safer to explore new beliefs. While back home faith was structured into their lives, in this new world faith becomes optional and voluntary. Back home, they went to church. In Portland, you have to make a choice to go to church.

Physical mobility doesn't *always* change one's beliefs—although in my experience it often does. Nor is moving necessarily deconstructive in nature. Sometimes transitions open us up to our deep need for God. In *To Spread the Power*, theologian George Hunter writes how simple acts of moving, transition, and crises can affect one's faith commitment:

> Individuals who have lost faith in anything—religion, a philosophy, a lover, a drug, a pipe dream, a utopian promise, or in themselves—tend to look for something new upon which to norm and inform their lives. The missionary congregation should constantly be on the lookout for people who are "between idols." A people experiencing major culture change tend to be very receptive . . . [be it a] decline of traditional values, or changes in marriage and family patterns or values, or changes in kinship structures or patterns. A range of changes in a society's political system, from being conquered to being liberated, from oppression imposed to oppression removed, from revolution to nationalism, have all contributed to the receptivity of a people. Major economic changes, such as unemployment, underemployment, runaway inflation, mergers, acquisitions, crop failures, and plant closings have all shaken people's false securities and opened them to the gospel.[23]

Transition—being "between idols"—affects one's faith. In the parable of the prodigal son, the prodigal "came to his senses" to want to return home only when there was a "severe famine in that whole country" (Luke 15:14, 17). By finding the end of himself, he yearned to go home. Indeed, losing faith in one thing can create a need for faith in something else. While painful, these experiences can awaken our need for something deeper, trustable, and sustaining. Transition causes us to look inward, to question the things we've held dear, to yearn for more secure securities.

My Deconstruction

I became a Christian in an odd way in my sophomore high school geometry class. Behind me sat two teenage girls arguing about Christ's return. They'd been reading something called the Left Behind series. These were the 1990s and just about everyone wondered which Russian dictator was the antichrist and how Visa was pining to write 666 on our foreheads. It was there that the gospel was accidentally shared with me. That lost, listless teenager—in the throes of the oppression of adolescence—sat and contemplated the reality of Jesus. I knew nothing of Jesus. I'd never even thought about Jesus. Yet something landed with a thud on my conscience. I went home, found a Bible, sat on my bedroom floor, and read. I asked God to speak to me. He did. My life was upended. I was a Christian.

My girlfriend at the time started taking me to her church. There I immersed myself in the Bible, a new life of faith, repentance, and Christian community. Whatever God was doing, I wanted to do it. Back then they called this "being on fire." Catapulted into evangelical culture, I was soon on a big yellow bus up to Seattle for an Acquire the Fire conference. I was all in. I bought every Newsboys and DC Talk CD at the local music store. I learned they don't serve breakfast in hell. I found out dating was a sin after reading *I Kissed Dating Goodbye*. In short, I'd acquired the fire.

After finishing a biblical studies degree in college, getting married, and receiving my first pastoral call as a college pastor, I enrolled in seminary to feed my hunger for God. Soon I was juggling a growing college ministry, married life, and seminary, where I enrolled in a full load of graduate work in Bible, theology, pastoral care, and preaching. I was a pastor by day, a seminary student by weekends, and a husband by night. It was a busy but rewarding season.

As it does for most, seminary affected me deeply. A number of things stand out. First, the diversity of students opened my mind to the width and depth of Christ's church. What immediately struck me was how many different kinds of Christians there were. *How could it be possible for there to be so many different Christians who thought differently than I did?* My still-young evangelical theology of the church tended to look suspiciously on Christians from other traditions: namely, Catholics, Anglicans, Episcopalians, and liberals. These seemingly exotic Christians from distant lands who seemed to love Jesus too caused me to begin to question my own views in the most subtle ways. I now saw a church that was far more expansive and far-reaching than my teenage mind could ever have dreamed.

Seminary also exposed me to a world of new ideas, knowledge, and concepts about the Bible, theology, and church history. Faith became far more complex than I'd ever known. This was amplified by my church history class where I learned about the chaotic origin of the church and its earliest beliefs. I also learned how the church had caused pain in the world through the Crusades and how the Reformation writings were used by the Third Reich as ideological crutches for their agenda. Faith wasn't as simple as it once was.

There was a personal dynamic as well. The experience of going to seminary on Mondays and pastoring the rest of the week led to a kind of cognitive dissonance. It was like I was becoming two people. There was seminary me and church me. As "church me," I grew uncomfortable preaching on topics I was being challenged by as "seminary me." That dissonance eventually led to deep frustrations with conservative Christians who were not asking the same questions as I was—or who came to different conclusions. I noticed a growing ire for those who believed the way I *used to* believe. It became enjoyable to poke fun at the certainty of conservative Christians who I saw as naive. It was fun. Nobody seems to have grace for those they used to be like.

I was also learning more about myself through counseling. Many of the personal struggles from my teenage years had not gone away—even though I'd hoped they would with the zeal of my new faith. I started coming to terms with my dark side, which conversion hadn't magically whisked away. A decade after conversion, I wrestled with many of the same struggles I'd had upon conversion—childhood trauma, gnawing loneliness, a struggle with alcohol, and unwanted sexual desires. This created a growing incongruence within. It felt like I had a choice to make: either change my behavior or change my theology. And by "change my theology," I really meant that I *needed* my theology to change so I wouldn't feel so much guilt about my struggles. I found changing my theology easier than changing my behavior. If I could just lighten up what I thought God had said in the Bible, I could stop being so hard on myself and the shame would be whisked away. These emotions were powerful. That teenage evangelical faith I'd first had was now on spin cycle. I had no language for it at the time—but I was in full-fledged deconstruction.

Around this time, I began experiencing some epiphanies around my evolving faith while beginning a PhD program in theology and starting a church in Portland the same year. Life was exciting during those years. I no longer took seminary classes. I now *taught* seminary classes. In the classroom, I relished leading graduate students into asking novel and exotic questions they'd never considered, like professors had done for me just a few years earlier. Mostly I loved how smart that provoking the questions made me feel. To this day, some of the most electric classroom experiences of mine were during those years when I gave extra space in the classroom to question and challenge traditional Christian beliefs.

I also discerned at that time a major shift in the student population of the seminaries where I taught. Students came to seminary less to learn theology and the Bible to serve their churches and more to dissect what they'd been taught in their churches. This was reflected in the fact that my course evaluations always seemed higher when I emphasized deconstruction in the classroom rather than construction. Whenever I took the time to articulate simple, historic, Christian doctrine, my evaluations fell flat. But when I challenged historic Christianity, the classes came alive. Then I noticed a shift within myself. For the first time, I began feeling uneasy about this insatiable hunger for deconstruction and critique within my students. Keep in mind, I was also a pastor. I wanted people to think through their faith. But I didn't want them to leave their faith. During this time, one of my closest friends finished seminary and left his Christian faith. The impact on me was devastating.

This was all compounded by the fact that so many of the people who had taught me how to follow Jesus, read my Bible, and serve the church as a sixteen-year-old no longer identified as a Christian. This includes my first Bible study leader, my first worship leader, and one of my first pastors.

I now began to see the dark side of deconstruction.

That was a major turning point for me, culminating in what I call "the" Bible study. During this time, I decided to lead a Bible study in our church on Exodus. During one of our first sessions, I decided to ask the class a provocative question: Did Moses really write this book? Can that be an important question to ask? Sure it can! But not always. The minute that question came out of my mouth I sensed something unsettling and nefarious in my gut. I wasn't raising this question because I wanted to serve the people in that Bible study. I raised the question because I was seeking to impress the group. I wanted the power of knowledge, of being able to hold my knowledge over Christians on the ground who simply wanted to follow Jesus. I wanted them to be as awed by me as I was by my seminary professors. The end result: I ended up spiritually wounding two young people in that group. I still regret that Bible study. I caused deep hurt—all because I wanted to appear smart, academic, and in the know.

Somewhere along the way, I came upon a writing by philosopher and theologian Simone Weil, who wrote, "People who are uprooted . . . hurl themselves in some form of activity necessarily designed to uproot, often by the most violent methods, those who are not yet uprooted, or only partly so. Whoever is uprooted himself uproots others. Whoever is rooted himself doesn't uproot others."[24] Weil's words hit the proverbial nail on the head. I'd needed to uproot others. The reason? I had been uprooted myself from what I'd been called to in that geometry class a decade and a half earlier. Hurt people hurt people. And uprooted people uproot people.

Things I Know Now

For ten years, I've been in reconstruction mode—of coming back to that old faith in a new way with a new set of lenses. I'm much less interested today in critiquing the faith than I am in actually having it. Today, I see so many around me deconstruct their faith—but with little humility or wisdom from those who have gone before them. There are some things I know now about deconstruction that I'd like to pass along.

I know now how important it is to distinguish my emotions from my theology. Can deconstruction be emotional? Even depressing? Can re-thinking beliefs be emotionally taxing? Without question! The by-product of doubt and deconstruction can easily lead to visceral emotional swings. There's room in the theological journey for emotions. We all have up days and down days in faith. What I've grown deeply wary of, however, are expressions of Christian faith that are no more than how we feel about God today. Jesus Christ is the same yesterday, today, and forever—whether I'm happy, sad, or perplexed about it. "Truth," the ever-astute Flannery O'Connor writes, "doesn't change according to my ability to stomach it emotionally."[25] I know now that emotions are central to the human experience. And that God is differentiated from my feelings.

I know now, also, that deconstruction can be a vital and life-giving part of following Jesus. I wouldn't undo my years of deconstruction for a moment. Many Christians like me, who accept historic Christian teachings, have good reason to be wary of and concerned for those deconstructing their faith. We have seen too many go too far in the deconstruction journey. But not all deconstruction leads to abandoned faith. There are many examples in Christian history of good and necessary deconstruction. The prophets of the Hebrew Bible, for one, deconstructed the pithy clichés of their day—using harsh words for those who lived by popular ethics rather than following Yahweh. They sought to deconstruct popular religion and hold God's people to true worship in the context of deceptive idolatry.

There's Martin Luther, whose deconstruction led to what we call Protestantism.[26] Standing at the door of a church with a hammer in his hand, he nailed his Ninety-Five Theses on the door of Wittenberg. He'd seen for too long the church's wanton abuse. He felt manipulated by religion for too long. He was fed up. Luther's critique of religious abuse eventually led to his German Bible being placed in the hands of the people. Protestantism, in essence, is a form of deconstructed Roman Catholicism—a movement within which I (and so many others) have had powerful encounters with the gospel of Jesus. The Russians have a word for people who ask too many questions: *pochemuchka*. Luther definitely embodied that word. Deconstruction *can* lead to a return to gospel truth, Scripture, and the original impulse of Christianity. I'm grateful Luther raised the questions.

Even Jesus Christ deconstructed the rigid interpretations of the Judaism of his own day. Matthew's Sermon on the Mount recounts Jesus standing against the religious interpretations prevalent in his time built on human tradition rather than on God's love, justice, and mercy. Critiquing religious codes and mores of his day, Jesus reinterpreted much of the biblical text with a refrain: "You have heard . . . but *I* say . . ." Jesus's deconstruction of religion upended all religious assumptions and reoriented everyone back to God's loving heart. Jesus deconstructed! And, by the Spirit, Jesus continues to deconstruct anything in the church today that goes contrary to his kingdom.[27]

Ecclesiastes puts it best: "There is a time for everything . . . a time to *tear down* and a time to *build*" (3:1, 3). There are times to tear down! Deconstruction is not bad in and of itself. Some forms of deconstruction have led to great life!

I know now, also, that deconstruction isn't the same thing as the rejection of Jesus or Christian truth. Quite the opposite. In walking with countless young people through their deconstruction process, I have seen that sometimes a rethought faith is the *only* way to keep faith alive. That brings us to an important vista: there's a fundamental difference between faith deconstruction and faith destruction. A healthy deconstruction of faith takes seriously the biblical command to "give careful thought to your ways" (Hag. 1:7) and "watch your life and doctrine closely" (1 Tim. 4:16). It is not only important—it is commanded—that we evaluate and refine what we believe about God and continually put it up to the sanctifying fire of the Holy Spirit and the pages of Scripture.

We are seeing a lot of people walk away from their faith right now. But I have a suspicion there's far more going on than meets the eye. This deconstruction and doubt could actually be a sign of emerging life. I think of it like this: My wife and I grow our own tomatoes. They're good. Proof-of-God good. When we have people over to our house, sometimes they won't eat the big, ripe, juicy heirlooms we picked twenty minutes earlier. They say they don't like tomatoes. Then I force them to try our tomatoes, which don't taste like the fake tomatoes you get from the grocery store. What I've learned is this: People don't hate tomatoes. People hate *fake* tomatoes. Truth is, maybe the "Christianity" so many in our culture today are rejecting isn't Christianity.[28] Often, they're rejecting false Christianity. They simply haven't tasted the real Jesus yet. Or they have tasted Jesus, and rigid religion has proven to be a poor substitute. Read Jesus and tell me he isn't worth following. Look at Christ and dare to say his way of life is not worth giving up everything to follow. I'm slowly beginning to believe that it isn't *true* Christianity that so many people are rejecting—although some are. More often, they are just doubting those things that could never bring them life.

Sometimes we're just "between idols."

Three

The Problem of "Freedom"

You Do You

A myriad of cultural, societal, and spiritual realities swirl beneath our age of deconstruction. Postwar philosophies—post-structuralism, post-modernism, and existential nihilism—set the stage for so much of our current reality. This is exacerbated by the church's struggle to formulate its identity in a fluid twenty-first-century world where instant communication, social media, and knowledge proliferation have given deconstruction a platform, common language, and shared experience. More than anywhere, deconstruction is embodied on the ground—in Instagram posts, Facebook updates, Bible studies, and just about every corner of the church.[1] The postwar West is rethinking the old "as is" doctrines, truths, and beliefs. What's left is a culture "haunted"[2] by Christianity—intrigued and inspired by its morals and dreams of justice while repulsed by and resentful of its absolutes, particulars, and ethical imperatives. Deconstruction isn't new. But the ways and means by which people are doing it has been lubricated by the ideas and engines of our cultural environment. We've all seen it. Or if not, we will soon.

In our first chapters, doubt and deconstruction were introduced as necessary parts of the theological journey. But to ignore how cultural forces have given rise to our deconstruction age would be foolhearted. Deconstruction isn't *just* undoing beliefs. Deconstruction and doubt can also be by-products of one's environment. Remember, it was Phil's physical move to Portland in chapter 1 that set the stage for his deconstruction experience. His new environment provoked new faith challenges. While there are undeniable spiritual and theological reasons behind deconstruction, there also remains a litany of environmental and cultural factors simultaneously playing into it. In this chapter, we will examine this relationship between deconstruction and our culture—particularly how expressive individualism, self-determination, and "freedom" have exacerbated it.

Before World War II, a Catholic priest named Adrian Van Kaam studied for the priesthood in the Netherlands. As the horrors of war began, Van Kaam found himself caught behind enemy lines as the Nazis commenced their unprovoked siege of Europe. Van Kaam spent the war obeying what he believed was God's call: supplying care and support to Jews who were experiencing systematic persecution, displacement, and murder. Van Kaam's harrowing stories of faithful discipleship continue to inspire many. When the war finally ended, he devoted the remainder of his life to psychology—particularly how psychology affects one's Christian formation. His writings (though admittedly dense and confusing) offer fascinating insights into how Christians think in relation to how they follow Jesus. In his book *Music of Eternity*, Van Kaam recounts the story of a volunteer nurse he'd encountered who cared for lepers. Van Kaam asks her some questions:

> I asked her if she *liked* what she was doing. She answered, "Liking is not the right word. . . . I feel appalled by the dirt, stench and disfiguration of the patients they carry in from the bush. Often, I feel like running away. But I stay for the love of God; I try to see Christ in their fractured bodies. This helps me to honor them with full attention in the midst of filth, groans, despair and death. In this sense, yes, I love my work, but I cannot as yet say that I *like* it."[3]

Around the time I read Van Kaam's account, I was delivering a series of lectures on Christian faithfulness and resiliency in the post-Christian

West. After one lecture, a student offhandedly commented, "Professor, if I'm honest, I don't *like* Christianity much anymore. Everyone seems to be running away from it. I'm struggling to find a reason to stay. Why should I stay?" Her statement landed awkwardly in the classroom—mostly a reflection of its brutal honesty. Searching within for some response, I struggled to locate a satisfying answer. Then Van Kaam's story of the woman who served lepers flashed before my mind. I ended class with a final question: "What if we were never called to *like* Jesus? What if we were called to follow him?"

How challenging it has become to faithfully follow Jesus in a *like* culture. Years of these interactions have revealed to me that students bring into the classroom a set of assumptions that are quite hostile to Christian faithfulness. How does one daily carry a cross in the context of a culture obsessed with chasing fame, likes, affirmation, and affluence? Sociologists have long described a litany of shifts in how Americans have identified with their faith following WWII. Robert Wuthnow's *After Heaven*, for one, noted a discernible shift in American spiritual beliefs since the 1950s, from obedience and submission to God to what he called "spiritual seeking."[4] This shift reflected something much broader than just a new way of thinking about authority. Robert Bellah's magisterial *Habits of the Heart* further unpacks how people in the modern world relate to their beliefs in vastly different ways than generations before them. Whereas Americans before the war hitched their beliefs to particular denominations, religions, or belief systems, postwar Americans now self-select their religious beliefs. Bellah calls this "expressive individualism." Long gone are the days when individuals would accept religious or spiritual beliefs as expressed through denominations, religions, or belief systems. Now we choose them ourselves. In this environment, individuals are encouraged to choose their own beliefs based almost exclusively on their desires, wants, and goals. Bellah points out that 80 percent of Americans affirm the statement, "An individual should arrive at his or her own religious beliefs independent of any church or synagogue."[5]

David Brooks—a columnist for the *New York Times*—illustrates how expressive individualism has become concretized within our education system. Sampling a series of college graduation speeches, Brooks discovers an ominously homogeneous echo resounding in the ears of graduates each graduation cycle:

> They are sent off into this world with [this] . . . theology ringing in their ears. If you sample some of the commencement addresses being broadcast on C-Span these days, you see that many graduates are told to: Follow *your* passion, chart *your* own course, march to the beat of *your* own drummer, follow *your* dreams and find *your*self. This is the litany of expressive individualism.[6]

And a powerful theology it has become. What we've been telling our graduates is exactly what we are getting in the marketplace, in the home, and in society. This is "freedom"—the expressive individualism that gives us the philosophical and societal permission to become everything we want to be.

As it relates to faith, expressive individualism greatly changes the ways many of my students relate to the Bible. In my Introduction to the Bible class, I give a yearly lecture on science and faith in which I discuss something called vasopressin. When two people have sexual intercourse, the brain releases a rush of chemicals called vasopressin. Those chemicals are the brain's way of helping people "bond" so that they might solidify nurturing, cooperative relationships that sustain life. However, when someone has multiple sexual partners, the vasopressin receptors in the brain stop working the way they should. They burn out. Neuroscience shows us that the human brain is wired for bonding and that promiscuity inhibits one's capacity for life-giving, long-term relationship. When I share this scientific tidbit with my students, they find it so interesting. Because it's neuroscience, it has authority in their minds. I mean, it's science, right! But when I show those same students a list of biblical texts that call us to sexual holiness within the boundaries of marital faithfulness, they look at me like I'm a time traveler visiting from the second century. When it's neuroscience, it's "interesting." When it's biblical truth, not so much. And these are students who identify as Christians.

In expressive individualism, the Bible becomes one of *many* means by which one arrives at meaning and truth. I finish my science and faith lecture by pointing to a number of findings the scientific community has historically articulated that the Bible has witnessed to for thousands of years. This all reveals a tremendous shift in how we relate to Christian faith in light of Western culture—a culture increasingly unhitched from religious truth entirely. Those described as the "nones" are known as such for their unwillingness to identify with *any* religious tradition. Yet, interestingly, the majority of these individuals self-identify as deeply spiritual people who long for transcendent meaning and desire to integrate spiritual practices into their lives. This obviously creates a tension. We've become religious "nones" but spiritual "somes"—picking from this or that spiritual stream tailor-made for our own tastes. This approach toward spirituality has been described as "theological eclecticism" by New Testament scholar Walter Liefeld:

> Eclecticism is a way of looking at religion and beliefs in which one is not committed to any one religious organization or belief system, but instead chooses aspects of these at will. Any teaching or ethical yardstick that is personally appealing is considered valid. Thus, many Catholics today accept traditional Catholic teachings about Mary but dismiss Catholic teachings on birth control. Religious authority and theological absolutism are dismissed.[7]

Theological eclecticism offers a framework for theological freedom. No one outside the self can dictate spiritual truth. Here the "thumbs-up" is emblematic of our privilege to surround ourselves with, commit ourselves to, and affirm and gravitate toward that which we emotionally like. Our capacity to self-select our own lifestyles, activities, relationships, and vocations is a distinctive mark of "free" Western capital societies— and has led to an ever-expanding world of expressive individualism where everyone can self-determine everything for themselves. This is "freedom." Our freedom of association allows us to self-determine the people and organizations with which we desire to affiliate. Our freedom of expression allows us to say what we want. Our freedom of choice permits us to embody our body as we wish. Taste is the new truth. You do you. I like, therefore, I am. You know the drill.

But this new norm has proven to be a profoundly inconsistent set of dogmas. On the one hand, we're required to be authentic and be ourselves. This demands that we abandon any restraint that might get in the way of that pursuit. Yet we are simultaneously required to conform to a set of values outside ourselves. If a person doesn't share the social vision, sexual ideology, or spiritual values of the prevailing, progressive worldview, they are written off as closed-minded, arrogant, and bigoted. How can authenticity to self and conformity to arbitrary external demands coincide? Indeed, these are confusing times. What is left is a judgment-free world that overtly condemns anyone daring to judge. Here, the most forbidden act is to forbid. This tension is best illustrated by the title of an article published in the *New York Times* by Adam Grant: "Unless You Are Oprah, 'Be Yourself' Is Terrible Advice." His point is that we want people to be themselves—so long as they are as good and moral as Oprah.

Still, wisdom invites balance. There are profound benefits to a world of freely chosen beliefs. Such freedom allows me to write this book. And this freedom permits you to buy it, read it, or burn it. We can't blithely ignore those past embarrassments when Christians force-baptized pagans, as Constantine and the conquistadors violently did. Nor should we look fondly upon those real places where nonbelief is forced—where claiming Christ's lordship or carrying a Bible could lead to the labor camps. Belief should never be compelled. Nor should nonbelief. The minute faith is forced, it is no longer faith. If we *are* to follow Jesus, we must do so as an act of the will and volition, not because we're compelled to. The freedom of our environment that allows us to deconstruct the Christian faith and walk away is the same freedom that gives room for the prisoner on death row to give their remaining life to the Lord their God and Maker. Spiritual freedom is not bad. Only false gods demand forced homage. If God is loved, he must be loved *willingly.*

We Serve No Sovereigns Here

History is important. Part of American identity is that our history entails throwing aside the reign of a distant king. A rebellion of British citizens against "taxation without representation" eventually would become what we know as the United States of America. America's formative identity was forged by rebellion. This history of rebellion *also* set into motion within just about every American a certain attitude, outlook, and perspective on life. America exists because it rejected external authority.

Years ago, I happened upon the story of John Guest. Guest was a well-known British evangelist and minister who came to America in the late 1960s to deliver a series of evangelistic talks. During this visit, Guest stopped at some of the earliest American colonial sites. Just outside Philadelphia, Guest entered a gift shop and encountered a host of signs showcasing the spirit of the early American revolution. "No taxation without representation." "Don't tread on me." Still, one particular sign caught Guest's attention: "We serve no sovereign here." Guest later reflected on that sign:

[That] sign stopped me in my tracks. I had left my native land and come across the Atlantic Ocean in response to a call, a vocation to be a minister of the gospel, to proclaim the kingdom of God. But on seeing this sign, I was filled with fear and consternation. I thought, "How can I possibly preach the kingdom of God to people who have a profound aversion to sovereignty?"[8]

Guest was onto something important. We *are* a nation who has rejected the very notion of the sovereign king who directs our affairs from afar. We rebelled. We protested. We dismantled. We deconstructed. We did away with anyone who told us what we must do.

Is it a stretch to suggest that our shared social and cultural history of throwing off external authority in the earthly realms has translated somehow to the spiritual realm? That King Henry is not the only one who should be dethroned? *All* kings should go. Guest's concern is clearer now than ever: *Is it possible for God to be understood by a people whose identity is defined by their aversion to sovereignty?* Walter Hooper, a friend of C. S. Lewis, echoed a similar concern in a foreword to one of Lewis's texts: "The contemporary preoccupation with 'individual freedom' and 'rights' has deceived so many of us into imagining that we can make up our *own* theology."[9] Hooper and Guest were discerning something afoot in our culture and at the heart of sinful humanity in rebellion against God. The very creatures who were made in God's own image have taken it into their hands to return the favor to God.

Does this mean freedom is wrong?[10] In no way! Freedom is God's creation. The fact that God's first sentence in the Bible begins with "Let there be . . ." reveals a God who makes things with freedom to become (Gen. 1:3). The word "let" is used some ten times in Genesis 1 alone. God *lets* animals teem. God *lets* Adam name animals. God *lets* creation flourish. God's first words to Adam are all the more revealing: "You are free . . ." (Gen. 2:16). This is a God who created freedom to love or rebel. Freedom is God's creation. What is the difference between our notion of freedom and God's? God's concept of freedom always occurs *within* obedience to God's covenant ways. Our Western, progressive, American concept of freedom has become freedom *from* any external established order. True obedience is possible only when we have the freedom to obey. And true freedom is possible only when we live within God's boundaries. Forced obedience is called coercion. Forced freedom is called America. God's ways are neither coerced nor libertine.

That brings us to deconstruction. I wonder if we now deconstruct Christianity simply because we don't *like* it anymore—it doesn't fit our preferences, wants, or goals. But this is our fatal error. We're called to follow Jesus, not like him.[11] This truth is both liberating and painful. To be a Christian is to receive the gospel message that has been faithfully guarded and passed down for two thousand years—often at the cost of the lives of those who bore it. This faith will inevitably present every person and every culture with realities and truths that it will not find sensible. Are we called to like the ways of Jesus? Or follow them?

Too often we will believe the things of God witnessed to in Scripture as long as they fit within the parameters of our sensibilities. We'll have faith in Jesus so long as that faith gives us what we want. Believing in Jesus is different than liking him. I don't like following Jesus. I don't like carrying a cross. I don't like hell. In fact, I *hate* hell. But I believe in hell because Jesus believed in hell. Jesus never tells me I have to like it. You know why? Because Jesus doesn't like hell. He hates it. And he doesn't get off on anyone going there. In fact, the people who like hell are the problem. They probably have someone in mind they wish were there.

Deconstruction as Privilege

The impulse to create gods in our own image is a perennial issue in history. The author of 2 Kings describes how every nation "made its own gods . . . and set them up in the shrines" (2 Kings 17:29). In that old world, each tribe forged its own god; each city had its own temple to its own idol; each family had its own religion. *You do you.* Nothing is new under the sun. As our new world returns to the ways of the old world, it finds at its fingerprints speed and power that the old world could only have dreamed of. As I've tried to articulate, there are acts of deconstruction that are ardent attempts at pursuing truth, goodness, and what is right. But there remains a darker form of deconstruction rising to the surface—an insidious deconstruction desiring not truth but power and control.

Thomas Jefferson—a framer of the US Constitution—professed a form of Christian faith known as Deism. Like many of his contemporaries, Jefferson adored the Jesus of morality, justice, and ethics but believed morality was the sole domain in which Jesus could have import. Jefferson deeply resented all the Bible's miracles, supernaturalism, and witness to Christ's divinity, which offended his European, Enlightenment sensibilities. Jefferson embraced the morality of Jesus while rejecting his supernatural divinity. Housed in the Smithsonian Institute in Washington, DC, is a lasting witness to his worldview—Jefferson's actual Bible. Perusing the pages of Jefferson's Bible, one discovers whole sections—those referencing miracles, Christ's claims of deity, and resurrection—cut out with scissors. Gone. What remained were the parts of Jesus's teaching and ministry that fit within his European sensibilities. Jesus was useful for Jefferson minus the "superstitious" miracles, claims to divinity, demons, and physical resurrection.

This same approach of editing the Bible was evidenced by slave owners around the same time. American slave owners liked portions of Scripture, notably how the Bible birthed hope and resilience among the slaves, in turn keeping them hard at work. But slave owners naturally rejected other portions of Scripture—like its call for slaves to be freed. Slave owners wanted to keep these parts of the Bible hidden from the slaves. This put slave owners in a tricky spot—they wanted the slaves to be spiritually inspired enough to have hope to keep up their work, but they didn't want the slaves to catch a vision for their own freedom. To alleviate this conundrum, slave owners edited a version of the Bible. Their version conveniently removed any verse hinting at freedom for slaves. This included the entire book of Exodus. These edited Bibles were called "slave Bibles."

Both Jefferson and the slave owners peddled their own version of a deconstructed Bible with its deconstructed faith. Now, I've never seen anyone take actual scissors to whole sections of the Bible they didn't like. But we cut out parts of the Bible all the time, emotionally—and culturally. Even intellectually and exegetically and spiritually. We've become adept at cutting out those parts of God's revelation that don't fit our modern sensibilities and convictions—or, worse yet, those parts that threaten our power and privilege and false sense of security. The slaves needed the *whole* Bible. Not parts of the Bible. And so did the slave owners. They needed to be confronted by God the way Pharaoh was confronted by God. Were a slave to read the whole Bible, they would find a God who not only wanted them to have hope but was actually fighting on their behalf for their freedom! The *whole* revelation of God was needed. Had Jefferson and the slave owners actually received the whole Bible as truth, perhaps they wouldn't have passed along a version of truth that protected them from God's judgment.

What is needed is the whole Bible for the whole world. Have you ever noticed God's word to Adam right after the woman was made? "That is why a man leaves his father and mother and is united to his wife" (Gen. 2:24). That's an odd statement to give to someone who had neither a father nor a mother. Adam was parentless. God said this not for Adam's sake but for the sake of everyone who would come after Adam. God's revelation to us isn't always for us directly. Sometimes what God has said is for *others* through us. This is why it is imperative we don't receive or pass along a fractured Bible. Jesus tells his disciples something similar: "Go and make disciples of all nations, . . . teaching them to obey *everything* I have commanded you" (Matt. 28:19–20). Jesus was telling the disciples to pass along all he had said. Not just the parts that prop up our current ways of living.

The worst forms of deconstruction are those that pass along a form of Christianity that fits our privilege, power, or current experiences. We pass along a version of faith that reflects our sensibilities more than God's heart. But the human soul needs all of God's revelation and all of the Bible—not the parts that conveniently fit—or else we will subtly massage our values into Scripture rather than let its values shape us.[12] We're all complicit in this. We all, like Jefferson, selectively slice out the parts of Scripture we find offensive to our culture, sensibilities, and time. But the big problem with this deconstructed gospel is that it lacks the message others may so desperately need. And this includes the very messages we need to be confronted by. Whenever we oppress the Bible's message, we end up oppressing others. This, in turn, unhinges our trust in what God has said and places it back in ourselves. To paraphrase Augustine, if we believe what we like in the Gospels, and reject what we don't like, it is not the gospel we believe, but ourselves.[13]

This is a critical point for students who come into my classes who reject the Bible because they think it endorses slavery. I do a whole lecture on Jefferson and the slave Bibles. Expectedly, I have a few students each year claim they can't trust the Bible because it was used to perpetuate slavery. Then I show them the hymns of the slaves. Guess what they reveal? Hymn after hymn filled with promises of freedom from Scripture. The slaves' hope in God and freedom rested on the Bible—that same book used by slave owners to perpetuate their evil. One twisted the Bible for evil. The other found hope and freedom within.

Each semester I propose the same thing: the real tool of oppression was a deconstructed, redacted, and edited Bible. The actual Bible was a tool for freedom. The actual Bible gave endless hope to the slaves. To deconstruct the Bible would be to rob the slaves of the only hope they had. The minute we say that the Bible is wrong, we better be prepared to go back and cut out everything that Martin Luther King Jr. said and where he found his entire hope. The Bible isn't the problem. We are the problem. You can imagine God's anger.[14] We need to return to the actual whole Bible and reject our deconstructed versions of the Bible that preach half the truth. I tell my students: the institution of slavery didn't end because people stopped reading the Bible. The institution of slavery started to end because people finally started reading the whole Bible.[15]

Somewhere along the winding road of church history we stopped reading the whole Bible for the whole world. Today, conservatives turn a blind eye to those parts of the Bible dealing with God's heart for social change, about turning swords into plowshares, about the love and care of creation, about God's heart for the refugee—and Jesus himself being a refugee! All the while progressives cover their ears to those parts of the Bible dealing with the inherent value of *every* life (born *and* unborn), its consistent themes of sexual purity and holiness, personal repentance, and evangelism. Shocking: both sides ignore the parts they aren't doing. But what if we let the *whole* Bible speak? If I—a white Christian male—were to take elements of someone else's culture and use them for my own purposes, they would call it "cultural appropriation." But if I take the ancient writings of the Bible and change them to fit my purposes with no regard for the intent with which they were written, they call me "enlightened" and "evolved." How could this be?

Deconstructing Christianity can be, more than anything else, a sign of our privilege. Consider the story of John Mbiti—an African Christian who was known to be able to heal. Mbiti was one of the first African pastors to travel to Europe and earn a doctorate in theology. Almost ten years later Mbiti returned to Africa after his European education. But he came back different. Mbiti had been taught by the Europeans that all that supernatural, miraculous stuff was nothing more than myth and superstition. Mbiti had become "enlightened" by Europe. It was said that when Mbiti returned, he no longer had the power he once had.

He no longer prayed for healing. The people reportedly said to Mbiti, "What is the use of studying in Europe? Before you could heal people; now you can't."[16]

We can be enlightened, or we can heal. We can't do both.

At the tail end of my deconstruction journey, I visited an African Muslim nation on a cultural exchange. When we arrived, our team was told that there were only twenty-five known Christians in the city of one million where we were staying. Our hosts told us that these radical Christians— who experienced extreme poverty, persecution, and social shaming for following Jesus—shared one Bible and a broken guitar and met secretly under cover of night. With their half-broken guitar, they sang simple songs to Jesus and loved one another, giving their lives for the gospel.

As a leader on the trip, I asked if we could meet these underground African Christians. I was so excited to see people loving God in their element. I was grieved when they told us we couldn't meet with them. Their reason was simple: they didn't want our consumerist, America-centric, Enlightenment faith to rub off on the African Christians. Our form of faith, they told us, was toxic for African Christians. They didn't want our Enlightenment to rub off on them.

That utterly broke me. That night, under the dark of the Tunisian sky, I lay there thinking about the twenty-five Christians who were awake, praying, hoping, reading, and singing quietly. Their hope was in Jesus. Nothing else.

That experience ruined me. All my critiques and challenges to Christianity were actually the enemy of those Christians in Africa. I did not come home the same. I found myself back in the seminary classroom where we'd been philosophizing about all our interesting "critiques" of the problematic elements of Christianity and the Bible. But I couldn't return to the same ways. I couldn't forget those twenty-five Christians who were literally *dying* so they could gather and read the very book I was being paid to deconstruct in the classroom.

I now believe that the kind of deconstructed Christianity the West is intoxicated with is the enemy of the poor, the enemy of the Christian on the ground, the enemy of those Christians singing quietly under the North

Africa sky. Jesus is their only hope. I weep thinking about those African Christians they never let me meet. I don't weep for them. I weep for me. I had forgotten the simple heart of Jesus. I had become a man who could critique everything wrong with Christianity. But I couldn't heal anymore. How could I say I loved the poor when I was trying to educate people out of the faith of the actual poor? If I loved the poor, I probably would have stopped trying to educate them to become more "enlightened" like me.

Lord, have mercy.

Just about every week now, I see another Facebook or Instagram deconstruction confession—one more young, white, progressive Westerner undoing or deconstructing their faith. It used to kill me seeing these. But I have a broader vision now because I've encountered the African Christians and their love for Jesus. And for every millennial, affluent, white college student who is choosing to deconstruct their Christian faith, there are five nonwhite people with less privilege in this world who are finding in the Bible the greatest message one could ever imagine.[17] This is the book and the faith of the poor. This is the book for the lost. This is the book for the hopeless. Maybe Jesus was right that it's nearly impossible for a rich person to enter the kingdom of heaven. God is coming to those who actually need him.

Jesus, heal us of our enlightenment.

Loving the God Who *Is*

God existed before us. And God will exist after us. The human life is meant to be a journey of learning how to love and embrace the God who is, not the God we wish he was. We often see "freedom" as the freedom to give ourselves our own story. But this way of thinking—that we can construct our own meaning—wrongheadedly conceives that there is no one beyond our existence who gives us a story. The core message of the Bible is that each part of creation, God's creation, is part of God's story. But we live as though we get to make up our own story. This is the heresy, the sin, the duplicity of our current way of thinking. At the end of the day, we have believed the lie that we get to create our own story. They call this *modernism*—the concept that there is no story and that our task is to come up with our own. Stanley Hauerwas writes, "We live at a time, you may call it modern . . . when we believe we should have no story, except the story we chose when we had no story. . . . We call this freedom."[18] Freedom, in the insanity that is modernism, is our ability to self-select our own story apart from the One who invented the very genre of story.

Never stop asking questions. The questions are good! But we should stop thinking that our questions can bring about a different God. Repentance is waking up to the fact that we don't get to love the God we *want*. True worship is loving the God who *is*.[19]

Now I can see, in some small way, what we mean when we say, "I could never believe in a God who . . ." Fill in the blank. That is our way of saying we'll love God as long as he's everything we like. At what point did we begin to think our opinions actually mattered? What we're really saying is that God is only worthy of our love and devotion so long as he believes, thinks, and is what *I* want him to believe, think, and be. God doesn't fit himself into my expectations: God is God. In the words of Paul, "Who are you, a human being, to talk back to God?" (Rom. 9:20).

God is God despite our beliefs about him. As William Alfred once said, "People who tell me there is no God are like a six-year-old boy saying there is no such thing as passionate love—they just haven't experienced it."[20] Just because we don't believe doesn't mean it isn't true. And so we must begin with a desire for the God who *is*. Do we want that God? Or do we want our own creation that will say what we wish he'd say?

We know we're worshiping God when our beliefs about God are subject to God. The sign of idolatry is when our beliefs have no room for God. That was the sin of the Pharisees: they had all the right theology with zero room for Jesus. The sign of true humility is that our faith can be broken around who God actually is, and not just who we want God to be. What a humbling thought—that before the living God we are all wrong. Every last one of us. Paul put it another way: "Let God be true, and every human being a liar" (Rom. 3:4). Every human includes me and you.

We won't be judged on whether we *liked* the Truth. We'll be judged on whether we followed him.

PART 2

FOLLOWING JESUS THROUGH DECONSTRUCTION AND DOUBT

Every single thing that Jesus taught us to do was something he had put into daily practice in circumstances just like ours.

—Dallas Willard, *The Great Omission*

Four

Knowing the Whole Self

The Forgotten Self

After exploring the experiences of doubt and deconstruction, in this second part of the book we turn our attention to practice—*how* can one go through doubt without losing faith? In this second part, we will examine eight core practices that can spiritually form the person walking in these experiences.

We begin with a story. There once was a theologian who, for twenty-five years, gave his life to studying God. His success was widely noted—he traveled to theological conferences, wrote in prestigious journals, and was admired by his peers in the academy. Then a personal crisis shattered his career. After losing his marriage and his prized teaching post, he endured the darkest crisis of faith one could imagine. Sitting in the rubble of life, he did something he'd never done before: he turned his attention from studying theology to studying himself through counseling, spiritual direction, silence, solitude, and group therapy. Waves of revelation ensued. He expressed varying levels of shock as he learned about the person he had become, and how difficult it must have been to be his spouse. While his nuanced knowledge of the doctrine of the Trinity and theories of atonement paved paths of success in theology, his lack of self-knowledge led to layers of narcissistic self-centeredness that eventually brought his marriage to a sudden end. Self-discovery revealed that his ardent study of God had actually become an unconscious escape from dealing with his own issues. He was transfixed by the irony: his obsession with God had served as an escape from dealing with himself.

Do we know ourselves?

For Christians, pursuing knowledge of God is standard fare. The Christian *should* seek God, growing in knowledge of his character. We do this part well. But rarer are Christians who passionately pursue a working knowledge of the self. It is often only after a personal crisis, failure, or loss of meaning that we begin the journey inward to learn about ourselves. But what if knowledge of the self was not an enemy of the knowledge of God? What if knowledge of our whole selves was part of our knowledge of the holy?[1]

Part of loving God is knowing ourselves as God's handiwork. We naturally enjoy being distracted by things outside ourselves. But constant external stimuli can create an internal deficit. Despite the fact that we can study the stars, map the galaxy, and peer into the endless face of the universe up above, we still know next to nothing of the human heart within. We go through so much of our lives ignorant of ourselves. Even the marketplace reveals this self-knowledge deficit. The emergence of— and seeming intoxication with—new technological options for mapping one's genealogy and ancestry are ubiquitous. Not only can we now discover our ancestry through the mail, we also have the Enneagram, StrengthsFinder, and a myriad of other methods to learn about who we are. One wonders if our obsession with genealogy, ancestry, and personality tests is symptomatic of a festering disease in the modern soul: we don't know who we are or where we come from.

When self-knowledge is ignored, the results can be devastating. Consider that famous story of the little boy who wanted to become an artist. His desire to be a creative is evidenced by the vast collection of drawings and sketches later found from his earliest years—many of which we have to this day. Despite the fact that his hard, disciplinary father wished him not to, the boy applied to the local art institute in Vienna to become an artist. His pursuit was met with great disappointment. While many of his own friends had been accepted, he was not. The rejection letter from the institute's directors said it all: his work was (in their words) "unsatisfactory." The combination of his father's cold demeanor with the message of being "unsatisfactory" led to a deep, seething anger that was never really dealt with. The boy would later write in his most widely read book that his hatred within had been born during that season of rejection in Vienna. Rejection shaped his entire life. And it reshaped the entire world. Of course, it is sobering to find out why Adolf Hitler could have hated so much. That kind of hatred doesn't come from nowhere. It's not unlikely that the death of millions of Jews under Hitler's tyrannical reign was the result of a man who never worked through his childhood pain.[2] Because of deep, lingering, unattended childhood wounds—in the words of Steven Pressfield—"it was easier for Hitler to start World War II than it was to face a blank square of canvas."[3] How true we know it to be: hurt people really can hurt people. Imagine what the world might look like today had Hitler undergone the inward journey of self-knowledge.

In mental health professions, increased attention has been given to the restorative power of self-knowledge for those who've endured trauma. Trauma, it is increasingly found, cannot be mended without the difficult work of integrating the very sources of pain into the life of the one traumatized. In his visceral account *What It Is Like to Go to War*, Karl Marlantes illustrates how remembering and self-knowledge have the potential to bring healing to the trauma, pain, and violence of the battlefield:

> The road to recovery requires learning to tell the truth, even if that truth is brutally painful. I'd never been able to tell anyone what was going on inside. So, I forced these images back, away, for years. I began [however] to reintegrate that split-off part of my experience.... Then, out came this overwhelming sadness and healing. Integrating the feelings of sadness, rage, or all of the above with the action should be standard operating procedure for all soldiers who have killed face-to-face. It requires no sophisticated psychological training.[4]

My colleagues in the counseling industry remind me that one of the most important actions someone can undertake who desires emotional healing is to intentionally (under the guidance of trained professionals) *remember* the trauma and pain—allowing it to become part of the individual's consciousness. Time itself doesn't heal. A part of healing can actually demand revisiting and replaying the pain.[5] Self-knowledge can even play a key role in spiritual conversion as well. It was only when C. S. Lewis began to pay attention to his heart—he called them "longings" for something he did not have—that he was led to the awareness of his deep longing for God.[6] This eventually blossomed into his conversion to Christianity.

What if knowing ourselves wasn't just about being healthy? What if it also included learning about God? "The glory of God is man fully alive," once wrote Irenaeus. Only when we find ourselves in him can we come alive. In his devotional classic *Imitation of Christ*, Thomas à Kempis sums up the importance of self-knowledge: "A humble understanding of yourself is a surer path to God than the deep inquiry into knowledge."[7] Imagine a world where Hitler took time to deal with childhood hurts. Or imagine a world where the Narnia series was never written because Lewis didn't listen to his longings. As Paul writes in Romans 2:12–15, God's reality and truth is "written" on the hearts of everyone in both conscience and intuition. Because our hearts and minds were formed by the living God, something of God can be learned by looking at what he made.

The Double Knowledge of God

Christians can often have a knee-jerk reaction against self-knowledge, a discomfort birthed from shame and guilt. If we give too much attention to the self, won't we ignore God? But this false dichotomy is found nowhere in Scripture. It also makes God sound like he's insecure and needy for attention. We must remember the invitation of Jesus: "Love the Lord your God with all your heart and with all your soul and with all your mind and with all your strength" (Mark 12:30). To love God with our actual heart, mind, soul, and strength means we must at least know about the very things with which we are loving God. We can't know how to love God with our mind and our strength until we understand what our mind and our strength actually are.

A lack of self-knowledge can construct false barriers between us and God. For several years, I pastored a young woman who did not identify as a Christian even while desiring to become one. At our preliminary coffee appointment, she expressed agitation and discomfort whenever I said the name Jesus. She believed in God. But the name Jesus stirred discomfort within her. Her rationale was simple: if God had a specific name, then that implied other religions must not be true. Our discussion eventually unearthed fears she had regarding her relationship with her parents, whom she loved deeply. She knew that if she became a Christian, naming God would be interpreted as a subtle slight against her parents' religious beliefs. This awareness of her fears actually led to her conversion to Christianity. In her relationship to God, she was, to borrow language from Paul, an enemy in her own mind (Col. 1:21). She began to identify that her discomfort with Jesus had nothing to do with his claims. She was simply afraid of hurting someone's feelings. She learned that there were ways to discuss her new faith in loving and nonjudgmental ways.

A lack of self-knowledge can also cause us to seek God for the wrong reasons. Dietrich Bonhoeffer, who led the Confessing Church during World War II, once confessed to a friend during one particular season that he was doing it all for the wrong reasons. His pursuit of the knowledge of God became a love for other things—to gain power, prestige, and advantage. His study of God, he suggests, was not actually a loving pursuit of God but a subtle self-preoccupation. And therein lay the irony. Bonhoeffer soon wrote a great deal against the use of theology for personal gain, which he concluded should never be used to further one's career. Theology must be in love of God and his people. Awakening to this, he writes, "I discovered the Bible. . . . I had often preached, I had seen a great deal of the church, spoken and preached about it—but I had not yet become a Christian."[8] Awakening to his own duplicity helped Bonhoeffer encounter God afresh.

The path of radical self-honesty—of naming truth as it is—is part of Christ's work in our lives. Truth is the name of his game. Yet radical honesty can often be exemplified more by those outside the church. Thomas Nagel, for example, is perhaps one of the most outspoken atheists in academia. In recent years, however, a deep honesty and self-awareness has begun to rise to the surface of his writings:

> I *want* atheism to be true, and I am made uneasy by the fact that some of the most intelligent and well-informed people I know are religious believers. It isn't just that I don't believe in God and, naturally, hope that I'm right in my belief. It's that I hope there is no God! I don't want there to be a God; I don't want the universe to be like that. My guess is that this cosmic authority problem is not a rare condition. I am curious . . . whether there is anyone who is genuinely indifferent as to whether there is a God.[9]

Nagel's honesty is exemplar. For Nagel, he admits that he *wants* there to be no God. This challenges me as a Christian. What things do I believe that are more about my wants than about the reality of God? I can't help but believe that Nagel's radical honesty and truth-telling will eventually lead him through the empty tomb to the God of truth.

Throughout church history there exists a long-standing theological tradition called *duplex cognitio Dei*, or the "double knowledge of God," defined as the knowledge of God as a means to understanding the self. We see this written into the Psalms, for example. In Psalm 139, the author writes, "Search me, God, and know my heart; test me and know my anxious thoughts. See if there is any offensive way in me, and lead me in the way everlasting" (vv. 23–24). David's plea before the Lord is to be known—nothing less. Many of the psalms reveal David's deep self-knowledge of his own brokenness, anxieties, depression, shortcomings, and limits. Our own unwillingness to follow Jesus to the knowledge of self is part of Jesus's warning of judgment in Matthew's Gospel: "Many will say to me on that day, 'Lord, Lord, did we not prophesy in your name and in your name drive out demons and in your name perform many miracles?' Then I will tell them plainly, 'I never *knew* you. Away from me, you evildoers'" (Matt. 7:22–23). It wasn't that Jesus didn't know *about* them. Instead, Jesus is saying that there was no intimacy with them. God knows about everyone, but God does not force intimacy. Jesus seems to reveal here that those who lack intimacy with God will continue to experience that separation after death. Paul's command to Timothy affirms all this—"Watch *your life* and doctrine closely" (1 Tim. 4:16). Good doctrine and self-knowledge are not mutually exclusive.

Some of the most important theologians and thinkers in Christian history have witnessed to this particular theology. In the first paragraph of *Institutes*, John Calvin writes that "without knowledge of self, there is no knowledge of God and without knowledge of God there is no knowledge of self."[10] Far before Calvin, Augustine writes in what is considered to be the first autobiography in Western history, *Confessions*, "Grant Lord that I might know myself, that I might know thee."[11] Even Thomas Aquinas, in *Summa Theologiae*, discusses how doctrine has as much to do with humans as it does with God: "Sacred doctrine is not concerned with God and the creatures equally. It is concerned with God fundamentally and with the creatures insofar as they relate to God as their beginning or end."[12] Thomas Merton beautifully blends together knowing God and self: "There is only one problem on which all my existence, my peace, and my happiness depend: to discover myself in discovering God. If I find Him, I will find myself and if I find my true self, I will find Him."[13]

Of course, self-knowledge is not an invitation to be obsessed with the self. As the rise of "selfie deaths" continues—deaths caught on camera as the distracted person snaps a photo of themselves—we must be reticent about outlooks of life that are narcissistically intoxicated with the self. Self-knowledge is not self-obsession. In self-obsession, we become like Eve in *Paradise Lost* who falls in love with herself as she looks at her own face in the reflection of a clear lake.[14] Self-obsession is not our point or goal. To borrow from the great theologian Hans Urs von Balthasar, we cannot truly see ourselves until we see ourselves in light of God's story. If we don't enter the *theo*-drama (God's story), we will always be an *ego*-drama (self-centered story).[15] A true knowledge of self is impossible *without* a true knowledge of the Creator.

In *Knowing God*, J. I. Packer illuminates one of the central problems of contemporary culture. Packer argues, "Christian minds have been confused by the modern skepticism."[16] That is, the confusion of our time is largely the result of our unwillingness to enter into intimacy and knowledge about God's character and nature. He further adds, "The [modern] spirit . . . spawns great thoughts of man and leaves room for only small thoughts of God."[17] The spirit of our age would love to see Christians obsessed with the self, with high views of the self and no view of God. That is not what we are after. What we need is not self-centered Christianity where God becomes a part of our story. We need an approach to spiritual formation that sees Christ as the center, in whose story we are a footnote.

John's Gospel beautifully teases this connection between self-knowledge and the love of God. Throughout his Gospel, the disciple John often inserts himself into the narrative of Jesus. John is there at many of the miracles, the transfiguration, the empty tomb, the Sea of Galilee before the ascension of Jesus. Yet, interestingly, John never gives us his real name in his Gospel. Rather, John gives us his nickname: "the disciple whom Jesus loved." It is comical that none of the other Gospel writers give John that same nickname, as if to say, "We had a nickname for him, but that definitely wasn't it!" John includes himself in his own story of Jesus. But he does so with a deep sense of self-knowledge. Self-knowledge can easily slip into self-obsession when *we* are the center of the story. John embodies the right approach. He knows himself only in light of the love of Jesus.

Projection

One of the gifts of growing in self-knowledge is awakening to *why* we make certain theological decisions. One story illustrates this. During a season when I was struggling personally, a trusted colleague started listening to my sermons online. He was considerably older (and more conservative) than me at the time. I trusted his voice. After listening to some of my sermons, he asked to meet with me. He complimented me on how much I preached on grace. I preached grace. A lot. Then my friend lovingly pointed out that grace was *all* I preached on. He asked me when I would start teaching on discipleship, holiness, sanctification, repentance, and bending one's life around God's call. I did grace really well. But sanctification not so much. It clicked. I knew what was going on. I had been preaching to others what I myself was most in need of. I was preaching "to save myself," in the words of Charles Spurgeon.[18] My struggle with sin was keeping me from ever talking about things like repentance, holiness, and discipleship. I couldn't preach those things because I wasn't doing them. I needed the Bible to arrange itself around my experience, not the other way around.

Self-knowledge is critical because we often make theological decisions based on where we are and what we are walking through. Scripture witnesses to this dynamic. It was only after my friend lovingly confronted me on my preaching that Hosea 5:4 made sense: "Their deeds do not permit them to return to their God." Our lives, our sin, our struggles actually cause us to rebel against God. There is an interesting line in the Old Testament that rarely gets attention: "To the pure you show yourself pure, but to the devious you show yourself shrewd" (Ps. 18:26). We often see God not as God is but as *we* are. If we live pure, good, righteous, holy, and loving lives, we will see God as pure, good, righteous, holy, and loving. But if we live selfish and devious lives, we will see God as selfish and devious. The theological truth is profoundly important for our conversation: who we are directly affects and informs the way we see God. In our sin, we start thinking God is like us. The psalmist records God's lament regarding this: "You thought I was exactly like you" (Ps. 50:21).

Counselors call this "projection." Sometimes we project ourselves onto others. For instance, when Israel is enslaved by Pharaoh, God tells Moses to confront Pharaoh about allowing God's people to worship God in the desert. Time and again, Pharaoh initially agrees but later recants. At one point, Pharaoh becomes so infuriated with the Israelites' request for freedom that he cries out, "Lazy, that's what you are—lazy!" (Exod. 5:17). We're left wondering how Pharaoh could tell the slaves that *they* were lazy. That is projection. It is the slave owner telling the slaves *they* aren't working hard enough.

We can also project ourselves onto God. Rather than loving the holy God for who God is, we see him as we see ourselves. Our problems with God probably have less to do with God than they do with our problems with ourselves. In his book *The Way of Paradox*, Cyprian Smith addresses how we often cannot rightly relate to God because we project our personal struggles and difficulties onto him: "A transcendent God is one who cannot be pinned down, controlled, or predicted. To cast oneself into the transcendent God is to cast oneself into the unknown. Many of our thoughts about God are projections. They say more about ourselves than they do God because they are distorted by our personal needs and our emotions and it takes time for all of that to be refined."[19]

These projections that we put onto God interfere with our intimacy with God. Rather than simply name the fact that we are not living as God has invited us to live, we project other rationale for our doubt and deconstruction. Tony Campolo used to tell a story when he taught sociology at a major university. As an outspoken Christian on campus, he was sought by one student who wanted to discuss his faith. The young man sits down and tells him that, after about six months of being at the school, he is having an existential crisis and no longer knows if he believes in God or the Bible. Without skipping a beat, and feeling led by the Spirit, Campolo asks this young man, "When did you start sleeping with your girlfriend?" The young man is surprised and wonders out loud how that could have anything to do with his existential crisis. But then he confesses: he had started sleeping with his girlfriend some two months before his faith crisis. Campolo says that what we mean by "faith crisis" is really just our doing something that does not align with God's ways.[20]

This isn't always the case. But our "faith crisis" might simply be our projections onto God of our own struggles—or even our sin. Rather than name our own unfaithfulness, we say God is unfaithful. Knowing ourselves allows us to understand *why* we have such a difficult time with the Bible and God. In the end, it is easier to try to change God and the

Bible than to change our lives. Usually we go for the more convenient option. It is always going to be easier to bend the ways of God around our lives than to bend our lives around the ways of God.

The Heart of the Question

Self-knowledge unearths so much about us—our experiences, goals, motivations, and questions we have about God. Teachers must learn early on the difference between a student's question and the *heart* behind the question. Throughout his earthly ministry, Jesus often refused to answer questions. We get a glimpse of why in Luke 20:19–26 when a group of teachers approach Jesus requesting an answer as to whether they should give taxes to the Roman Empire. Jesus gives an answer, but not to the question they asked. Luke says their question was dishonest— "they hoped to *catch Jesus* in something he said" (20:20). They weren't after truth. They were trying to trap. Any teacher today could learn from the master. Like Lord Peter Whimsey in Dorothy Sayers's *Whose Body?*, Jesus was a master at answering the thought, not the words.[21]

The heart of our question changes the response we'll get. Jesus will lovingly make space for our honest questions. But not for our critical skepticism, nor dishonest questions or attempts to trap him. The same goes with Scripture. The Bible can handle our integrous, honest, difficult questions birthed out of a true and right desire to discover truth. But the minute we approach the Bible to trap it, we won't find what we are looking for. In these moments, we find no answers that will satisfy. God won't be put to the test. In the wise reflections of C. S. Lewis in his *A Grief Observed*, "Can a mortal ask questions which God finds unanswerable? Quite easily, I should think. All non-sense questions are unanswerable. How many hours are there in a mile? Is yellow square or round? Probably half the questions we ask—half our great theological and metaphysical problems—are like that."[22]

Martin Luther—when asked by a student what God was doing on the eighth day—is reported to have answered that God was creating hell for people who ask silly questions.

Our heart's posture changes the response. Consider that moment in the New Testament when Jesus hears of Lazarus's death. After reaching Bethany, Jesus is confronted by Lazarus's two sisters—Martha and Mary. Martha's confrontation just outside the city is rife with frustration: "Lord, if you had been here, my brother would not have died" (John 11:21). Jesus entirely sidesteps her critique: "Your brother will rise again" (v. 23). Then comes Mary with the exact same word-for-word confrontation: "Lord, if you had been here, my brother would not have died." Mary's and Martha's words are the same. Yet, astonishingly, Jesus doesn't sidestep Mary's response. He receives her words tenderly. Then Jesus weeps. Both sisters offer the same words. Yet only one receives a word of comfort. While Martha may have been asking the same question as Mary, her question was birthed not out of love and compassion but from a compulsive sense of obligation for what Jesus should have done.

We often see Jesus for who *we* are rather than for who he is. We may be asking an altogether sensible question on the surface but below rages subterranean anger or resentment. What may appear on the surface to be a genuine search for the truth through the deconstruction experience is really just at its core our deep desire to finally get to do whatever we want with our lives. To be free. To not have constraints. To live as we really want to live.

Everyone in the Lazarus story critiques Jesus. The disciples question his travel plans to Bethany. The sisters both ask Jesus deep existential questions in their loss. And the religious leaders critique him for his actions. *Everyone has some critique of Jesus.* Except for one person: Lazarus! We can find all the questions and critiques for Jesus and his church we want to find. We will find the dirt we are looking for. There will likely be no end to our Western, secular, post-Christian critiques of Jesus, the Bible, and the church. But the ones who have no critiques are the ones who are finding resurrection life—the broken, the hurting, the despised. Our deconstruction culture has less to do with who Jesus is than with the kind of people we have become. It isn't always about him. Sometimes it is more about us.

Go to Thyself

Questions in our relationship with God can be good. In Genesis 1–3, we hear God's very first words to Adam and Eve after their disobedience. Approaching them hiding in the trees, God says, "Where are you?" (Gen. 3:9). Likewise, in the New Testament, the first story of Jesus's childhood tells of him lost in the temple as his parents look for him. When they find him, Jesus's first words are a question: "Why were you searching for me?" (Luke 2:49). These questions are not happenstance. The Bible is not primarily a record of God's answers to people's questions. First and foremost, the Bible is a record of how humans respond to God's divine questions.

Later on, God comes to a man named Abram in Genesis 12 and invites him to follow him into the promised land. God tells Abram: *lekh lekha*. Literally, this means "go to thyself." God is taking Abram on a journey. God wants to use him. God wants to know him. For God to do this, Abram must go inward. *Go to thyself.*

How can we do this? There are many tools at the disposal of the Christ-follower. To begin, counseling, therapy, and trusted mental health professionals can help us toward self-knowledge. Consider sitting down with a therapist or counselor who can help you see yourself truthfully. Even the process of finding a counselor, setting up an appointment, getting ready, driving there, and paying to see a trained professional who simply listens is a miniature act of the process of discipleship. In discipleship, we go to great ends to seek Jesus only to find him sitting there looking at us lovingly in the quiet. The very act of speaking to someone and listening to yourself speak is critical—often the process itself gives language to our experience before we even knew how to talk about it.

Alongside this is the ancient art of spiritual direction—a practice Christians have been undertaking since earliest Christianity. In spiritual direction, an individual submits their spiritual journey to the loving guidance of someone who is "over you in the Lord" (1 Thess. 5:12 ESV). As with counseling, there's a lot of listening. The important component of spiritual direction is that the person who has walked through deconstruction can offer wisdom and insight on how to journey through it. There *are* profound benefits to walking alongside someone who has gone further down the theological journey than us. Of course, the best mechanics are the ones who've taken an engine apart. We need people who have had enough experience to help us with ours.

Likewise, there remain many personality tools for self-examination, like the Enneagram, StrengthsFinder, and the like. These tools offer *an* important word about who we are, but they never offer a *final* word over who we are. They can help us learn about ourselves. But they must not take a higher place than the words of Scripture in our lives.

Reflection and honest self-critique are also important. Critique is not bad. The biblical prophets standing against evil are a model for us. Wherever there's darkness, they held out the light. Critique of that which is evil, as such, is inherently Christian.[23] But critique is not to be extended to the external world alone. We need to turn critique inward as well. Looking at Paul's writings—particularly Romans 5–6—we see a man critiquing his own desires that wage within him. But sadly, the weapons of critique are now being turned on their source, God—we are critiquing that which gives us the power and ideas to critique. Catch the irony: we now use the tools of Christianity not to defeat evil but to defeat Christianity. Our capacity and ability to take our critiques too far is voiced in the ever-prophetic insight of Friedrich Nietzsche, who asks: What is it that has conquered Christianity and its God? "Christian morality itself, the concept of truthfulness taken more and more strictly. The confessional subtlety of the Christian conscience translated and sublimated into the scientific conscience, into intellectual cleanliness at any price."[24]

The Christian virtue of self-critique is now eating Christianity from the inside—taking self-critique to the end point of self-hatred and self-annihilation. It is indeed possible to take self-critique too far. What is needed is not to critique to destroy or to critique for critique's sake—what is needed is self-critique expressed in love as part of the process of repentance, grace, justice, and mercy. Or, to borrow the words of Miroslav Volf and Matthew Croasmun, "We need an 'I have a dream' speech, not an 'I have a complaint' speech."[25] Critique that crucifies hope is never the heart of Jesus.

This doesn't mean we beat ourselves up. Self-talk is normative for all of us—those speeches we tell ourselves and often repeat in our conception of the self. But healthy self-critique is not self-flagellation. When we speak poorly to ourselves about ourselves, we fail to take seriously what Christ says over us as his beloved. We are loved by Jesus. Truth be told, if we had friends or family members who talked to us the same way we often talk down to ourselves, we might very well be able to categorize that as abuse. Self-abuse is *never* the geography of healthy spiritual formation. That said, the more we begin to walk in the presence of Christ, the more we become aware of the false self and the sin that lurks in our souls. Often, the closer we come to Jesus, the further Jesus feels from us. The light really does illuminate the darkness. We do not overcome the darkness of the self by beating up the self.

The hardest person to love is the one we used to be like. Which is why we often hate the old us. Have you ever looked back over your life and found something you hate? In the earlier stages of our journey, all of us made decisions that harmed ourselves or harmed others. Nothing hurts more than thinking back to those immature patterns from our past. But even there lies a chance for grace. We must learn to forgive the old us. If we don't, we will have little room for grace for anyone who is like the old us.

It is easy during times of deconstruction to give in to the temptation of finding and naming what's wrong with everyone else. But God desires us to become radically honest and self-reflective, learning to grasp the light and darkness in our own hearts. The goal in all of this is that we approach self-knowledge as a way to worship and love God more fully. It is an exercise in learning about the kind of God who loves people like us.

Five

Going to Church

Finding Jesus in the Church

Abraham Kuyper—the nineteenth-century Dutch preeminent theologian, cultural transformer, and journalist—somehow also found time to be the prime minister of his homeland. Kuyper's early life connects with the ideas we've been discussing. While Kuyper was studying theology at the famed Leiden University under the tutelage of the finest theologians of his time, his intellectual rigor eventually morphed into a full-blown deconstruction of his childhood faith. Yet all his new questions and critiques of Christianity left him unsatisfied. A chance reading of *The Heir of Redclyffe* by Christian novelist Charlotte Yonge turned his faith around, provoking Kuyper to reconsider historic Christianity. This happenstance reading coincided with a recent pastoral assignment to a homely village among a world of rural, humble, and simple Christians. Kuyper's encounter with everyday farmers, mothers, fathers, businessmen, watchmakers, and shoemakers who lived with a simple love for Jesus had a resounding impact that eventually led to his reconversion to Christianity.[1]

Kuyper's return to Christ paralleled his return to church. As we often see, deconstruction reorients our relationship with the church. This can lead to leaving the church. But isolation doesn't fix everything. After some personal crisis, a growing sense of aloneness, the need for help, or the desire to find companionship, one's hunger for God, community, and tradition begin to awaken again. Even a crisis like childbearing can awaken one's hunger for God. I can't count on two hands the number of new parents I know who've come back to church and God after having their first child! Parenting has a way of illuminating our deep need for a supernatural God (or, at the least, our desperate need for babysitting one hour every Sunday morning). Returning to the church often plays a foundational role in the renewal of one's faith.

The overlap between loving God and loving his people is established throughout Scripture. The epistle to the Hebrews, for instance, addresses Christians who've "fallen away" from the faith. In that context, the author writes, "God is not unjust; he will not forget your work and the love you have shown him as you have helped *his people* and continue to help *them*" (Heb. 6:10). Apparently, one's love for God's people (the church) is counted as love toward Jesus. This principle is echoed in the words of the ascended Christ to Saul as he travels to Damascus to persecute Christians there: "Saul, Saul, why do you persecute *me*?" (Acts 9:4). The message of Acts and Hebrews is the same. Notice that Jesus doesn't say, "Why do you persecute *the church*?" He says, "Why do you persecute *me*?" To persecute the church is to persecute Jesus.[2] Consider how this affects Saul. In subsequent letters to Christians following his conversion, Paul repeatedly confesses "longing" to be with them, "wishing" he could travel to them, even blaming Satan, who stands in his way to get there. The shift in Paul's posture toward the church is both astounding and instructive. The same Saul who traveled to critique, kill, and persecute Christians has become the Paul who gives his life to serve them. Apparently, being Jesus's friend means befriending Jesus's friends.[3]

We're told in Matthew's parable of the sheep and the goats that we are caring for Jesus as we care for the "least of these" (Matt. 25:31–46). Rightly so, this is interpreted as caring for the poor and downtrodden. Indeed, to care for the poor is to care for Jesus! But we limit the scope and weight of Christ's words when we ignore that the "least of these" can also include the brothers and sisters in the faith. Again, back to Paul, who confesses that he cares for the church as a "nursing mother cares for her children" (1 Thess. 2:7–8). Indeed, a bold metaphor used by a single guy without children, womb, or breasts with which to nurse.[4] Paul undoubtedly had to have loved the church to risk such a feminine metaphor in a patriarchal world!

Doubt and deconstruction can easily travel alongside anger and angst toward the church—much of it justified! This experience may entail a season of taking a break from church to heal and reevaluate. Indeed, this *can* be healing. But it should not be the end of the process. At some point, God will invite us to love the church *through* that pain again—to return to the body. Our healing process before Christ is played out in our love for the church as we begin to love her again, to be with her, and to *go* to her.

Listening to the whispers of Western culture, one gets the impression that God can essentially be found everywhere *but* church—in the woods, in activism, and in silence. It's as though we believe abandoning the church is our best way of loving God. Perhaps this reaction is justified in light of past generations who overemphasized churchgoing as the sole means of encountering the living God. But ignoring the historical and biblical witness regarding the importance of being among God's people is, itself, entirely unjustifiable. There's literally no expression of covenant faith in the Bible—in Israel or the church—that disconnects faith formation from the community of God's people. Loving God but hating his people has no historical precedent. Part of loving God is loving the church and being present with her.

Does this mean that we shut up, leaving our critiques at the door? No. The prophet is the immune system of the church. We need words of truth. But playing the prophetic role is best done from *within* the church in love—not from *outside* the church as finger-pointing. When we do this, we embody great power from God's Spirit to heal our mother, the church. Consider this: if a mother suffers organ damage during pregnancy, the baby in the womb can actually send stem cells repairing the mother's damaged organ. The miracle of God's design is so breathtaking that even in our precritical, unborn state, we're designed to help our mother in need when she is hurting. I can't help but think of the church. She hurts. She has made many mistakes and errors. And she's been beaten, rejected, hated, abused, and despised. And many beat her down even further. Do we come as a Saul or a Paul? Much is learned about how we love our mother in her time of need. Do we come to serve her and love her? Or do we kick her while she's down?

I and We

The way in which Christians relate to the church has gone through many iterations. Before the sixteenth-century Reformation, Roman Catholic Christians largely equated salvation with being in the church. One was saved *through* the church. *Sacerdotalism*—the idea that one is saved through churchgoing and connection to the institutional church—was one of the very theological assumptions Martin Luther vehemently sought to deconstruct. Salvation, for Luther, was not received through church-going, liturgy, or the Eucharist. It was only through faith in Christ's unmerited grace. This is the gospel! The Reformers even coined a phrase mocking the popular notion that one was rendered righteous through participation in church—*fides carbonaria*. This literally meant "faith in the charcoal burner."[5] I am grateful for the Reformers' critique of sacerdotalism with its suggestion that one can be made right with God through liturgy, the Eucharist, or ritual alone.

But Western deconstruction has taken these ideas too far. The problem Western Christianity faces today is now the exact opposite of Luther's. Long gone are the days we thought salvation was secured through churchgoing. A new generation of Christians articulate a love for Jesus, grace, and mercy with a dwindling commitment to the body of Christ— the church. I hear replaying in my mind hundreds of conversations that follow the same script: "I love Jesus, listen to podcasts, pray, and do justice. I'm following Jesus! But church just isn't my thing." We have replaced the bad idea that God was found *only* in church with another bad idea that God can be found everywhere *but* church. What a devastating trade! What began as Luther's call to reform institutional Christianity has become its very rejection. We must recover—in the prophetic words of theologian Thomas Oden—the "sense of the active work of the Spirit in history, through living communities. Our modern individualism too easily tempts us to take our Bible and remove ourselves from the wider believing community. We end up with a Bible and a radio, but no church."[6] Or now simply a Bible and our favorite podcast.

The lure to abandon church does not come by a predictable route. The tactics of the devil aren't always by overt power and coercion. Demons opt for the subtle, the titillating, the suggestive. More often, the spirits of this world operate by means of a soft power that beckons and whispers and suggests how naive we must be to even need the church. *Only weaklings need the church*, they say. One pastor told me that the young have stopped coming to church because of sin and evil and disobedience. It's rarely that overt. Usually, they have been lured away from church on Sunday because of brunch.[7] Plain and simple. When it comes to the difficult work of getting out of bed, putting on clothes, and going to hear a message about sin and salvation, we'd rather have bacon, French toast, and an extra hour of sleep. God's people have traded in church for a mimosa.

But why *should* we go to church? For some, there's the ritual and predictability—a sense of perpetuity in a liquid world of tumult. For others, it's the sense of community and inclusiveness in a world of separateness and isolation. J. D. Vance, in his widely read *Hillbilly Elegy*, poignantly describes how it was his childhood experience of being adopted by a churchgoing family member that gave his childhood consistency and meaning.[8] Or we go to church simply because we always have—it structures life. During the release of the 2017 film *First Reformed*—a story of a pastor played by Ethan Hawke—the director Paul Schrader admitted to why he liked going to church. Long having disconnected from the faith of his childhood, Schrader confessed that church gave him the gift of boredom. "For me," Schrader said, "I like to go to church on Sunday mornings to organize my thoughts, organize my week, and be quiet. And you don't walk out of a church because you're bored. You go to church to be bored—to have that time. And you can have it in your room in the lotus position or you can have it in a pew. It's essentially the same sort of thing for me and that's what I enjoy about it."[9]

Society even benefits from churchgoing. The National Bureau of Economic Research published one study entitled "Is Religion Good for You?" examining the benefits of attending religious services. Surprisingly, the study revealed that regular church attendance can be transformative to the individual and society as a whole. Research shows that "doubling the rate of religious attendance raises household income by 9.1 percent, decreases welfare participation by 16 percent from baseline rates, decreases the odds of being divorced by 4 percent, and increases the odds of being married by 4.4 percent."[10] We now have empirical research showing that individuals and the whole of society benefit from churchgoing.

There are a thousand rational reasons to go to church. But that becomes a problem—we go to get something. Do we really go to church just for the benefits? Doesn't doing so merely perpetuate the consumerist culture that has caused so many to abandon church? The reasons shared above might be good reasons for churchgoing. But they are all utilitarian and consumeristic in nature—we go to *get* something. There must be a far more beautiful and deeply meaningful rationale for going to church beyond what we get out of it. Right?

Allow me to draw your attention to something from the creeds of the early church. The early church curated a number of creeds (Apostles', Nicene, Athanasian, etc.) that served as theological statements articulating what the first Christians believed. They represented, in a way, the founding documents of the Christian movement. While the New Testament writings had circulated for some time, a deep need was growing for clarity about right and wrong beliefs. There were two kinds of creeds. One creed, the Apostles' Creed, served as a confessional statement for new Christians in conversion. After spending nearly three years preparing to be baptized into the faith, the convert would memorize the Apostles' Creed for their baptism. It begins with the words "I believe" (Latin *credo*). It is the only creed beginning with that phrase, "I believe." This leads us to the second kind of creed. The Nicene Creed (written in the fourth century) represents a remarkably concise, dense, and nuanced statement about the nature of Christ as both fully human and fully divine man. These communal creeds represent the beliefs of the whole church, for all Christians everywhere. These creeds begin with the phrase "We believe" (Latin *credimus*).

There are two kinds of creeds: an "I believe" creed and "we believe" creeds.

Creeds offer theological boundaries around true and untrue Christian beliefs. They define "orthodoxy"—or what C. S. Lewis calls "mere Christianity."[11] But the creeds weren't simply about *what* to believe. They were also about *how* to believe. On the one hand, we're called to believe in Jesus, personally following him, repenting, and giving our lives in fidelity to Christ. But this is only half the story. We're simultaneously invited to believe alongside the rest of the church in history, in eternity, and on earth. To be a Christian is to believe personally and corporately with the rest of the church.

This is notable: both types of creeds unequivocally affirm belief in the church as a part of historic Christian faith. One reads, "I believe in the holy, catholic church." The other reads, "We believe in the holy, catholic church." *I* and *we*! Just as belief in the Trinity, Christ's death and resurrection, and the incarnation is part of the core of Christian belief, so is belief in the church. In the same way that we are called to believe in the resurrection, the Trinity, and the existence of God, we are called to believe in the church! Belief in Jesus cannot be unhitched from belief in the church. Churchless Christianity is fundamentally different from historic Christianity.[12]

My friend tells a story about how we have forgotten this component of historic Christianity. He's an evangelical pastor and wanted to lead his church into a deeper understanding of where Christians get their theology. To that end, he began leading the entire congregation in reading the Apostles' Creed at the beginning of their corporate worship gatherings. Each Sunday, they'd also read the Nicene Creed together out loud. However, he noticed something odd: his evangelical congregation got a little quieter when they came to the place that read, "We believe in the holy, *catholic* church." Soon the emails started rolling in. *Are we secretly becoming Roman Catholics?* He recognized a problem. People didn't know what "catholic" meant. They thought it meant the Roman

Catholic church. Nobody had taught them that "catholic" means "according to the whole"—the historic, global church that has followed Jesus through history. This isn't a belief in a specific institution, denomination, or iteration of the church. It is a belief in the global and historic Christian church that has been following Jesus since the days of Peter.

Processing this, my friend wrestled with what to do. Should they say the creed at all? Or maybe he should edit the creed? He decided to edit the creed and remove the part about believing in the church. With a pen in hand, he started to mark out the phrase on the creed in front of him. Then he was stopped in his tracks. It hit him. He was about to change what Christians had been confessing for two thousand years all because his church didn't understand it. With the swipe of a pen, he was about to do away with what has been a central part of what Christians worldwide believe together. That led my friend on a journey with his church. Rather than changing what Christians have always believed, he began to teach the people what Christians have always believed, everywhere.

Isn't it terrifying that one can change the essence of Christianity with the swipe of a pen?

We desperately need to recapture the communal aspect of historic Christianity. I suspect one reason young evangelicals deconstruct their childhood faith is that they come to reject the overly individualistic forms of faith in which they were raised that ignored the "we" part of Christianity. For so many, the whole "I accepted Jesus" framework becomes a signpost for consumeristic individuality. This obsessive individuality is a problem, but we respond against these individualistic impulses by leaving the church. What an odd way to critique individualistic Christianity—by leaving the church. In rejecting and leaving those churches that embodied individualized conversionism, we turn, perplexingly, away from the beliefs of historic Christianity from the last two thousand years. In the name of rejecting individualism, we individualize our faith outside the church. This drips with irony. If we end up deconstructing individualistic Christianity by self-made, self-selected individualistic theology, we merely trade in one form of individualism for another. It seems odd to leave Christian community as a protest against individualistic Christianity.

We all need the church. I need the church. I need to know that there's a community of people in my city who could be on my doorstep at a moment's notice with pitchforks, tar, and feathers if I chose to walk away from Jesus or use his name for my own power. I'm dead without the "we." We all need to be accountable for our words. We need to be held to the Bible. We need to be held to Jesus.

This can't be stressed enough—there's no room for do-it-yourself Christianity. The entire palate of Christian discipleship to Jesus requires others. The unconverted cannot believe alone—the gospel must be preached and heard. We don't call ourselves. God initiates that call. Self-baptism isn't an option. We need someone to bring us up from the watery grave. Even Christ required his cousin to baptize him. The disciples didn't wash their own feet. Jesus did it for them. Communion is to be served, not individually unwrapped. Time and again, Jesus borrowed people's things. Cups of water. Boats. Donkeys to ride into town with. He was even buried in a borrowed grave. And Jesus had the angels move the rock off the empty grave. He didn't lift a finger. Until we can be helped, loved, and served, faith will never be understood or received.

The "I" is nothing without the "we."

Inherited and Accepted Belief

For two millennia, Christian faith has been formed in the context of the church. Humans need a place where they can not only learn how to believe but also bring their difficulties, struggles, and doubts. The place of community in faith formation has been modeled by the Amish practice of Rumspringa, or the "running around." On their sixteenth birthday, each Amish teenager is sent into the world to do as they please—party, experiment, taste the pleasures of the world. For many, this is their first engagement with the outside world. Then they are given a choice to return. They can choose to leave the community or to return. The statistics are remarkable. Over 95 percent of those who go through Rumspringa return home to their communities after "running around."[13]

Why do they return to these communities? In his book *Tribe*, journalist Sebastian Junger examines the stories of the frontiersmen of early European expansion across the North American landscape. Traveling across the sprawling space, many frontiersmen were not only impressed by but drawn to the tight-knit tribalism of the indigenous peoples. As Junger points out, there are thousands of recorded incidents of early frontiersmen leaving their Western culture to join the culture of indigenous peoples. However, there are almost no accounts of indigenous peoples leaving their community by choice to join white European culture. Junger quotes an eighteenth-century Frenchman: "Thousands of Europeans are Indians, and we have no examples of even one of those Aborigines having from choice become European. There must be in their social bond something singularly captivating and far superior to anything to be boasted of among us."[14] What attracted people so deeply to the culture of indigenous peoples? Easy. There was a pervading sense of tribe and community that Western European culture lacked.

That's why over 95 percent of Amish kids come back and get baptized in the Amish communities of their childhood. The relational and social dynamics of a Christ-centered community really do matter. God desires faith to have "genuineness" (1 Pet. 1:7). To make that happen, God places us in the community of God's people. Genuine faith isn't forged alone. There is a tension here between one's *inherited* beliefs (those we've been taught) and one's *accepted* beliefs (those we've accepted). In *The Evolving Self*, Robert Kegan discusses three stages one goes through in having faith—confirmation, contradiction, and continuity.[15] Confirmation is the faith handed to us by a community—a church, family, even a culture. Continuity is following Jesus as an adult. We may have inherited as children, in the safe environment of our home, the historic Christian belief that Jesus is the only way to God. But that same belief may feel more difficult to receive down the road when we are relating to beloved coworkers and friends who want little to do with Jesus or the church in urban Portland. Jesus is the same everywhere, indeed. But though that theological truth is true no matter where we are, believing as children can feel different than believing as adults.

I think that the way to move from *inherited* faith to *accepted* faith is to surround ourselves with people who keep us going. Why? Because we are far more social as creatures than we're comfortable admitting. What if it is true that we often end up believing what those around us believe? That we think and believe in tribes? How good it is that we articulate and pass along to the young good beliefs. We do that well. But the gospel wasn't intended to be divorced from gospel environments. As we're finding, beliefs can easily be replaced because of new environments. All it took for Phil (from chapter 1) to go through a faith crisis was a move. Sadly, American Christianity has a form of Rumspringa—and it is neither intentional nor effective. It's called college. As a college professor, I'm no longer surprised each fall semester to see a whole new group of young students in my Bible and theology classes who were raised in churches and homes that did not prepare them for the world outside. I walk them through facing this new, scary, big world. Usually they come out the other side with faith. But not every professor is as in love with Jesus as I am.

Researchers continue to inform us that deep Christian community plays a disproportionate role in one's lifelong formation. In her book *Almost Christian*, Kenda Creasy Dean identifies two factors that help someone remain a lifelong follower of Christ.[16] First, their parents have walked through their own faith challenges and remained faithful to God through those difficulties. And second, the child has no less than five adult Christians in their life who love them, care, and instill a commitment to Jesus into them. A tribe! The tribe gives the young a chance to believe for themselves. But they package that belief in a rich and committed community—a great cloud of saints—that one would be crazy to deconstruct.

Perhaps Jesus knew exactly what he was saying when he said, "By this everyone will know that you are my disciples, if you love one another" (John 13:35). What Jesus said is actually happening. We have a generation deconstructing their beliefs not because those beliefs are wrong but because they never saw those beliefs actually *done* in a loving community of commitment and sacrifice. I'm convinced that until we return to the radical, tribal roots of a church community that lives, believes, and dies together, we will simply see each generation enter their Rumspringa with far worse statistics than the Amish. The famed British missionary Lesslie Newbigin prophetically said that there is only one real way to see the gospel: through "a congregation which believes it."[17]

History has a way of retweeting itself. In the 1970s, an unexpected spiritual revival swept the American landscape as thousands of disenfranchised hippies were baptized in oceans and rivers, hungry for Jesus. What had once seemed an impossible mission field, the countercultural, weed-smoking, sexually liberated hippies flocked to Jesus in what became known as the "Jesus people" movement. The Jesus people, interestingly, became a revival comprising baby boomers who rejected their parents' expression of church but received the basic elements of their faith. It was a move of God. But it was also a strong critique *against* the perceived religious rigidity of the previous generation. That same posture is being repeated today. And we are surprised that this generation is repeating what their parents' generation did to *their* parents? It is striking to watch the young in our current context reject certain aspects of the faith of their boomer parents and flock to mainline, liberal Protestant and Catholic churches—doing ominously what their parents did to their grandparents. Just as the Jesus people accepted the faith of their parents but rejected their forms of church, the young today are hungry for the God of their parents but want nothing to do with their churches and are returning (ironically) to the churches that their grandparents would likely have attended.

God must desire a movement that runs deeper than being "against" the last generation of saints.[18] In the end, our children will do to us what we did to our parents. This doesn't mean we ought not take seriously the wrongs of the previous generation. As has been said, we may have Jesus in our hearts, but we have our mother and father in our bones.[19] We must learn to walk humbly and graciously in how we look upon the past. We must learn to walk a different path than simply reacting against everything we were given. We are born again. Not born *against*.

The Church Is Not a Hospital

How we imagine the church changes the way we engage the church. Metaphors are important and powerful. In the 1950s, Elizabeth Gordon edited a magazine entitled *House Beautiful* espousing the idea that the architecture of suburban landscapes had become the backbone and the engine of individualism, greed, and selfishness. She said, "Architecture . . . will encourage the development of individualism."[20] Suburbia—that matrix of self-contained homes, garage doors, sheds, and fences—is not just the result of individualism; its very architecture feeds individualism. Gordon's point was simply profound: individualism had built suburbia, and suburbia was making us individualistic. We shape our buildings, Gordon suggests, and our buildings shape us back.[21]

The metaphors we use shape us. Consider our typical language about the church: "I want to *plug into* a church." Listen to that metaphor. We—the congregants—are akin to electronic devices to be plugged into the outlet of the church. Not only does the metaphor break down, it actually breaks us down. People aren't machines. Nor are people always "filled up" by churchgoing. We perpetuate this message when we talk about "installing a new pastor," which mirrors how we treat pastors, as appliances. Once they burn out, break down, or stop working, we just get a new one.

Or consider the metaphor of the church as a hospital. Certainly, it is beautiful to imagine the church as a space for the broken. In that sense, the church as a hospital is true to the New Testament message. But think through the underlying message of that metaphor, which implies two things we ought not convey. For one, it suggests that the church is an institution employing a class of elite professionals who are different from the sick. All the more, the metaphor suggests that the church is a place someone goes to until they are no longer sick. Once we are healthy, we no longer need it. The sign of health then becomes our leaving it—once you're better, more mature, healthy, evolved, or no longer in need of its services, you have no place for it. Sadly, this is precisely the way many Christians think about and imagine their relationship to God's church. The metaphor has shaped us.

We should not be surprised when people stop going to church after having heard for years the statement, "You don't *go* to church; you *are* the church." No wonder we have a generation of people who follow Jesus without the church. They're just enacting the metaphor we gave them. Of course, in the end, it is both. We *are* the church. But because we *are* the church, we *gather* as a church. A body dismembered will no longer live. Remaining connected is absolutely necessary. These aren't mutually exclusive—being and gathering. Our sermons have not returned void. We're becoming our bad metaphors.

The metaphors for the church have actually already been built—those found in the New Testament. Consider Paul's metaphor of God's church as a *mysterion*, a "mystery" (Eph. 3:3–6). The church is a mystery. It isn't something we enter to get something from. The mystery doesn't exist to provide us with good feelings or put our adrenal glands on overdrive. A mystery is something you simply enter. When we enter within, subterraneous and hidden things take place that neither you, I, nor the awkward person next to you at greeting time rationally categorize. It's simply a *mystery*.

When it's a mystery, friends, the sermon might as well be in Italian; it doesn't matter. When it's a mystery, the *way* the music is done becomes far less important than the fact that we are singing. A mystery is a mystery. A mystery is not understandable, rational, manageable, or logical. A mystery is entered into simply because it is a mystery. The church is a bit like Narnia's wardrobe. Outside it looks like a tiny, useless upstairs closet with little noteworthy inside. But inside awaits a whole new world of wonder and life and difficulties that will change your entire story. Our task is simple: enter.

Or consider Paul's metaphor for the church as the bride of Christ (Eph. 5:25–27). In this instance, the church is a being, a person, a body, a beautiful woman on her wedding day. If we adopt Paul's metaphor, I suspect it might reshape the way we engage the church. Because the church is a person—a two-thousand-year-old person—we must love her as such. Old women move slower than we wish. She isn't as fast as the world. She's behind on the times. She isn't up to date. Which is okay.

We need one group of people who don't keep the same time with the rest of the world. When we critique her for not having sermons that are as evolved or nuanced as NPR; or when she isn't doing what the people on Twitter are doing; or when she says odd things in her prayers—we can take a deep breath. We are with a very old bride with a diversity of weird people. Christ loves this woman, warts and all. Can we?

When we forget who the church is, we dole out endless grace for everyone in the world except the very community that taught us the mysteries of grace. We soon have endless streams of grace for the sinner—but none for the saint. When it comes to the sins of the church, we're Pharisees—rocks in hand.

Bringing and Borrowing

There's healing in worshiping God with the firstfruits of our questions, doubts, and difficulties. "Praising God," writes Eugene Peterson, "does not inoculate us from doubts about God."[22] One could say those doubts are part of praising God. This separation of church and doubt has harmed too many.

I want to push this further. We should be invited to bring our difficulties. What's more, what if the church was the place where we were introduced to the difficulties of belief? A healthy family, it seems, is one that knows and names its challenges, problems, and systemic issues. When those difficulties and challenges are named *within* the safe confines of the family, trust is built. But when these same difficulties are discovered outside the family through YouTube or a college professor, it builds resentment. The developer of the children's church curriculum Godly Play built something utterly majestic into its curriculum to accomplish this. After reading the Scripture, the leader asks: *How did you see yourself in the story? What was your favorite part?* Then comes the surprising question: *What part of the story did you not like?* What happens next is powerful as the children are invited to bring their questions and doubts and problems into the presence of God and others. Even more powerful is that the leader is not allowed to resolve the tension. It just has to be.

Imagine the impact that has on a child's faith development. Imagine coming to learn early on that the church is the safest place to take your questions. It may even be the place to learn the questions themselves!

When we do bring our questions as adults, we must not do so with a bombastic, rude, or provoking spirit. If we want loving responses, we need loving questions. Sadly, I've experienced that those in deconstruction can—from time to time—bear questions and critiques with abundant judgmentalism and arrogance. But there is a way to bring our questions to others in the church in a Christlike way. Which circles us back to Job: in preparing his questions for God, "Job did not sin by charging God with wrongdoing" (Job 1:22). Apparently, there's a line Job refused to cross. Job's anger, challenge, and frustration with God's divine judgments never led Job to judge God as a bad guy. The posture of Job's heart allowed him to point out the problem without pointing his finger at God as the source of that problem.

Among God's people, we bring each other to Jesus right where we are. In one scene from Matthew's Gospel, Jesus sits and teaches in a living room. So many are there that no one else can enter. One man is outside— a paralytic desperately in need of Jesus's healing touch. His friends think up a solution. They carry him to the roof where they make an opening, strap a rope on the paralytic, and lower him before Jesus. Looking up, Jesus sees the man being lowered. Matthew then writes something peculiar: "Jesus saw *their* faith" (Matt. 9:2). Whose faith? Not the paralytic's faith. Jesus saw the faith of his friends who lowered him to Jesus. Jesus saw *their* faith. Because of their faith, the man was healed and set free.

Sometimes the best thing I can do—when I struggle with my faith—is surround myself with the faithful the way the blind would with those who see.[23] We all need a group around us who believes *for* us when we struggle to believe on our own. For those deconstructing their faith, this can be their deepest need—someone's faith to borrow. Sometimes we just keep showing up to borrow others' faith when we don't have enough of our own.

This was the hardest chapter in this book to write. My intuition tells me that many of us have deep wounds from the church. Name those wounds. Don't run from them. And have hope that those wounds can heal. Could God be inviting you to forgive the church? In the parable of the prodigal son, there are two sons. One squanders his father's inheritance in a foreign land. As Thomas Oden writes, "The prodigal son had to try out every wrong path in a far country before he found the right path home. Only after his testing of futile ways was he ready to come home."[24] The son needed to run away to truly see his need for home. But the other son squanders his father's grace having never left home. No longer do I call it the parable of the prodigal son. It's the parable of the prodigal *sons*. Both are lost. It's sobering to realize one can be lost without ever having left home.

But what if we saw this parable in a different way? Maybe we're sometimes like the father and the church is the younger brother. Perhaps at some point along the way you felt like the church came to you, used your gifts, used your skills, used your resources, used your story, and ran off to squander them in a foreign land. I can understand that maybe you would never want to be around the church again. But what if part of God's invitation is learning to welcome the church home, back into your life again? Just the way the Father has for you.

Six

Feeling Everything

Little Speeches

Before entering a vocation of teaching, I was a pastor. In 2009, my wife and I moved to Portland, Oregon, and founded a church. It was a miracle. God showed himself. People met God.

Then the assignment abruptly ended.

During a sabbatical, my wife and I began naming what appeared to be a subterranean shift in our sense of calling. We wondered if our time of pastoring in Portland was coming to a close. Waves of devastation and shame overwhelmed us over our even wondering about this shift. Returning from the sabbatical, we tried white-knuckling ministry for a few months in hopes that the feelings might dissipate—only to face the inevitable reality of what we had sensed during our time of rest. The grace God had given us for pastoral work in Portland had been lifted. Submitting our resignation and announcing our departure to the staff and church, we said goodbye to the very people we'd first brought together in our living room a decade earlier.

The emotions that came with that vocational loss were the most horrific and excruciating we've ever experienced. How does one walk away from something they assumed they'd do their whole life? Who are you when you don't do what you do anymore?

My father wisely told me during that season, "If you are what you do, and you don't, then you aren't." That represented much of our experience during that season. The problem wasn't that we'd been pastors. The problem was that being pastors was *all* we were. We were what we did. With that core identity swept away from us, we had little choice but to spend the next nine months crawling back to Jesus like babes. Without knowing what was ahead, we endured a long winter of waiting and lament. The Bible read differently to me during those months. I saw things I hadn't seen before. As I read Paul's letters, it became clear why he started so many churches and then left them in a few months. Leaving is unimaginably painful, even for an apostle.

Naturally our friends and family asked what we planned on doing next. Whenever the question came up, I caught myself jesting, "I'm going to work at Costco." I probably voiced this promise a thousand times, thinking little of it until my friend John asked me to pause and think about what I was saying. John confronted me: I wouldn't get a job at Costco. Actually, I think he said I "couldn't" get a job at Costco. I wasn't qualified. My training in academic theology and pastoral experience were great, but one has to actually know how to work hard at Costco. I hesitantly agreed. Then John lovingly wondered if something lay underneath that little speech of mine. John asked if that speech was perhaps made out of self-pity and feeling sorry for myself.

Until then, the feelings behind my words had not been clearly identified. I was sad. I felt sorry for myself. More than anything, that little speech had become a ruse, a cover, a front for deep hurt and woundedness that I'd been afraid to explore. It's unlikely I'm alone in my speechwriting abilities. At some point in life, we all write little speeches with the ink of pain and self-pity. Then came another breakthrough in my reading of Scripture—it was the parable of the prodigal son I referenced earlier. As the younger son walks home after years of blowing his inheritance and wanton living, he prepares *his* own little speech. He practices out loud his speech for his father: "Make me like one of your hired servants" (Luke 15:19). That little speech never made sense to me. Then a thud in my spirit. That was me! Not until my own identity crisis did that boy's speech make sense. The prodigal was promising to work at Costco. He was sad. He felt sorry for himself. He couldn't imagine that there was a difference between a momentary chapter of mistakes and an entire unified story of redemption. He came home with his tail between his legs. He couldn't fathom the party that awaited.

I soon traded in my speech-writing career for the hard work of attending to the wounded emotions lying within. This led me to honestly examine that slew of shame and sorrow and self-pity I'd been enslaved to for feeling like I couldn't handle pastoral work. For the first time I saw that maybe I hadn't failed. Maybe God was in our loss, the very creator and nurturer of it. It was then that God began inviting us to envision a future glory he'd dreamed of in the midst of our lament, doubt, and destruction. There was a party to come. With this Father, there's *always* a fatted calf.

Tremendous emotions often accompany deconstruction and doubt and can actually be the undercurrent beneath our faith difficulties. In this chapter on emotions, we want to aim for two things. First, to learn to feel everything—and feel it to the most of our ability. And second, to learn that God is far more faithful and real than those emotions often let on. Tending to our emotions can actually help us learn about ourselves and the very God who seeks to throw a party on our behalf. When we do this, we might be more sensitive to the fact that our doubts and deconstructions can be a front for deep-seated resentment toward our parents, for hurts from church, for jealousies that others got more than us, or for the angst of unrealized dreams. Deconstruction is not *merely* emotionalism, but emotions do play a role. When we don't attend to those deep emotions of anger or resentment, our actions become extensions of those dark emotions. The cycle can be vicious.

Feeling Rightly

Does God have feelings? Religion has long wrestled with this question. Before Jesus, ancient Near Eastern religions generally believed the gods (and there were many "gods") to be more or less emotional, fickle,

93

capricious deities swayed by their willy-nilly emotions. Later, the Greco-Roman view swung to the opposite extreme, largely believing the gods to be unemotional. For them, emotions meant someone was changing. If there *was* one God, Aristotle would suggest, that God certainly couldn't be swayed by emotion. Aristotle called God "the unmoved Mover."

The gods were fickle. Or the gods were stoic. Then along came a peasant, homeless, Jewish Messianic upstart from Nazareth named Jesus who claimed to be God in flesh. The incarnation revealed something eye-opening: If Jesus was God, then God was emotional. Jesus experienced all the emotions. Jesus wept. Jesus endured physical pain. Jesus looked lovingly upon people. Jesus got enraged with anger. Jesus knew anxiety. Jesus enjoyed friendship. Every human emotion can be found in the God who becomes a human being. No doubt this would've stuck out like a sore thumb in an ancient world unable to relate emotions to the deities.

Scripture consistently witnesses to a Creator God who not only *has* emotions but *creates* beings with emotions. Emotions reflect *imago Dei*—human beings made in God's image. The Psalms, noticeably, canonize this full spectrum of emotions as part and parcel of authentic spirituality. Affection for God. Hatred for enemies. Warm fuzzies. Cold apathy. Anxiety. Worry. Joy. Rage. Melancholy. Name it, it's there. The borderline neurotic emotionality of the authors of the Psalms upends so many of our stoic assumptions about the Christian faith. Granted, this biblical emotionalism is a turnoff to many. But rather than terrify us, it should comfort us. Emotional beings serve an emotional God. And the rough edges around the psalmists' erratic emotions don't diminish for a second their truthfulness. "Even if the Psalms were written by neurotics," C. S. Lewis comments, "that would not make them irrelevant."[1]

The problem occurs when we equate who God is with our feelings about God. Deconstruction can be the life-giving process of clarifying one's beliefs based on Scripture reading, theological reflection, meditation, confrontation, repentance, or study. But far too often, deconstruction becomes a series of theological reactions based solely on the shifting sands of our emotions. Consider one young man raised in a Christian home. In his upbringing, exclusive emphasis was placed on knowledge of the Bible and good doctrine above all other aspects of Christian formation. This left the lingering impression within him that Christianity was solely about belief. Though his family of origin had handed him good beliefs, they were no match for the hurt caused by the ungenerous, harsh, reactionary, uptight, and controlling environment where he'd received them. This created a lasting disconnect in his perception of Christianity. While the beliefs he'd been handed may have been good and true, the emotional woundedness of not feeling loved in childhood led to deconstruction after college. What that man needed was permission to find God in his wounds. His wounds alienated him from God, and so he, like many others, made a series of theological decisions with emotional motivations.

I can identify with this. During one season I obsessively critiqued and deconstructed the penal substitutionary atonement theory I had been handed in the early years of my faith journey. I angrily critiqued it. In my anger, I failed to recognize that it was a *theory*—one of many utilized in church history as a way to describe how the blood of Jesus worked. It took me a few years of spiritual direction and reflection to further realize that I was actually furiously jealous of a pastor just down the street who regularly affirmed penal substitutionary theory and whose church was growing faster than my own. It wasn't that I hated the penal substitutionary atonement theory. I was jealous. And in my jealousy, I blindly curated a half-baked theological critique as a means to mitigate feelings of inadequacy and failure in light of another's ministry.

Our theological critiques can easily be less about the theology we're critiquing than the wounds we carry from those who espouse those theologies. Regardless of my former critiques, I finally returned to my understanding of atonement with a far more generous spirit. And regardless of disagreements on how the atonement precisely works, I came to agree that the blood of Jesus is nonnegotiable. I basically landed where Flannery O'Connor landed: that the blood of Jesus was entirely necessary because nobody would have paid attention to Jesus had he died at eighty of athlete's foot.[2] The cross is that absolutely scandalous, obscene, gross, painful story of a man who trusted God and got the cross for it—and showed us how to do the same. The blood of Christ is essential—regardless of one's critique of our theories about it.

We need to always be cautious of allowing hurt feelings to push us away from true beliefs. Walter Rauschenbusch (1861–1918) was a Christian at the turn of the twentieth century who believed Christians played a disproportionate role in changing society through proclaiming the gospel. When we look deeper, Rauschenbusch's "social gospel" was part of a broader critique of what he saw as a conservative Christianity that was overly spiritual and otherworldly. Rauschenbusch openly eschewed doctrinal arguments around things like atonement theories because he believed them to lead to un-Christlike arguments between Christians. As a result, Rauschenbusch's trajectory privileged Christlikeness over doctrine, lived Christology over believed Christology, action over belief. The same reaction is common for those in deconstruction today. Watching Christians argue over fine doctrinal points may indeed be off-putting. But does that mean doctrine doesn't matter? Indeed, we must hold to and articulate that which is good and true. Right beliefs matter greatly. Being unclear about them—being unfaithful to what we have received—can lead to a form of Christianity that is practiced in the present but not articulated for the future.

Three things remain noteworthy regarding the relationship between our beliefs and emotions. First, we should be cautious about building theological beliefs on feelings. The great saint François Fenelon remarks, "Faith which is built on emotion is resting on a very changeable foundation."[3] Fenelon's invitation was not to avoid feeling or having emotions. A cursory reading of Fenelon's devotional work reveals the opposite: a belief that God meets us at the core of our emotional experience. But our belief, our faith, our trust is not built *on* emotions.

In Christian spirituality, there are historically three dimensions to Christian formation: orthodoxy, orthopraxy, and orthopathy. Orthodoxy is "right beliefs"—those core, historic Christian beliefs handed down since the apostolic age. Orthopraxy is those ways of "right living" that echo the life of Jesus in this world. But there is a third: orthopathy, or "right feeling" or "right affection."[4] Orthopathy relates to our emotions and heart. We need to feel. Emotions shouldn't be denied. But our affections and emotions need to always be hitched to good and true beliefs. In the end, emotions are real. But who God is, is a reflection of who we feel he is. The Protestant doctrine of *sola Scriptura* is critical, for it reminds us that the final authority on God's nature is to be found in the pages of our Bible—not the neuro-wiring of our minds or the secretion of our glands.

We see Jesus masterfully modeling human relationships by simultaneously exhibiting unprecedented compassion and a fidelity to truth and reality. Encountering the Samaritan woman in John 4, Jesus looks lovingly upon this woman caught in sexual sin and marital chaos. Yet he's clear: "You Samaritans worship what you do not know; we worship what we do know" (4:22). Jesus confronts a marginalized woman with compassion and offers her great truth. What stands out is Christ's unwillingness to privilege truth *over* compassion or compassion *over* truth. He always weds truth to compassion. The tension Christians feel today is thinking that either truth or compassion has to be chosen to the exclusion of the other. Many have idolized compassion, making it a false god. Others have idolized truth, worshiping ideals over the living God.

Second, emotions come and go. In my tribe of charismatic Christianity, emotions play a central role in worship. We're the adrenal gland of the body of Christ. A single emotional encounter with Jesus can have a lasting impact on one's faith. However, these experiences can also betray us. I've experienced that God *can* remove the feelings of our youth—not because God is mean, harsh, or unfeeling but because God intends to move us from an emotional relationship to a deeper, whole-being relationship. When those feelings wane—when life gets hard and we hit what Eugene Peterson calls the "badlands"—it is easy to assume God has abandoned us.[5]

Sometimes God removes the good feelings. Many of the early church fathers and mothers who gave themselves wholly to Christ wrote of the experience of long periods of time when God seemed quiet, if not entirely absent. They wrote that it was almost like God had emotionally abandoned them. This experience was first called "the dark night of the soul" by St. John of the Cross, a phrase for when the means and methods one has employed to cultivate intimacy with God no longer seem to work. Their writings sometimes reveal a fear that God is dead or not even real.

Why would God do this? Here's how I think about it. For years I've been in counseling. And I've noticed that my counselor never calls me to set up our next appointment. And I mean *never*. The responsibility is always mine. Perturbed by what I originally sensed to be a lack of interest on his part, I prodded: Why do I always have to be the one who initiates? He shared something insightful with me pertaining to counseling ethics. He told me that counselors are not supposed to initiate. If they do, he told me, it can easily become enablement or babysitting rather than counseling. The power of counseling is at its greatest when the person in need of counseling takes responsibility for their life, therapy, and process of healing. True healing is possible when the one in need of healing is required to take responsibility for the work of healing.

God's silence is not the same as God's absence. God's sensory distance is not actual distance. In fact, often God is revealing his true intimacy with us if he can make himself known in the absence. As Jesus said, "Unless I go away, the Advocate will not come to you" (John 16:7). God has not abandoned you; he is just revealing another side of himself. Silence is just one of many mysterious chords God likes to sing.

Third, emotions need to be discerned. Emotions can serve as an indicator light, but something bad happens when emotions become our engine.[6] Rather than listening to our emotions, we can begin to worship them. Philosopher Alasdair MacIntyre once wrote about what he called "emotivism," his word to describe the worship of emotions and feelings as the sole compass for what is good or bad in human existence.[7] Emotivism is codified as, "If it feels good, do it!" Some of our greatest Christian thinkers have openly lamented the trajectory of emotivism among even the Christian faithful. "One of the ironies in the story of Western theology during my lifetime," writes N. T. Wright, "has been the way in which the 'liberal' tradition, which used to pride itself above all on clear, rational thinking, has quietly been taken over by *emotivism*, not least in the area of ethics."[8] What Wright and MacIntyre bemoan is a Western tradition that has slowly moved from ethics to feelings as the orienting basis for right and wrong.

When we equate emotions with belief, our feelings can lure us away from right beliefs. This is now commonplace—we check social media or the news cycle and take in some painful story that flares up our rage at injustice. Again, emotions are good and created by God. But they take the wrong place when they become the engine for our action. Were we to take action simply because of the emotions, we would not do the hard work of actually discerning with Christ how we are to respond. When we read yet another story of abuse in the church, our gut reaction is to lose all hope and trust in the church. You can play this out for yourself. Our current environment—where we are faced with a world of diversity, difference, and readily visible injustice through social media—constantly tempts us to trade in Christian beliefs in order to ease emotional discomfort. One particular young man whom I pastored was prone to emotional manipulation. He lived his life on social media—and as a result, every time I would meet him for a pastoral coffee, he was newly angry about some injustice he had seen in the world. I affirmed his deep compassion for the world and agreed with his critiques of the church. But at one point I had to establish boundaries: I was having difficulty meeting with him without walking away from my own faith. His every crisis became my every crisis. Boundaries desperately needed to be established.

The Christian life should be triangulated between right belief, right action, and right feeling. God invites us to all three at the same time. If I am believing in Jesus rightly, it will *always* lead me to having a deeper emotional love and compassion for the world and a deeper practice of God's kingdom in the world. If I am feeling deep compassion for a person or a people, it needs to be connected to a deepened sense of theological faithfulness to who God is. Our emotions are not intended to cause us to abandon God's truth. Right belief, living, and feeling, when played together, become the beautiful symphony of Christian faithfulness. But keeping these three parts of our lives faithful to the living God is indeed challenging. There's a relational side to theology we too easily overlook. We need to learn this painful lesson from Solomon in the Old Testament.

When 1 Kings tells us that he had 700 wives and 1,200 concubines, we should not be shocked to find that these new relationships were having a spiritual impact on him. All that pillow talk "turned his heart after other gods" (1 Kings 11:4).

From Deconstruction to Deconstructor

When emotions become the engine for deconstruction, its purpose can be lost. Emotions hijack the car. Our posture of deconstruction shapes our character: perpetual acts of deconstruction can make us into destructive individuals. We morph from doing *deconstruction* to being *deconstructors*. One of the inherent problems with deconstruction is when we don't have the wisdom to know where it should stop. If we deconstruct certain biblical interpretations, when do we stop? If we deconstruct Christian theology, where do we pause before undoing the entire system? If we chuck one part of orthodoxy, where do we stop? Therein lies the danger: Once we begin deconstructing, when is the right moment to put down the sledgehammer?

Every action can become a precedent. C. S. Lewis describes in vivid detail the power that decisions and actions have on transforming the story of our lives. In *The Great Divorce*, Lewis depicts a person in hell whose unforgivable spirit took root first in early decisions to not forgive. Lewis hauntingly describes the effect of willingly choosing not to forgive time and again: first they *will not* forgive, then they *cannot* forgive. We might call this *character solidification*, the idea that our character is most formed by how we act and live—we become our actions. In Lewis's story, what was an initial choice of unforgiveness became an entire life centered around an inability to extend mercy and kindness to others. This principle directly applies to the danger of basing a Christian spirituality on deconstruction alone. Something dark happens within us when we give our energies only to tearing down.

Character solidification is found throughout history. November 9, 1938, has been called Kristallnacht—"the night of the broken glass." One fateful evening, the German gestapo burned down countless synagogues throughout Germany. The Jews were mocked and spit upon, their scrolls of Scripture dragged into the streets and burned. Soon the whole German nation would be drunk with hatred for the Jews—blaming them for whatever social or national ills they could think of. In towns big and small, synagogues were destroyed. For some German towns without a synagogue, there was a problem: What could be burned down? This was the case in the Pomeranian town of Ratzeburg where no synagogue was available to destroy. The angry mob had nothing to aim its hatred toward. Then someone discovered that Ratzeburg had once had a Jewish synagogue. What was now an egg market once was a place of Jewish worship. To satiate their hatred toward the Jews, the locals retroactively annulled the sale of the synagogue, removed the egg market, and restored the synagogue so that the citizens of Ratzeburg had something to burn down. In the words of one scholar, "What was a locality without a burned synagogue?"[9] Once the floodgates of hatred began, every German *needed* a synagogue to deconstruct.

Whenever we are perpetually given to hate, we actually *become* hateful. Of course, my own nation isn't free of this tendency. In 2015, the Public Policy Polling Institute surveyed 532 American voters if they would support the bombing of the city of Agrabah. While 54 percent said they weren't sure what should be done, a sizable 30 percent said they supported bombing the city. The problem? It would prove challenging to take military action against Agrabah given it was the fictional city depicted in Disney's movie *Aladdin*. The lesson is terrifying: 30 percent of those polled were not interested in bombing an *actual* city that posed a threat. They wanted to destroy a fictional city because it sounded like a Muslim city.[10]

Over time, we become our actions. A Christianity disproportionately centered on deconstruction creates a certain kind of Christian. When we're constantly tearing down, we become destructive. Then there is no end. Everything must come down. We deconstruct, but less and less because something needs to be deconstructed and more because we've become the kind of people who *need* to deconstruct. To the immature kid who's been given a hammer, everything starts looking like a nail.

Don't fall in love with the hammer. The spirit of our actions becomes the spirit of our very being. Not *all* acts of deconstruction inevitably lead to bitterness, cynicism, and a critical spirit, but our current intoxication with deconstruction is creating a community of deconstructors with theological tar, feathers, and pitchforks at the ready. This very spirit, prevalent among postmodern thinkers of his time, greatly concerned philosopher Paul Ricoeur—the terrors of what he called "unbounded deconstruction."[11] This kind of deconstruction tears down not because something needs to be dismantled—but rather because we have become deconstructors. A cursory reading of any biography of the French post-modern existentialist philosopher Michel Foucault illustrates a life of wanton pleasure, illicit drug use, boundless lust, pedophilia, and existential meaninglessness—all, ironically, in the name of "deconstructing" truth.

Building is harder, is more time consuming, and requires more intentionality than critique does. Theologians Miroslav Volf and Matthew Croasmun tear down our current fascination with tearing everything down. "Critique," they surmise, "is often infinite; it applies to everything—to biblical texts and biblical figures, to the church today and throughout its history, to God and to all aspects of modern societies—and it never stops."[12] It won't stop anytime soon. Undoubtedly, we must admit, something within all of us quietly longs to see things come down to the ground. We are jealous of those who have the confidence we used to have. We have hatred for those who represent what we used to believe. We hold disdain for those whose theological beliefs have hurt us or our loved ones. These are real feelings. But if we deconstruct without love, we become the very thing we hate and are seeking to deconstruct. *We become our hatred.* Still, the soils of hatred cannot grow the fruit of the Spirit.

What underlies so much of this is not a desire to deconstruct Christianity because the claims of Jesus are wrong. Rather, there is deep anger toward Christians. We have been hurt in the "name of Jesus." We have grown weary of the church. We want to escape the family systems that damaged our hearts. Someone needs to pay for the pain. So we use theology as a front for what is often real emotional pain. Rather than acknowledge the ways we have been emotionally hurt by our pastors or leaders in the church, we use theology to hurt them back. Or, worse yet, we use the pain we've received from a particular tribe or particular kind of Christian as a way to assume that all who hold their theological positions must be as unhealthy and sick as they are. But this kind of stereotyping just creates more division and hatred. The end result is failing to confront reality—we use theology as a cover for our emotional wounds. Puffing out our chests, we run to the life of the mind to make a judgment rather than acknowledge the tears and the hurts that harbor deep within. Perhaps the best thing someone in pain can do is put down the hammer for a while and learn to cry a little.

There's another dynamic for those who've been hurt. Hurting back is often our only way of finding agency and dignity. We hurt because we need to be seen. I wonder if we sometimes hurt the church after being hurt by the church to know that we still have power or agency. Maybe this is why we hurt God. Each member of the Trinity can be wounded. The Father was rejected by the prodigal. Jesus was crucified by his own. Even the Spirit can be grieved.[13] God can be hurt. Sometimes our desire to hurt is a question in the dark: Do I still matter? Perhaps as we enter glory, we will recognize Christ by the scars on his hands as he wipes away the tears from our eyes. I think that's how we'll know it's him. No other God would dare wear scars. Charles Spurgeon says, "A Jesus who never wept could never wipe away my tears."[14] We can't really follow God unless we know we can hurt him. And though we have hurt God, our tears have been wiped away by the very hands that saved us.

A Tale of Two Sisters

Coming to terms with our emotions includes coming to terms with hidden resentments we hold toward other Christians or the church. After the latest gun violence tragedy, you may have sensed resentment between those who offer "prayers and thoughts" and those who seek to change laws. This tension reveals a growing distrust between those who "have faith" and those who "do." A similar disconnect swirled in the New

Testament between Christians who emphasized "faith" and those who emphasized "deeds." James corrects both, saying, "Faith without works is useless" (James 2:20). Biblical faith can't be sequestered into either disconnected internal belief or externalized activism. Believing *is* action. Luke illustrates this resentment in a story of two sisters hosting Jesus for dinner. Mary sits in contemplation at Jesus's feet. Martha furiously prepares a meal. The words of Martha reveal a growing resentment toward Mary: "Lord, don't you care that my sister has left me to do the work by myself? *Tell her to help me!*" (Luke 10:40). Martha resents her sister, who lingers in the presence of the King while she herself is stuck with dinner and the dishes.

Similar resentments percolate between today's Mary Christians and Martha Christians. Some of us might even swing from one extreme to the other. In environments where salvation is understood solely in terms of "going to heaven," little attention is given to doing justice in the real world. The result can be the rejection of one for the extreme of the other. James K. A. Smith writes, "Many evangelicals are reacting to the dualism of their fundamental heritage that seemed only to value 'heaven' and offered no functional affirmation of the importance of 'this life.' Their rejection of this finds expression in a new emphasis on 'the goodness of creation' and the importance of social justice."[15] Many are reacting against their pietist upbringings and swinging toward the other extreme: activist Christianity. The resentment comes from suspicion that those spiritual practices were actually a way to avoid facing the pain of the world.

Deconstruction often presents with passionate pleas and calls for social justice and the dismantling of injustice. A life of Bible reading, spiritual fervor, prayer, worship, and evangelism is good—but it can also buffer us from the pain and suffering of the world. It can even feel as though the "spiritual life" of evangelicalism has been used as a way to escape doing justice in the world—even if it hasn't. I would often witness, and be able to predict, that the deconstruction journey of the young would almost universally lead to their headlong pursuit of justice, service in nonprofit organizations, and a heightened awareness of justice issues on social media.

Our pursuit of justice is good and right. Balance is also paramount. Our world *is* hurting. And we need followers of Jesus who act. But not at the expense of mocking those who sit at the feet of Jesus. In a world desperately in need of Martha Christians who fight for justice, it is easy to resent our upbringing among the Mary Christians who taught us to sit at the feet of Jesus. It is *easy*, but it is not the better way. One such man in the throes of deconstruction gave me the gift of allowing me to hear his story. He expressed a deep anger that his parents and church of origin had *talked* about the love of the poor his entire childhood but had never done a thing about it. He may have learned about the ideal of justice in the church, but he didn't see the church doing it. In his later years, he began to see the role a Christian can play in the world to bear witness and do justice. But he also came to appreciate that it was his upbringing that gave him the disciplines and practices necessary to do it with love. What a sacred and important epiphany!

Deconstruction too often trades in the spirituality of Mary for the new spirituality of Martha. But these are sisters serving the same Jesus. Each played her own role in this Jesus dinner party. I've come to resent our reading of the Martha/Mary narrative because Martha is made out to be the bad guy. She isn't. Someone had to make lunch. Someone has to do the good and worthy work. The sickness in the church goes malignant when Martha *looks down* on Mary for her devotion. Christ calls us to be a church where Martha and Mary work together in mutual respect and honor. Someone needs to pray too! There are *justified* Christians and *justice* Christians—followers of Jesus who emphasize being made right with God and followers of Jesus who emphasize making the world right. But they need each other, desperately.

I can't express how difficult it is in this moment to lead a church of Marthas and Marys who work together. It may seem idealistic and cool to say we need churches where activists and prayer warriors worship together. But it can be hell, and it can reveal our hypocrisy. After a mass shooting, I noticed that the progressives in the church demanded that I preach about changing our gun laws. And when the March for Life protest came to town, I noticed that the conservatives wanted me to implore the church to come and stand for the unborn. But when the shooting took place in a church or at a country music festival, the progressives were quiet. And the conservatives were entirely silent about the lives of refugees. It revealed to all of us that even our sense of justice is perverted—that we advocate for justice so long as it resonates with our ideological and political preferences. We all had to learn humility. We all had to see the church as a church of Marthas and Marys who work together. In fact, Jesus became the only reason they could continue to worship together. The minute we replace Jesus with anything—whether justice, prayer, or whatever—we lose our way. Jesus is the center of the church. Nothing else.

Everyone wants to change the world. The world needs changing. But when we fail to address deep emotional resentments harbored against brothers and sisters in Jesus, we can do justice for the wrong reasons. This can lead to less-than-loving motivations that cause us to, rather than actually change the world, only desire to be *known* for changing the world.[16] Soon enough our justice is no longer enacted in love for God's creatures as much as it is a statement to the other Christians who we despise. Our justice ceases to be loving. When we blindly ignore our resentment toward those other Christians who are just sitting around and praying, justice simply becomes a middle finger. It becomes a middle finger to the parents who raised us, to the churches that we feel aren't as passionate as we want them to be about the things we care about. Instead of doing justice, we are really just rejecting others. It's like we're saying, *We are doing justice. Where are you?*

There's an old revolutionary saying: "Everyone wants a revolution. But nobody wants to do the dishes." Every follower of Jesus carries some part of the yoke of Christ. No one carries the whole burden. Everything starts to break down when we allow our emotions to cause us to look down at the other who isn't doing what God is asking us to do. But few in activist cultures want to do the hard work of sitting at the feet of Jesus anymore to hear how he might want us to change our world. And too often our prayer warriors use prayer as a cover for cultural disengagement. We need both Mary and Martha. We need Marthas who do the work of activism, calling their senators and collecting signatures. And we need Marys who quietly sit, pray, and contemplate the goodness of Jesus.

What if we learned to see Christ's work through both sisters?

Needing a Place to Cry

Our goal must be to receive *all* emotions as part of our journey toward Jesus. Emotions matter. Denying them serves no one. Dan Allender and Tremper Longman III wisely write, "Ignoring our emotions is turning our back on reality; listening to our emotions ushers us into reality. And reality is where we meet God."[17] We desperately need to encounter God in our emotions. At the same time, we need a love for God that goes beyond emotion.

A good starting place is refusing to anesthetize it all. "Feeling better," writes Larry Crabb, "has become more important than finding God. And worse, we assume that people who find God always feel better."[18] Recognizing that pain is a necessary part of the Christian experience frees us from needing to do away with it. Jesus Christ is not always a solution to pain. He is often the cause of it. Jesus Christ solves the sin issue—not the pain issue. To follow Jesus is to follow him *into* the pain, *into* the dark emotions, *into* the difficulty. How we ever deceived ourselves into believing that "picking up your cross" could be a solution to pain is perplexing. Crosses hurt.

I began this chapter recounting my vocational crisis. Since I left pastoring, the pain has been immense, overwhelming. In my darker moments, I wished I were no longer alive. The pain never seemed to end. For our family, transitioning out of a pastoral assignment meant we needed to leave that church. The new pastor needed room to become their own self. So we faced a challenge: Where should we go to church?

The best advice I received in the grieving process was to find a place to go to church, sit in the back, and just be. Don't serve. Don't preach. Don't lead. Don't anything. Just be. We sensed the Spirit of Jesus in that. After nearly twenty years of pastoral leadership, my little family showed up one Sunday morning at a church where we had deep relational connections but no assignment, no clarity, and no sense of direction. We sat in the back. We just cried. The whole service.

Let me tell you: it's embarrassing crying in the back of a church service when everyone knows you used to be a pastor. I worried they would think I had an affair. I was embarrassed that they saw me being vulnerable. I felt like a failure. Mostly, I noticed the impact it had on my seven-year-old son. He sat in the back with us. He would try to comfort me—he didn't understand why we were crying at church. That experience, though painful, was (I believe) the greatest gift we have ever given our son. I love that my son will always know that the church is a place where you are allowed and invited to cry your deepest tears. He would say we cried too much. We did. But he'll also always remember Mom and Dad weeping in the back, and he'll remember that when his crisis hits, he can do the same. God welcomes the tears.

When John describes heaven in the book of Revelation, he says that heaven will be a place where Jesus will wipe every tear from our eyes. But that implies we enter heaven *having been* crying. We all need a place to cry. But we also need a place to cry where there are others who might help wipe away the tears.

In heaven, someone else wipes away our tears. May it also be in the church. We need a church where we can come and cry. I wonder, in our efforts at marketing a form of Christianity that appears appealing and victorious to the world, if we've created a church culture where we publicly put ourselves together. It isn't a place where we can cry anymore. In public we smile. In private we fall apart. I'll tell you: I've sat in the back and cried in the presence of Jesus. It's liberating. It's life-giving to simply be in the presence of God, who has emotions just like you.

Seven

Learning to Tend

Reflective Poverty

The Uber driver was named Jusef. Our short drive to the airport provided just enough time for introductions. Jusef moved from his Muslim homeland to come to the "land of the free." My work as a pastor and professor didn't hide itself for long. He perked up. Peering in the rearview mirror, he asked if I was a Christian. I nodded. Jusef confessed in broken English, "I've been interested in Christianity. I've met great Christians. But I have no time to study God. Uber, three jobs, kids, wife. God is interesting. Just no time." Then I perked up—a chance to talk about Jesus, with a stranger! Christian folks like me live for these interactions. Our ride then ended abruptly. Coming to a stop, he thanked me. I was suddenly standing at the airport's curb.

This is the new drill in the modern world where microinteractions are normative for a lightning-speed culture. Jusef represents many who are interested in deep, ultimate questions about God, eternity, and the good life—but who don't have time to ponder them. The by-product of this environment is that we're inundated with increasing knowledge and decreasing margin to process it. Our proliferating knowledge is matched by scant wisdom, space, and energy.

David Foster Wallace insightfully opined that this fast-paced, fluid culture actually nurtures lifestyles hostile to life's big questions: "We don't even seem to be able to focus for a very long time on the question."[1] Andrew Sullivan—considered a thought leader on modern distraction— has widely written how this time crunch affects our relationship with religion and faith. When we no longer have space to reflect, Sullivan suggests, we stop asking about meaning and the good life. Sullivan describes our situation in dark terms:

> If the churches came to understand that the greatest threat to faith today is not hedonism but distraction, perhaps they might begin to appeal anew to a frazzled digital generation. Christian leaders seem to think that they need more distraction to counter the distraction. Their services have degenerated into emotional spasms, their spaces drowned with light and noise and locked shut throughout the day, when their darkness and silence might actually draw those whose minds and souls have grown web weary.[2]

The greatest enemy to faith is not hedonism but distraction? Could this be true? While the modern person may be evoked to spiritual hunger and curiosity about God, there's rarely time for such activities. The spirit is willing but the schedule is not. Our lack of margin to think through and reflect on life's big questions is glaringly evident. In their wildly popular undergraduate course at Yale—Life Worth Living—theologians Miroslav Volf and Matthew Croasmun highlight one of their student's comments: "The world's greatest traditions have been trying to answer this question for 3,000+ years. And now I'm supposed to work out my own answer—in my spare time?"[3]

Modern existence systematically fills the "tiny cracks of inactivity," borrowing from Sullivan's piece on distraction.[4] Kill boredom. Sanitize it of silence. Fill everything with something. Ear buds in. This cultural mantra is best epitomized by a statement from Reed Hastings, the CEO of Netflix, on the purpose of the company: "Fundamentally we're about eliminating loneliness and boredom."[5] In a Netflix world, we're haunted by the big questions and ashamed we have few moorings to attach them to, even though we find time to binge-watch our favorite shows.

I'm whisked back to that moment my freshman high school teacher concluded his explanation of both sides to a complex political issue: "My task is to present the facts. *Your* job is to determine the truth." I still can't believe they thought freshmen could determine truth. I'd barely finished puberty. I couldn't see it then, but an embryonic form of the "my truth" worldview was gently sown in my generation's soul. We were taught that determining truth was our responsibility. But how does one know what is true? Without Christ or Scripture, we're left to build whatever we wish. Salman Rushdie—a brilliant agnostic—identifies the building materials of most: "Meaning is a shaky edifice we build out of scraps of dogma, childhood injuries, newspaper articles, chance remarks, old films, small victories, people hated, people loved; perhaps it is because our sense of what is the case is constructed from such inadequate materials that we defend it so fiercely, even to the death."[6] No wonder we're so anxious.

This is the toxic trinity of our moment: a hunger for truth, a belief that we determine it for ourselves, and the never-ending task of juggling family, hobbies, kids, friends, sports, and, yes, Uber deliveries at night. We suffer from a kind of reflective poverty. This is particularly heightened for those in the throes of deconstruction. I can think of countless examples of young people who try to follow Jesus in this context, exhausted by rethinking and reframing one's faith every few weeks (even hours) in light of everything they are learning.

Reflective poverty reframes our search for truth. What took years of deep, arduous thought and prayer in the past is replaced with the easy, the succinct, the tweetable. A lifetime of painstaking effort at reflection, risk, and error is replaced by a TED talk. And the modern "expert" is the one who read an article about something once.[7] Yet even in those rare moments that ultimate questions of meaning do make it onto the public stage, they're undertaken with speed, efficiency, and economics in mind. Money, sex, and religion can be discussed so long as they cast the widest nets possible—the risk of offense driving us to the lowest common denominator. And when a bold soul offers something counter to the prevailing cultural opinion? We kill them by cancelling them. We're a Cain culture. We'd rather murder Abel than humbly sit and learn about how he might be right. If we can't be the victors, we kill the whole conversation and tear down everyone else. It's called the "revenge of failure"—if we can't have the whole truth to ourselves, then we deconstruct any who claim to have any truth.[8] We've become Jude's greatest fear: "people [who] slander whatever they do not understand" (Jude 10).

Theologian Wolfhart Pannenberg once remarked that "criticism is *easier* than reconstruction."[9] Deconstruction can often be our way of entering a discussion without having to risk any answers. Listen: it's easy to find everything wrong with everyone else. Armchair ethics offers a powerful seat at the table. You look smart up there. With the combination of our time crunch and anxiety, we don't take the time to build, construct, or receive good, beautiful, and worthwhile beliefs. We only have time to pull others down. No wonder my students are terrified to risk a response in class anymore. To risk answering gets you killed these days.

God's Backside

There's a way forward: the risk of patience. Deconstruction and doubt can produce fervor within—we want answers, justice, resolution, and truth. We want them *now*. As Voltaire writes, "Doubt is not a pleasant condition." How true! Doubt can be excruciating and the itch of unsettled questions unbearable. One congregant of mine started listening to a podcast that began to open her eyes to the complexities of how the Bible was put together in antiquity. These new concepts awakened her to how much more dynamic the whole process was than she had thought. But it also created a real angst within her. She sat with me in an almost pressing anger—"We need to start talking about this from the pulpit. We need to hear more about this." Over time, the discomfort of these questions led to a full-blown deconstruction experience. Her new awareness of a very old set of conversations birthed a faith crisis she barely survived. She needed answers *now*.

These are what Dallas Willard called "the hard questions that smother faith."[10] Many of these questions are old questions. But what's new is our inability to sit and be refined by the questions over an extended period of time. Reading the saints of Christian history, we discover how many of them asked the same questions we have—issues of theology, injustice, spiritual difficulties, doubts, even deconstruction. What is different is that they often took an entire lifetime to wrestle with them. Our obsession with the quick fix and immediate response does not permit us to ask the big questions over a long period of time. Patient reflection is gone. Rather than going deep, we go wide. In our fervor to scratch our soul's itches, we rush to the podcast, YouTube channel, or favorite celebrity to help ease the pain of the unanswered questions. We opt for quick answers to our hard questions rather than hard answers that result from long, difficult, toilsome reflection. We've traded the wise for the quick.

In our impatience, we forget that God's greatest gifts are often wrapped in unanswered questions.[11] Could God solve all our epistemic problems? Of course. God is sovereign and holds exhaustive knowledge. But he doesn't rush to fix. Consider Jesus's response in finding out that his friend Lazarus was dying. Jesus did not *rush off* to heal Lazarus. Instead, Jesus waited four days before journeying toward Lazarus, arriving after his death. By the story's end, Jesus had resurrected his friend. But the fact that Jesus didn't drop everything, rush off, and provide a quick fix reveals something of God's nature. Could it be that God doesn't seem shackled by the priorities and demands of our timetable?

Patience is so uncomfortable to us because we assume a compassionate God is obliged to alleviate suffering instantaneously. But Jesus isn't obligated to do anything. Ever. Sometimes, in his compassion, God allows pain and difficulty to remain to deepen us, his people. Like Thomas, we have no framework to understand a God who would not rush in to resolve our theological and spiritual struggles: "Unless I see the nail marks in his hands and put my finger where the nails were, and put my hand into his side, I will not believe" (John 20:25). We demand that God resolve difficulty or we'll withhold the gift of our belief. But, as Jesus does with Thomas, there is no rushing off. Jesus eventually shows Thomas his scars, but a whole week later! Yes, Thomas will believe. But not before having to, borrowing from Willard, "stew" on his doubt for a week.[12]

Risking patience means looking longer and deeper. Scripture often distinguishes between *seeing* and *looking*. John writes in one of his letters, "We have *seen* with our eyes. . . . We have *looked* at [Jesus]" (1 John 1:1). Many saw Jesus, but John *looked* at Jesus. Consider the New Testament words *pondering* and *amazement*.[13] When Mary is informed that she's pregnant, she "pondered what sort of greeting this might be" (Luke 1:29 NRSV). After the birth, the shepherds come to Jesus. What does Mary do? "Mary treasured up all these things and pondered them in her heart" (Luke 2:19). She even follows him to the cross, pondering the death of her son. Mary doesn't just see Jesus—she *ponders* Jesus. Juxtaposed to Mary in the Gospels are the crowds who are "amazed" at Jesus—jaws dropping, fainting at his every word, and following Jesus from miracle to miracle the way a groupie follows a band. They were blown out of the water by how interesting he was. But they would never follow him to his death.

Jesus even warns Nicodemus to "not be amazed" (John 3:7 NASB) at what he has said. Jesus didn't want groupies who just loved the show. To "ponder" with Mary is to receive the story of Jesus for what it is. The ultimate difference between pondering and amazement appears in Luke's contrast between Zechariah and Elizabeth. An angel informs Zechariah that his wife will give birth. By all indicators, he is amazed. In response, the angel silences Zechariah. But Elizabeth responds to the same news with just a few questions, and then she self-mutes. She lets it be. She ponders. Her voice was not taken away.

To follow Jesus is to patiently follow him to his death. At times in the Christian journey, we will be given the gift of God's silence in the face of an immeasurable challenge. In Matthew 15, we read of a Canaanite woman who approaches Jesus to heal her demon-possessed daughter. She pleads for help. How does Jesus respond? "Jesus did not answer a word" (Matt. 15:23). Silence. Don't miss it—Jesus is being intentional. His verbal nonresponse is an intentional spiritual response. He's not being evasive, cruel, or passive. Jesus knows what he's doing. *What does someone do when it seems like Jesus isn't listening or responding?* The Canaanite woman, facing this silence, breaks through, falls at her feet, and cries out all the more, "Lord, help me!" The result? Her daughter was healed. To *see* Jesus is to let him pass by when we don't get what we want. To *look* longingly on Jesus, however, is to press in even when he's silent—when it seems he is ignoring you. God's Word isn't the only thing that we believe to be inspired. His silence is too.

The book of Proverbs puts it another way: "It is the glory of God to conceal a matter; to search out a matter is the glory of kings" (Prov. 25:2). Sometimes God hides from us. He is seeking to create a kind of person whose patient persistence can actually handle truth. God won't ruin us with truth if we don't have the character to handle it. God does not always hide things from us. Sometimes he hides them *for* us. God loves a desperate heart. Martin Luther had a phrase for this: *posteriora Dei,* or "God's backside." From time to time in the Bible, God shows us only his backside. Moses experienced this. God does this because if we can't handle God's backside, we certainly can't handle his face. If we can never understand his silence, we'll certainly never understand his words.

God doesn't dole out his answers. Sometimes we're not ready for the truth. Throughout *The Lord of the Rings,* J. R. R. Tolkien masterfully weaves an entire story around Frodo Baggins, the unlikely, humble, nothing of a hobbit who has to be the one to carry the ring. The ring would destroy everyone else. They'd use it for self and power. Only a hobbit could carry it. God desires us to have truth. But God isn't going to give us something so powerful that it would destroy us. The same God who tells us to "not give dogs what is sacred" (Matt. 7:6) is the same God who wisely gives us truth when we can handle it.

Parents know the importance of readiness: there's a reason a good parent won't explain all the details of sexual intercourse to their four-year-old child. They can't handle that stuff yet. At some point, you tell them. But our knowledge of the truth must be matched by our maturity to receive it. God is a good parent. Just as a good parent refuses to give the unfit child the "naked truth" in the wrong time, God knows there are some things we aren't ready for. Timing is everything. And it's also why there is danger in sex before marriage. Not that sex is bad. It's just that we haven't become the kind of people who can handle it yet. Patience makes us the kind of people who can.

Faith, writes Doris Betts, "is not synonymous with certainty—but a decision to keep your eyes open."[14]

Theological Impatience

The role of patience is built into the writings of the New Testament. Scholars generally believe we have thirteen of the letters that Paul wrote. He probably wrote more. Each letter had a purpose, context, and rationale. They weren't accidental—letters were written at great personal cost in the ancient world. Who knows what the production cost would be if Luke were to write both his Gospel and Acts today? Perhaps thousands of dollars. This may explain why both are dedicated to a man named Theophilus, who may have helped finance their production. The time, money, and papyrus needed to write these letters were outside Paul's own cash flow.

Paul sent letters when he couldn't go. Each letter would have been a response to a letter that a particular church or individual would have written to Paul with their questions and concerns about following Jesus in their context. When Paul wrote the letter to the Romans, he was answering questions the Romans had. When Paul penned the two known letters to Corinth, he addressed issues they faced. When Paul wrote Ephesians, he provided feedback on the issues that church was facing. Each letter addresses different questions. Each was written for a different church with different problems in different spaces.

Ancient letter writing has become an exciting area in New Testament studies. One thing we know: a letter would travel a long time to get where it was going. There was no postal service. Each letter required some risk-taking adventurer to carry it to the intended destination. When Paul wrote to Rome, or Corinth, or Ephesus, the letter would be given to a trusted person who *personally* carried that letter to its destination. This is why Paul ends so many of his letters glowingly thanking the person who carried it. These communications came at a great cost both financially and personally. Because of unforeseen tragedy, some likely never made it to their destination.

If you had written to Paul with your faith question, waiting for that answer would require great patience. Months. Even years. The very context of theological formation in the early church was framed by lots and lots of waiting and in-between time. The truths of the New Testament took tremendous time, cost, and risk. When a church needed an answer or issue addressed, they were not privileged to write a quick email, send a text, or find a helpful podcast on the topic. They didn't even have a New Testament they could open and read. Until they got their answer, where would they go? They would pray. And debate. And disagree. And talk. And wrestle out their question. And read the Old Testament. The letter from Paul or Peter or John would eventually arrive. The answer would come. But not for a long time.

Why is this important in Christian formation? Something beautiful happens in the in-between. History teaches us that the theological problems the church faced were met with patience, perseverance, community, prayer, and trust. Our earliest theology was done patiently.[15] This process of sending expensive letters at the risk of personal harm, and then waiting months (even years) for a response—while difficult, no doubt—I believe had a powerful effect on the early Christians. They couldn't get fast answers.[16] They were even waiting for the New Testament to be written, the very letters they were receiving. This whole process forced the church to its knees in fervent prayer and deep dialogue with one another. The waiting pushed them toward one another and toward God. They became a theologically patient people.

We no longer have any need to wait for theological answers or to pray patiently or to endure painstaking dialogue with other members of our church. We no longer need to be patient for the long-awaited voice of God through prayer or Paul's letter. We can get answers *immediately*. We rush to podcasts, books, or quick texts for answers. We YouTube it. Rather than dig into the real, the blood, the guts, the problems of *actual* life in a community of worshipers, we replace it with digital environments that allow us to validate our doubts without needing to confess them to others who can bear them with us. Our modern existence is not set up for any kind of patient prayer that waits for the answer over a lifetime. Rather, we can have all the answers without having to form the character that can handle them well.

Living with the Heretics

Can you hear the spirit of Pontius Pilate in all of this? We stand before the one who called himself "the way and the truth and the life" (John 14:6). Before him, we have the boldness to ask the question, "What is truth?"—just as Pilate did. We stand before Truth with the most important question in history, a right and good question. What *is* truth? But rather than asking the question and doing the hard work of sitting down, reflecting, and pondering what Jesus might have to say—or has said—we do what Pilate does. We present the question, only to turn away without having time to hear a response. "With this [Pilate] went out again to the Jews gathered there" (John 18:38). Pilate had the right question. He just didn't have time to stick around to hear the response. In the words of the philosopher Francis Bacon, "Pilate . . . would not stay for an answer."[17]

Neither do we.

The word *Israel* literally means "wrestles with God." Our very identity as God's people is to struggle with God and others over long periods of time—to stay long enough to be shaped by the waiting for an answer. I suspect this is why sexuality often provokes so many to wrestle with—and often deconstruct—their theology. The sexuality dialogue is painful, emotional, and feels like it must be resolved immediately. There aren't always easy answers. Things demand nuance, sensitivity, and a lot of clarification. A friend of mine wrestled for years with sexuality and his Christian faith. The pain he felt was deep. He decided to spend a year reading everything on the topic, gain some perspective, and arrive on the other side with some answers. Eventually the experience changed his theology.

I applauded his fervent desire for truth. He modeled a tenacity that I think everyone needs to have. But I confessed two problems I had with his process. First, I told him that in his year of reading and listening to people he had never met, I felt useless as his pastor. I felt replaced. Second, I expressed surprise at the time frame. One year, that's it? Why not forty years? Or how about two thousand years, as the church has? I told him that I thought it was silly he could fit into one year what has been a two-thousand-year theological dialogue. While I respect him and his decision, I felt frustrated at the method and speed with which he undertook it.

It seems like we end up becoming somewhat like the people we read and listen to. I did an experiment recently. I spent one week getting my information from Fox News. The following week, I got my news from CNN. Something astonishing happened. After week one, I was certain the Democrats were the essence of evil and the problem behind all things. But in the following week, I was all but certain that the Republicans were the end of our fine nation and our president the serpent incarnate. What did I learn? We are who we listen to. We are where we go for our information. We become the podcasts we listen to. We become the books we read. We become the people we go to for our answers.

An obscure monk by the name of Chame gave advice to Christians under his care: "Don't live with the heretics."[18] His point was don't spend the majority of your time with those whose theology alienates you from Jesus. Not don't *know* the heretics. Not don't *love* them. Don't *live* with them. Use caution in discerning who you live with and spend your time with. When we spend time listening to those who deconstruct and question Christianity, we shouldn't wonder why we're deconstructing our faith. When we run into the arms of conservative fundamentalism to answer our questions, we shouldn't be surprised we become fundamentalists who write off everyone we disagree with. Chame should be heard. Though we need the voices of the left and the right, may we first go to our knees and the community with whom we follow Jesus.

We are shaped less by our questions than by the community with whom we wrestle with those questions. We must not be satisfied with replacing church and community and Eucharist with podcasts. Open yourself to the question that may take decades to pray through—even eternity. And do it with some people until you all have wrinkles. Critique the immediate and instead hunger for the wise. Order your pizzas and books and music online, but don't take your deepest doubts and questions there. Bring them to us, God's people on the ground. Please don't replace us. Question the assumption that a PhD is the same as being wise, or the assumption that "most viewed" or "viral" has anything to do with veracity. Tenure and holiness aren't the same thing. They never have been. And, for God's sake, give the Bible a chance. In a world of lemmings, we need one book that doesn't bow to the pressures of peer review.

Tending

The quintessential picture of pondering is seen in Exodus 3. Moses walks through the desert "tending the flock of Jethro his father-in-law" (Exod. 3:1). Moses comes upon a burning bush. Naturally, he stops, looks, and ponders. Then the bush speaks. God reveals his personal, holy name. *Elyeh asher elyeh.* Roughly, it means "I AM WHO I AM." God tells Moses to take off his shoes. He's on holy ground.

Rabbis have long believed that Moses wasn't the first person to pass by the bush. What was special about Moses was his willingness to stop. What distinguished Moses and so many other biblical characters was not that God spoke to them. Rather, they had what Jesus called "eyes to see" and "ears to hear." Moses was prepared for this. Look at Moses's occupation: he *tended* Jethro's flocks. Tending was an essential part of ancient life and the story of Scripture. "Tending" (or *ra'ah* in Hebrew) is a common image in the Bible.[19] In Genesis 2, God assigns the man and woman to "tend" Eden's garden, name animals, and create culture. Abel "tends" the flocks in the fields before he is murdered by his brother. Jacob "tends" sheep to be able to have his wife. David "tends" sheep before becoming king. Aaron, the first priest, "tends" the tabernacle lamp where God is worshiped. Even the New Testament shepherds "tend" their flocks before hearing the angel's proclamation. Ancient life was a *tending* life—looking, paying attention, giving yourself to something, taking your assignment seriously enough to stick to it for the long haul.[20]

Ours is a Tinder world that struggles giving the monogamy of our attention to anything—we crave and chase whatever looks best. Giving our attention to anything is almost impossible. Now an entire academic field studies distraction and our modern loss of attention. "Attention studies" are increasingly articulating ways in which our screen-based culture not only steals our attention but actually builds an entire economy upon it. All the rings, advertisements, offers, messages, and opportunities have created a people who have what one scholar calls "plasticity of attention."[21] We no longer attend to anything because we are attending to *everything*. In this frenetic culture of clickbait and distraction, we give the highest bidder our attention for the payoff of little hits of dopamine and adrenaline.

Have you noticed how different reading has become? Nicholas Carr, in his 2008 article "Is Google Making Us Stupid?" expresses disdain over his inability to read anymore:

> Immersing myself in a book or a lengthy article used to be easy. My mind would get caught up in the narrative or the turns of the argument, and I'd spend hours strolling through long stretches of prose. That's rarely the case anymore. Now my concentration often starts to drift after two or three pages. I get fidgety, lose the thread, begin looking for something else to do. I feel as if I'm always dragging my wayward brain back to the text. . . . Once I was a scuba diver in the sea of words. Now I zip along the surface like a guy on a Jet Ski.[22]

This distraction economy banks on our willingness to be distractible. A daily economy of billions of dollars depends entirely on clicks. Nothing more, just clicks. In the old world, economies were built on building things. In the new world, economies are built on the ability to grab and steal attention. Lives are being changed. Distracted driving accidents and alcohol-related accidents now happen at nearly the same rate. Babies are dying, forgotten in sweltering cars as parents aloofly purchase a gallon of milk. Congressmen play solitaire on their phones in congressional meetings that decide whether we'll bomb a nation. Distraction isn't a nuisance. Distraction is life and death.

Most at risk is our ability to attend to God. Back to Moses who *tended* sheep. Why could it be that so many biblical characters who had life-altering encounters with God tended things beforehand? Here's my hunch: the fact that the ancients didn't carry screens in their pockets made them a certain kind of people. Their lives were given to one craft, one marriage, one job until their death. When Moses spends his life tending sheep, he's perfectly prepared to hear God when God speaks. Moses paid attention to the burning bush because he'd spent years tending to the sheep of Jethro.

The human soul withers under the avalanche of distraction that our attentionally promiscuous culture has curated. We have not yet learned the skills of attention that would allow us to hear God when he does speak. Our soul pays a price when we throw around our attention willy-nilly to every little thing of slightest interest on our screens, to the buzzes in our pockets, to notifications, or to news articles. We lose what Augustine called a "virginity of our mind."[23] When we're promiscuous with our attention, we're promiscuous with our soul. Practicing attentional discipline is challenging business. Curating a tending heart in a Tinder world requires far more than goodwill and nostalgia. It means missing out. Being ignorant. Falling behind. Not reading what everyone else is reading. Not watching what everyone else is watching. And maybe even being on the wrong side of history.

Had Moses owned an iPhone, he wouldn't have stopped and looked at the burning bush.[24] Giving God the monogamy of our attention—what Scripture calls "single-heartedness" and "purity of heart"—requires ruthless discipline around what we give our attention to. Brother Lawrence must have known this when he titled his book *The Practice of the Presence of God*. God's presence doesn't just happen. We *practice* preparing for it.

Alan Fadling offers a beautiful image to help us understand tending to Jesus. In winemaking, Fadling points out, the wine's quality is directly related to the quality of the grapes. In turn, the quality of the grapes is related to the quality of the vines and their roots. Fadling asks, How does one grow healthy grapes in harsh and unpredictable environments? In order to cultivate deep roots, the winemaker must intentionally *not* artificially water the grapevines. If the vines are watered by sprinklers or artificial means, something bad happens—their roots are not forced to go deep. When water is intentionally withheld, the roots *must* go down in order to find deeper sources of refreshment. The connection between surface-level roots and overwatering is long established: "Vines that grow with irrigation develop a relatively small, onion-shaped root ball since they don't need to reach any farther for the water they need."[25]

The deepest people are the ones who attend to Jesus even before he speaks—those who have *practiced* for God's presence. I've long noted something different about people like C. S. Lewis, Henri Nouwen, Brennan Manning, and Flannery O'Connor. Each of these endured excruciating seasons of difficulty in their faith. Lewis struggled with bouts of grief and depression after his wife's death. Nouwen struggled with his sexuality. Manning was a drunk who never really got clean. O'Connor spent her entire adult life with lupus, making even standing for long periods of time impossible—and eventually it took her life. What do these writers have? They have *patina*—those brown stains that appear on a baking sheet after seventy years of putting it in the oven. Patina is the sign of grit, of long-suffering, of endurance, of having been through the fire. You can smell the writers who have patina. Their writings reflect the faith of those who didn't get everything they wanted. Yet they continued. They *long* suffered. They remained. They would not have traded their struggle for anything. Ask a mother in labor who pushes a little child out of her body how she is feeling. She'd scream in pain—but she would keep going. Why? Because of the glory that is to come. The Christian heroes who speak most to us are always the ones who *didn't* get everything they wanted out of this life.

Want to hear God? Practice tending. Put down your phone when you're with one another. People are made in the image of God; iPhones are not. Give the person in front of you the attention they deserve as beloved, image-bearing creations of God. Leave those earbuds behind and walk alone in silence. Leave the phone in the car. No screens at the table. Take Dietrich Bonhoeffer seriously: "He who no longer listens to his brother will not listen to God."[26] If you're in deconstruction, be intentional about spending far less time on your phone, on social media, and with earphones in. Instead, sit in the questions. Let them give you your God-given patina. Hear the wisdom of Evelyn Underhill: "For lack of attention, a thousand forms of loveliness elude us every day."[27]

But there is one final detail: the shoes. Take them off! Why would God tell Moses to take off his shoes? I never understood this. But then we had a child. For years, when I returned from work, Elliot would run up to me and say, "Papa, papa, take off your shoes!" I never got it. I even asked other parents if their kids did this. Then I finally asked him. Why did he insist I take off my shoes? His answer wasn't complex. "When your shoes are on," Elliot said, "you have somewhere else to be. When your shoes are off, you've got nowhere else to be."

It isn't merely that we're distracted. It's that we privilege everywhere else over right here. God came to me through my son. He's a burning bush. Only now I'm starting to see.

Until we learn to see the bush, we're just pretenders.

Eight

Practicing Being Wrong

Conversion and Repentance

The New Testament describes two different types of encounters with God: conversion and repentance. Conversion is turning to God in faith. Repentance, however, is turning back to God in faith through a changed mind and action. Pagans convert; Christians repent. Oddly enough, Scripture doesn't describe these as mutually exclusive experiences. Consider Luke's portrayal of Saul's conversion to Christianity. Our first glimpse of Saul is as persecutor of the church. Following the death of the first Christian martyr, responsibility is placed on young Saul: "The witnesses laid their coats at the feet of a young man named Saul" (Acts 7:58). It shouldn't surprise us to see Saul traveling to Damascus to persecute Christians there after consenting to Stephen's murder. Saul is a man on a dark mission to zealously persecute Christians. Luke ominously writes that Saul was "breathing out murderous threats against the Lord's disciples" (Acts 9:1).

But then something surprising happens. Nearing Damascus, Saul hears Christ's voice: "Saul, Saul, why do you persecute me?" (Acts 9:4). Hard-hearted Saul—cut to the heart—falls to the ground blinded. He sees his own folly. Underscoring the surprise, Luke employs one of his favorite words: "suddenly" a light shines around Saul.[1] Saul lies in the dirt, heart shattered, a life undone. As the adage goes, God often births humility through humiliation. This is a painful birth.

Looking carefully, we see reverberations of a creation event afoot. Consider the parallel imagery between Acts 9 and Genesis 1–2. God "breathed into" Adam his Spirit; Saul "breathes out" hate against Spirit-bearing covenant people. God created the light *ex nihilo* ("out of nothing") in Genesis; the light appears "suddenly" around Saul in Acts. We even hear echoes from God's first recorded words to Adam in his disobedience, "Where are you?" (Gen. 3:9). Saul hears a question: "Why do you persecute me?" God doesn't accuse. God invites confession. A final sign of new creation: just as Adam rises from the dust, Saul is brought down to the dust. We've come full circle. "For dust you are and to dust you will return" (3:19). The Hebrew word for "return" is *shuv*, the same as "repentance." No wonder Paul would have so much to say about new creation in his letters. He was a new creation.

Consider, as well, the weight of the phrase, "They led [Saul] *by the hand* into Damascus" (Acts 9:8). The vicious leader is now being led. The one who saw is blinded. The one who hated Jesus is forgiven by him. Everything is now upside down. The self-sustaining, self-referential, self-sufficient religious leader is now being led blindly into God's kingdom. Jesus, Paul later writes, has "made foolish the wisdom of the world" (1 Cor. 1:20). Paul knows this because he has experienced it. Conversion and humility go hand in hand. Saul is invited to submit—to Christ, to church, to the cross. Being raised to life in this way violently threatens one's sense of self-resurrection. As the #MeToo movement swept Hollywood, convicted rapist Harvey Weinstein emailed a friend pleading for grace. He could make an early comeback if he could just go away for a while. Weinstein writes, "My board is thinking of firing me. All I'm asking for is, let me take a leave of absence and get into heavy therapy and counseling whether it be in a facility or somewhere else, and allow me to *resurrect myself* with a second chance."[2] Oh, the spirit of our time. We love resurrection as long as we're in control of it. But real resurrection can't be controlled or self-attained.

The essence of Christlikeness is in receiving, a truism unexplored by too many Christians. In baptism, someone *else* brings us out of the water. In foot washing, someone else washes our feet. "Unless I wash you," Jesus tells Peter, "you have no part with me" (John 13:8). There is simply no room in the inn for self-sufficiency in the journey of Christian discipleship. Christlikeness is death to DIY spirituality.

Unbeknownst to Saul, that same ascended Christ was speaking to a man in Damascus named Ananias. Little is known about Ananias. His name means "God is gracious." He was a follower of Jesus. And he kept up on the news—knowing that Saul was a threat to the Christians in his hometown. Some early church fathers believed Ananias was the pastor of the little church in Damascus. If true, what a startling image for those ordained into pastoral work: there was a time when pastors could just sit around and do whatever God told them to do that day. This illustrates the power of the obedient, available disciple. Ananias greets Saul in the appointed home on Straight Street and lays his hands on him. Saul's sight returns, he's converted and baptized, and he starts preaching.

Ananias's legacy isn't his fame but his faith. Look at his first words to his enemy Saul. He calls him "brother." Two things are happening here. As Saul is converting, Ananias is repenting. Saul opens himself up to Christ as Ananias opens himself up to the enemy Saul. That's the way God's economy often works. As Christians repent, the world sees Christ afresh. For the scales to fall from Saul's eyes, they had to fall from the hearts of God's people, just like they did for Ananias.

We need each other in God's kingdom. Through Saul, Ananias sees God's heart for his enemies. Through Ananias, Saul enters the church and his baptism. Saul's conversion and Ananias's repentance are intertwined, almost symbiotic. In God's kingdom, people in different places of the theological journey need each other to wholly pursue Jesus. Those in construction need vital conversations with those who've gone ahead. And likewise—we need people who wrestle with doubt to push us to ask good questions. In God's kingdom, we help carry one another's theological burdens. Everyone becomes a winner when churches become a place where those in construction, deconstruction, and reconstruction can pray together and lay their hands on one another. Saul needs Ananias. Ananias needs Saul. We need places where doubters can embrace faith and the faithful can honestly embrace their doubts.[3] Without these spaces, there would be no reason for Jude to write, "Be merciful to those who doubt" (v. 22). The command implies our need of one another.

Broken on the Floor

"Paul's conversion," opines historian William Placher, "sounds more like a nervous breakdown than a successful religious conversion."[4] Conversion is messy. But being humbled and brought to the ground was not unique to Paul. Moses and Joshua removed their shoes to touch the soil in their encounter of the divine. Abraham "falls to the ground" as God reestablishes the covenant in Genesis 17. Daniel and Ezekiel fall on their faces when they see God. Peter, James, and John are leveled to their faces in the transfiguration. John describes that he "fell at his feet as though dead" (Rev. 1:17) after seeing Jesus. Seeing God is a humbling experience. The word "humble" is derived from the Latin word *humus*—meaning "dirt." Being humbled is being brought down to who we are.

In our contemporary world, pride has often won over humility. Research consistently shows that evangelical Christians are increasingly known for being narrow-minded, prideful, and deeply intolerant.[5] How could any Christian be known for this? It hasn't always been the case. In the ancient church, as theologians finished their writing careers, they compiled a list of ideas that they no longer believed. To clear the air, their final writing would be an anthology of the things they now disagreed with. They were called *retractions*. For example, Augustine's *Retractions* talks about how he reversed his views on many things but refused to retract his belief in miracles. He'd seen too many to recant. Christians naming their follies in public: Can you imagine that? Imagine if Christians were known for their witness to the saving work of Christ and for recounting all the silly things they were now humble enough to amend.

Following Jesus should humble us. But, perplexingly, it can have the opposite effect. I've observed that when Christians believe something passionately, it can lead to a posture of pride and arrogance. There is a kind of arrogance that often comes with having the truth. Rather than allowing the truth to humble us, we use the truth as a weapon. Truth should always first and foremost be turned toward ourselves—never as a rod with which we beat others. What we need is truth matched with great humility. "We need a return to *gentle* dogmatism," writes A. W. Tozer, "that smiles while it stands stubborn and firm on the Word of God."[6]

This arrogance is the very reason that so many are disenfranchised with conservative and progressive Christianity. Those two sides of Western Christianity are often so full of themselves. What do you do when you see non-Christians who are humbler than Christians? What do you do when those who passionately proclaim the name of Jesus do so with such arrogance and pride? But something transformative can happen when a person encounters a follower of Jesus who passionately holds to the truth of Scripture yet does so gently. I once heard my theological hero say in a room full of people, "At any given moment, I have to be at peace with the fact that 80 percent of my theology is probably wrong. The problem is I just don't know what parts are wrong." When I first heard that, it made me mad at him. He was my hero! Now I think I admire him all the more. He believes deeply in Jesus, but he has the humility to know he has a long way to go. Ah, the glory of gentle dogmatism.

The journey toward humility comes by honestly knowing our history. Chuck Klosterman's excellent little book *But What If We're Wrong?* details the endless ways societies have been utterly wrong.[7] We were wrong about gravity, philosophy, worldview, Pluto, slavery, the earth-centered universe. Time and again, we were wrong. Everything that we now believe to be "true" at some point we were utterly wrong about. Klosterman's work raises a big question: What are we wrong about right now? The goal of this thought experiment is humility. Klosterman even invites us to "think about the present as if it were the distant past."[8] What do we hold dearly to today that in three hundred years will be found to be entirely wrong? It is a mark of humanity to think that we are right at this very moment. We are full of pride. We assume our progressive, secular values of today can't be wrong. How could they be? We believe them to be true. But we do not want to confront the ways in which we might be wrong.

Humans have an incredible capacity to avoid looking reality in the face. We never want to look wrong. One could argue that the most broken among us are the ones most capable of looking at reality and looking it in the face. In her groundbreaking research on depression, Kathryn Schulz writes about how depressed individuals seem to exhibit a greater capacity to deal with reality in a more honest and truthful way than those who live in the illusion of constant happiness and success. In her book *Being Wrong*, Schulz writes, "Countless studies have shown that people who suffer from depression have a more accurate worldview than nondepressed people. Depressed people do not nurture the cheering illusion that they can control the course of their lives. . . . That outlook is known as depressive realism."⁹ Our happiness, Schulz suggests, can actually shield us from reality. Rather than wanting to see reality for what it is, we protect our happiness at all costs.

One point of tension in my life as a Christian academic is this conflicting desire within to appear humble and smart at the same time. I never want to be shown to be wrong, but I want to be humble too. Teachers now have to deal with the fact that anything they say can be immediately corrected in the classroom by any student with access to Wikipedia on their phone. It's bound to happen. I'll get the names and dates wrong. This is normal. And the most difficult thing for me to say in the classroom is, "I was wrong." I lose sleep over this stuff.

The core problem is my assumption that being a Christian means having to constantly prove that I'm always right. I'm slowly coming around. I'm starting to see differently. I wonder if the gift of the Christian to the world is their willingness to boldly witness to their deepest, silliest, stupidest, clumsiest mistakes. The world doesn't know how to be wrong. Maybe we can show them how to be. Like Paul, Isaiah, Jeremiah, Ezekiel, and the rest of the gang.

We are allowed to be the only people in the world who are eternally loved at the core of our being and who simultaneously do *not* have adequate responses to all the questions.

What if being wrong was actually an important part of following Jesus? What if it was actually the sign that we were being humbled—a sign of the Spirit's work within?

Leah Libresco was an atheist who converted to Christianity in college. Libresco was a debater and spent a good portion of her years in college arguing ideas with others in sparring dialogue. Libresco talks about how debate is set up for one person to win and one person to lose. No one wants to be wrong. But the mark of a good debater, as outlined by the Yale Political Union, is not whether one wins every debate. Rather, can someone be humble enough to lose a debate? They call this being "broken on the floor." Why is this important? Because a good debater is not one who can only win an argument. A good debater is so committed to truth that they are willing to be broken by its presence.[10] They are willing to lose face to protect truth.

Resisting Brokenness

A human is an odd thing. People can do just about anything to avoid coming to terms with their wrongness. In the years following World War II as Allied forces liberated Europe, they discovered a major problem. Seas of captured Nazi soldiers not only did not believe that the Holocaust happened—they *refused* to believe it happened. To this day, Holocaust denialism is illegal in twenty countries as a result of the fact that so many continue to disbelieve that six million Jews were persecuted, murdered, and incinerated in ovens. The Allies took drastic measures to curb this denialism. In parts of Europe, the Allies would rent a movie theater, gather the captured Nazi soldiers, and show footage from Auschwitz. In one of my classes I show a picture of a group of Nazis taking in the movie. Many stoically watch, refusing to accept what they are seeing. Why would someone refuse to believe? To believe the truth was to admit guilt. Because they would be complicit if it were true, they had a vested interest in not believing the Holocaust. They *needed* their illusion.

Neuroscience tells us that the human mind can actually prefer resisting truth and reality.[11] We don't like facing truth. For many in the chaplain community, this is a normative experience. Chaplains often report that when the news is broken to a patient that they have a terminal illness, something peculiar happens—the patient, the patient's family, and even the doctor will often bring up other unrelated subjects. Rather than talk about impending death, anything else will be discussed—weather, basketball, summer vacation, bad hospital food. This phenomenon has been called "mutual pretense."

While the natural mind may be hostile to truth and reality, the spiritual person is called to turn toward it at all costs. In Christian theology, *repentance* means facing reality head-on. Repentance is difficult to ignore throughout the Bible. The first word out of John the Baptist's mouth is "repent" (Matt. 3:2). The first word of Jesus's first sermon is "repent" (Matt. 4:17). Repentance is critical to Christian life. The joy of being a Christian is that Jesus actually invites us to explore our wrongness. To look at our sin. To come to terms. To not look the other way. Mincing words does not help—repentance can be painful and life-shattering. But that shattering is counted as good and necessary for Christians. Repentance is not only about changed actions; it is also about changing our minds. From time to time, we need to repent in how we think about God. Repentance is exactly what the Greek word *metanoia* means—"to change one's mind."

The process of repentance includes allowing God the freedom to shatter our thoughts of him. When C. S. Lewis's wife Joy died, he penned a book on suffering and loss called *A Grief Observed*. In one penetrating section, Lewis reflects on his "memory" of Joy. Lewis admits that he finds himself falling in love with his memories of Joy. He sees it almost as a kind of adultery—to love the memories of Joy more than Joy herself. Then Lewis applies this to theology. In our thoughts of God, Lewis writes, we often love our ideas of God more than God himself. When we do this, we run the risk of idolatry, of loving that which looks like God rather than God himself. Lewis writes:

> I need Christ, not something that resembles Him. A really good photograph might become in the end a snare, a horror, and an obstacle. . . . Images of the Holy easily become holy images—sacrosanct. My idea of

God is not a divine idea. *It has to be shattered time after time.* He shatters it Himself. He is the great iconoclast. Could we not almost say that this shattering is one of the marks of His presence? The Incarnation is the supreme example; it leaves all previous ideas of the Messiah in ruins.[12]

God will from "time to time" shatter our thoughts of him in order that we might love him more. Lewis knew that Scripture warns that we can worship our ideas of God over God—*idolatry*. In Lewis's words, God is the "great iconoclast" who disrupts our theology so that we can stop loving our words about God more than God himself. Too many love their idea of God. And too few love God.

When Moses comes down Mount Sinai and Israel is worshiping the golden calf, he discovers that Aaron the priest led the rebellion. Idolatry is a constant temptation among the faithful—to forge our love around what we think rather than a passionate pursuit of Yahweh. When our words become our gods, Paul writes, God will frustrate "the intelligence of the intelligent" (1 Cor. 1:19). True faith journeys to Jesus—a journey that must take us through the first two commandments: worship God alone and renounce graven images. The order of these commands is instructive. Worship is first loving God, but worship also includes deconstructing any graven images. *In order* to love God properly, we must absolutely annihilate the false images we erect in his place.

By God's Spirit, we are to ground up and deconstruct the graven images. That's the task of discipleship: to love God with one's *whole* heart, mind, soul, and strength. We might from time to time have our dearly held beliefs shattered so that we can worship God more than our ideas. Jesus didn't come to save our faith. Jesus came to save *us*. To save us he must destroy our false faiths from time to time.

Part of being a Christian is being wrong. I'm reminded of Karl Barth's dictum, "Only Christians sin."[13] What Barth means is that Christians alone have a belief system that can account for their own wrongness. The joy of following Jesus is that not only are we allowed to be wrong, our continual acknowledgment that we *are* wrong is the sign that we're on the right path. Oh, the irony. And how freeing! The Christian gospel is an invitation to humility. In our deconstruction age, this humility liberates us. Petrarch once said, "I am so afraid of being wrong that I keep hurling myself into the arms of doubt rather than the arms of truth." Yet, in Christian faith, we don't have to be afraid of being wrong. We are called to be wrong. But being aware of our wrongness leads many to deconstruct the faith rather than construct it. In knowing that we might be wrong about any number of things, we can end up tearing down belief. The Christian gospel invites us not only to be wrong but to *risk* belief. To *wager* our minds and our hearts for something greater than ourselves. Don't allow your knowledge of your wrongness to keep you from the joy of belief.

I've heard it said that we build a box in the first half of life where we place our understanding of God. That box is good. We need a box. But in the second half of life, we need a much bigger box in which to hold those thoughts. That is one way to think about it. But I've come to like the image of Hannah in the Old Testament. In 1 Samuel 1, we see Hannah bring a new pair of clothes for her little boy Samuel who has been dedicated to work before the Lord in a religious space. Why is Hannah making and delivering clothes to her son? In the ancient world, moms made clothes for their sons. But kids grow up. Hannah did this every year—bringing new clothes to fit her growing child. Undoubtedly, Mary would have done the same for her son, Jesus Christ. Except her son was God in the flesh. As Jesus grew, Mary would have made new clothes to cover his growing body. In making new clothes for her son, she was simply keeping up with who Jesus was. Jesus was the same person. But he grew up before her very eyes. The clothing had to keep up.

Don't confuse God with our thoughts. Theology is just the clothing we put on God—the words we use to wrap the Word. But the two should never be confused. The clothes of Jesus don't save. It is the man inside them who saves us.

Isms

The classic 1994 film *Forrest Gump* starring Tom Hanks features Robin Wright as his beloved crush, Jenny. Jenny is portrayed as a young girl who goes into the world and gets caught up in a world of political activism and protest against the Vietnam War. Her boyfriend captures the timeless effort of so much of the spirit of the 1960s when the young were caught in the fervor of fighting the Republican president's decision to take the US to war. In one gruesome scene, Jenny's hippy boyfriend beats her up. The scene is difficult to watch. What does Jenny's beloved friend Forrest do? He beats up the boyfriend. The next morning, everyone is stepping onto a bus to head to the next protest. There the boyfriend tries to apologize, to make right his violence toward Jenny. In his attempts at saying sorry, he stops, exasperated, and mutters, "This is all President Lyndon Johnson's fault anyway."

The scene in *Forrest Gump* captures the sixties, but it also captures today. Today's young are captured by dreams of changing systems, activism, and protesting the brokenness. And praise God! God dreams of a just, merciful, and peaceful world, akin to what Martin Luther King Jr. called "the beloved community." But unabated, our efforts at changing the system out there can cause us to overlook the darkness within. Christopher Derrick, in his timeless essay "Trimming the Ark," suggests that external focus can keep us from character-building: "But in general we shall seem to have surrendered pretty completely to the political and *activist* illusion of the time, placing our trust in policy and insight and arrangement, in the human wisdom of our managerial elite, in our new fine cleverness."[14] What Derrick suggests is that when we focus exclusively on external arrangements, *who* we are becomes secondary. Everything becomes President Johnson's fault. Our hands become clean.

Undeniably, the most difficult week of pastoral work I've ever experienced was the Sunday after President Trump won the 2016 election. The day after, I walked my Portland neighborhood and saw people weeping in the streets, grieving and worried. That Sunday, I attempted to find some way to bridge the chasm for a congregation at ideological odds with itself.

Portland was a painful place to be after the election. Ronald Reagan once called it "little Beirut." It has taken on a reputation for being a hotbed for angry protests between the extreme right and left. I carefully read our newspapers that week to see how our city was processing everything that was taking place. I was struck by one particular article in the local *Willamette Week*. In an editorial, one writer sought to comfort Portlanders who were facing a new world. One line in the editorial caught my attention: "We won't allow hatred to come into *our* city." Epiphanies show up late in my life. But when they do, I pay attention. Not long after, the implication hit me: Hatred isn't *us*. Hatred isn't Portland. Hatred isn't inside of our broken hearts. It is out there. It is some other people. Hatred is always everywhere *else*.

That editorial troubled me. So much of our sense of injustice had become about what was happening *out there*. Not in here. And as we've seen, this externalized vision of evil has deeply reshaped our relationships. I could see it in how people's relationships with their parents changed after the election. The twenty-first century has given us a front-row view of all the injustices in our world. From the bird's-eye view of social media and the never-ending news cycle, we observe evil in a way we never have before. The world is not eviler; we just have the videos. I am meeting more atheists who believe in evil than ever before. *Everyone can see this thing isn't working.* The way we now talk about these evils is almost exclusively in terms of "isms": sexism, Islamophobism, homophobism, intersectionalism, racism. Thank God we are talking about these things that must be faced head-on. We need to deal with sexism and the rampant, entrenched, systemic subjugation of women in Western culture. And Islamophobism with its entirely unfair prejudice and hatred. Homophobism is never the answer. Gay and lesbian people should never be treated with disrespect or dishonor, especially by those who claim to disagree with them in love. And talking openly about racism is now the new norm—not just personal racism but institutional racism. Thank God the bandage has been ripped off.

Everything is on the table now. As a follower of Jesus, I can't help but celebrate the cultural backlash we are seeing against forms of evil that have lurked in our laws and culture for far too long. But it simultaneously terrifies me—in broader Western culture, among my friends, in the church, and among Christians. Whenever we talk about racism—and I see this in myself—it is always *someone else* who is racist. We rail against racism but only in others. It is never us. No one ever says, "Hey, there's this big problem of racism, and it's me!" It is always other people. Other people are sexist. Other people are homophobic. Other people are Islamophobic. It is never, ever me. The echo reverberates: evil is all "out there." And we won't let evil in here.

The selectivity of the kinds of isms we are willing to face is insanely embarrassing. In a culture that is obsessed with facing the isms, we so quickly reject the thoughts and ideas of the generations who have gone before us because they don't agree or don't have our same educational pedigree. We may be facing racism and sexism and homophobism, but we are committing ageism at the moment we do so.

We are good at facing the evil *out there*.

When the *Times* in London posed a question to its readers, "What is wrong with the world?" it received a lot of responses. The (possibly apocryphal) response of G. K. Chesterton would have stuck out:

Dear sir,
I am.
Yours, G. K. Chesterton[15]

It is an easy temptation for the person who is deconstructing their faith to come into their new belief structure and assume that everything they believe on the other side of deconstruction is all of a sudden true. The dark side of this is that we believe we are right in our deconstruction and everyone who is not in deconstruction is wrong—specifically those who have not yet walked through it. Healthy deconstruction entails a person's willingness to deconstruct their deconstruction! Doubt your doubts. Suspend your disbelief. Just because you are deconstructing something right now does not mean you are right or have arrived.

Biblical humility starts with the confession that God is right and we are wrong. Full stop. "Let God be true," writes St. Paul, "and every human being a liar" (Rom. 3:4). Every human being includes you and me.

Are we humble enough to see ourselves as the problem? Or is it just "out there"?

The dark side of deconstruction is pride—as it can be of every stage of the theological journey. After the presidential election, I learned that when the community loses a posture of humility and brokenness, the whole thing can easily fall apart. By God's grace it didn't. As long as we're all open to being wrong, learning, growing, and being corrected, we can continue. I started preaching that the Christ-shaped church was a church that continued to convert and repent over and over. This meant seeking to create a church culture where it was okay to be wrong. This kind of environment—and attitude—must be fostered. It doesn't just happen. Any church that fosters arrogance, pride, and self-sufficiency could *not* be a safe place for a person to repent. When we read the letters of the New Testament, we discover that Paul, Peter, and John (and any other writer) simultaneously write about truth and humble postures toward one another. These are not mutually exclusive. The consistent invitation of the New Testament is toward a life of humility marked by having the humility of Jesus.

Whenever our pride demands that the church conform to our ideals and sensibilities, the enemy wins. This is Christ's church, not ours. On October 1, 1960, the famed contemplative and Catholic priest Thomas Merton wrote to a friend, English scholar and fellow priest Bruno Scott James. The two were collaborating on a project about the life and writings of St. Bernard of Clairvaux. After the introduction to the letter, Merton expresses—as is representative of so much of his writing—innumerable joy for knowing the depths of Christ's love. Then a break. Merton seems to get angry. He confesses there's a brewing problem in his parish: there's a "group of fanatics who are crying for a dialogue Mass." The meaning of "dialogue Mass" is difficult to assess, but Merton is clearly perturbed by a group coming to Mass who seem to want to change the liturgy. They don't want Mass. They want to sit around and dialogue during Mass—a more decentered, less top-down approach to the Lord's Supper. Merton grieves:

This they want after Lauds, at four in the morning, between Lauds and Prime, when there should be a quiet interval of reading, a lot of liturgical novelty and excitement. Understand my groans. They call themselves *liturgists*.[16]

Merton's agitation with what he called the "liturgists" stood out to me. His proverbial groans seem aimed at those who desired to reshape the ancient liturgy around their own wants and sensibilities. Something of Merton's tone strikes me. He rarely seems upset, and so this is out of the ordinary. Merton isn't being an academic here. He's being a pastor. He is seeking to bring people to the Lord's Supper. But they want *more*. They aren't content with Christ as he is. They don't want a church shaped and broken by Jesus. They want Jesus and the church shaped by their newfound ideals.

"The church we want," writes Eugene Peterson, "becomes the enemy of the church we have."[17] Anyone can be a liturgist—conservatives, progressives, Baptists, Episcopalians, egalitarians, complementarians, traditionalists, the open and affirming. We become liturgists the minute we seek to shape the church around our desires. When we succeed, we rob the church of its church-ness and turn it into a club. In our culture of deconstruction, we need to make it our goal to be humble no matter where we are on the theological journey. We need humble progressives who can still learn to listen to the theological views of Christians from the Global South who are conservative in theology and practice. And we need humble conservatives who don't beat down progressives with their orthodoxy but humbly offer it as a gift.

As long as we are willing to be "broken on the floor," there is hope.

Nine

Discerning the Truth

Discerning

We now turn to the practice of discernment. *Discernment* is a New Testament word meaning "weigh." The Greek word, *dokimazō*, refers to the weighing of metals as a means to decipher which were real or fake. The New Testament writings connect discernment with the weighing of truth and falsehood.

How do we know what's true? Discernment was particularly critical in the early church as Christians encountered environments where hostile ideas threatened to undermine the gospel's spread. Discernment was how the church distinguished between the Spirit of Christ and the spirits of the world. One writing, the *Didache*, instructs local congregations on how to identify the validity of a prophet's claim. The writing offers a (at times hilarious) metric to discern this. If the prophet did not practice what they preached, they were deemed a false prophet. Or, if they asked for money, they were not of the Lord. Or—and this is the best—they were a false prophet if they stayed in town for longer than three days!

Other church fathers emphasized discernment. Ignatius writes, "I urge you, therefore . . . partake only of Christian food, and keep away from every strange plant, which is heresy. These people, while pretending to be trustworthy, mix Jesus Christ with themselves—like those who administer a deadly drug with honeyed wine, which the unsuspecting victim accepts without fear, and so with fatal pleasure drinks down death."[1] Discernment, as such, was the plucking of the "strange plants" of heresy from the communities of faith. This task was as important then as it is now. Like the children in Narnia, the church is in a world of great beauty that is also the domain of the witch.[2] Caution is critical.

Paul offers an important prayer for the Philippians: "that your love may abound more and more in knowledge and depth of insight, so that you may be able to *discern* what is best and may be pure and blameless for the day of Christ" (Phil. 1:9–10). As it often does, Paul's writing reflects great anticipation for Christ's return. Discernment not only distinguished truth from falsehood but also led to a deepening love of God and his people. Paul prayed, and taught, that the church might be a discerning church able to recognize truth when it sees it. As Jesus prayed, "May your will be done" (Matt. 26:42). The emphasis is on God's will being done on earth, here, in the present. This can be done through our Spirit-led discernment.

Theologian Sinclair Ferguson defines discernment as "the ability to make discriminating judgments, to distinguish between, and recognize the moral implications of, different situations and courses of action. It includes, apparently, the ability to 'weigh up' and assess the moral and spiritual status of individuals, groups and even movements."[3] Discernment is to make theological judgment calls. This isn't the same as judgmentalism or condemnation. To discern is to judge, to discriminate, to be willing to name what is true and what is not. "The person with the Spirit," Paul writes, "makes judgments about *all* things" (1 Cor. 2:15). And thank God the spiritual person does discern and judge. Without judgment, the most vulnerable among us are exposed to the greatest harm. When my son needed a babysitter, we never went to Craigslist to find someone who was free for an evening. We found people who we knew where they lived and could be found and held to account. This is good judgment! Without good judgment, the least of these are put in harm's way.

Still, it's become unfashionable to do any judging in our contemporary context—least of all in the realm of theological or doctrinal belief. In our postjudgment world, the church has grown too afraid to name lies as *lies* and heresies as *heresies*. In one of his finest essays, theologian Stanley Hauerwas explores this growing hesitancy to discern truth and falsehood in the church by offering a medical analogy. If a medical student told his advisor, "I'm not into anatomy this year. I am really into people" and asked to skip anatomy class to focus on people, the medical school would reply, "Who do you think you are, kid? . . . You're going to take anatomy. If you don't like it, that's tough." Hauerwas delivers his crucial point: "Now what that shows you is that people believe incompetent physicians can hurt them. Therefore, people expect medical schools to hold their students responsible for the kind of training that's necessary to be competent physicians. On the other hand, few people believe an incompetent minister can damage their salvation."[4] Bad doctrine can actually harm the human soul. Just as we would not give a degree in medicine to someone who did not know the human body, we should not be willing to put people in power who preach and teach false ideas about God that can kill the soul. Just as an ill-equipped doctor can make people more ill, so the dissemination of lies can harm the soul. Ideas matter. Truth brings life. Lies kill, isolate, and give birth to spiritual death.

In discernment, we learn what we can trust and what we can't trust. This is tricky business. Paul further warned that in the last days, the church would find itself in an environment with great contempt for truth. In his second letter to Timothy, Paul writes, "To suit their own desires, [people] will gather around them a great number of teachers to say what their itching ears want to hear. They will turn their ears away from the truth and turn aside to myths" (2 Tim. 4:3–4). This is one of the marks of the end of days. The train is coming to the station.

Paul saw what was coming. In Neil Postman's introduction to his book *Amusing Ourselves to Death*, he prophetically contrasts two cultural views: that of George Orwell's *1984* and Aldous Huxley's *Brave New World*. Orwell's *1984* had looked to the dystopian future and anticipated that books would be banned by the government as a result of censorship. But Huxley's view was different. In *Brave New World*, Huxley held that books, rather than being banned, would become marginalized by a torrent of new information. One saw the dystopian future in terms of censorship. The other saw the dystopian future as one marked by access to too much information, where one could not discern falsehood from truth because of *too much* knowledge and information. Postman writes, "Orwell feared those who would deprive us of information. Huxley feared those who would give us so much information that we would be reduced to passivity and egoism. Orwell feared that the truth would be concealed from us. Huxley feared that the truth would be drowned in a sea of irrelevance."[5]

To illustrate the troubling nature of the moment, I invite my students to Google people who deny that the Holocaust happened. What they find terrifies them—and me. The number of people with PhDs who deny that the Holocaust ever happened is astounding and jaw-dropping. The point is one that I hope haunts them after they finish my class: that one can now find anyone with credentials who can articulate just about *anything* someone might want to believe. It seems like Huxley saw the future. So did Paul. The challenge for Christians in this matrix of clickbait and Google searches is not that we lack knowledge—it's that our excess of knowledge drowns out the truth in the screaming loudness of culture, pundits, and critics. As Charles Hartshorne once wrote, "We live in a century in which everything has been said. The challenge today is to learn which statements to deny."[6] Discernment helps us learn what *not* to accept.

John and Discernment

No apostolic writer discusses discernment more than John. Perhaps the most important text on the topic, 1 John 4 reads, "Dear friends, do not believe every spirit, but test [*dokimazō*] the spirits to see whether they are from God, because many false prophets have gone out into the world. This is how you can recognize the Spirit of God: every spirit that acknowledges that Jesus Christ has come in the flesh is from God, but every spirit that does not acknowledge Jesus is not from God" (vv. 1–3). What can we learn from John about discernment?

Three core ideas are noteworthy. First, John portrays the universe as an entirely spiritual universe. "Many false prophets have gone out into the world," John writes. It is as though he is saying, "They are here. Ours is a world bathed in spirituality." Everything *is* spiritual! Philosopher Charles Taylor—in his book *A Secular Age*—writes about what he calls *disenchantment*, the idea that our secular environment prides itself on living in a world devoid of the spiritual. We've become disenchanted. As a result, we are haunted by transcendence.[7] Humming behind this secular myth is the gnawing knowledge that there is more to this world. Indeed—this is a very spiritual world. There are spirits. And there is the Spirit. For John, secularity is a total myth. This is a spiritual world in which we must learn how to discern that which is of God and that which is not.

The fact that the world is spiritual—John argues—doesn't mean those spirits are inherently good or trustworthy. The common truism of our time is that everyone is spiritual but not religious. For John, being spiritual wasn't the goal. As New Testament scholar Gordon Fee points out, John may actually be critiquing those envisioning themselves as spiritual but without fidelity to Christ. Fee indicates that the New Testament use of "spiritual" (*pneumatikos*) is always related to the personal Spirit of God. What's important is not being spiritual. What's important is being born of the Spirit through faith in Christ.[8] One can be "spiritual" and still be a child of the devil. John Stott would say, "Behind every profit is a spirit, and behind every spirit is either God or the devil."[9] Similarly, Martin Luther was fond of saying, "Everyone is a horse that either Jesus or the devil rides."[10] For John, we are *either* spiritual or born of the Spirit. Nobody is *not* spiritual. But few are born of the Holy Spirit. When one does believe in Christ, that person is clothed by the Spirit, as was the Old Testament prophet Gideon (Judg. 6:34).[11]

For the person in deconstruction or doubt, it's important to remember that just because something *feels* spiritual or enjoyable or liberating doesn't mean it's permissible, good, or wise. In fact, the most beautiful things are often *not* for human consumption. The forbidden tree in Eden was "good for food and pleasing to the eye" (Gen. 3:6). Was the fruit bad?

No! Was the tree evil? No! God created it. Did the fruit probably taste good? Absolutely! The problem wasn't the tree's badness. God simply had not given the humans permission to experience it. In a culture of emotivity, we assume that anything good, beautiful, tasty, and enjoyable is for human consumption. I mean *we were made for this*, right? But the early chapters of Genesis actually offer a critique of beauty and taste as the sole metric for discerning good from bad.

Second, John ardently distinguishes between the spirits (plural) and the Spirit (singular). This speaks volumes. Unlike God, the spirits of this age send a blizzard of conflicting messages, temptations, and ideas. The spirits of this age are not unified. They are torn asunder by the chaotic reign of Satan operating in chaos and disorder. One minute they tell us one thing, the next another. Their words are shifting sands. But the Holy Spirit is unlike the spirits. God's Spirit is one, unified with the Father and the Son. The Trinity's unified purpose means that God is consistent and coherent. God doesn't mix up his messages. The Spirit of Jesus will never tell us anything that does not align with what Jesus himself said. The Father, the Son, and the Spirit never conflict with one another. This is a helpful framework for discernment. Put simply: the voice of God that we may hear in our hearts or minds will never contradict the words of God that have already been written. God is consistent with himself and doesn't contradict himself.

Third, and most importantly, John writes that the Spirit points to Jesus. John's claim is clear and concise. If the spirits don't "acknowledge" Jesus—that he came in the flesh, died, and resurrected—they aren't to be trusted. The implication is that the spirits of the demonic will never point us toward Jesus. What a spirit points *to* matters.

Let's play this out. J. B. Phillips was likely the most reputed Bible scholar and translator of the twentieth century, having shaped some of the most important Bible translations of the modern era. Near his life's end, Phillips shared an experience that he'd kept quiet for years. Phillips claimed in written testimony that three days after C. S. Lewis's death, Lewis visited Phillips as an apparition. The claim rattled many in the Christian world. What's to be made of such an audacious claim from a

most revered Bible translator? Phillips's book *Ring of Truth* agrees the
story is odd. Still, he insists it happened:

> The late C. S. Lewis, whom I did not know very well . . . gave me an unusual
> experience. A few days after his death, while I was watching television,
> he "appeared" sitting in a chair within a few feet of me and spoke a few
> words which were particularly relevant to the difficult circumstances
> through which I was passing. He was ruddier in complexion than ever,
> grinning all over his face and, as the old-fashioned saying has it, positively
> glowing with health. The interesting thing to me was that I had not been
> thinking about him at all. I was neither alarmed nor surprised. . . . He
> was just *there*—"large as life and twice as natural"! A week later . . . he
> appeared again, even more rosily radiant than before, and repeated the
> same message.[12]

What do we do with C. S. Lewis visiting someone after his death?
Whenever I share this with my class, they are usually divided on the
issue. Some say it could happen, some say it couldn't. I often play devil's
advocate: Didn't Moses and Elijah appear at the Mount of Transfiguration? Why couldn't one of the modern-day saints appear today?

Discernment asks important questions in such matters. While students articulate both sides of the debate, I ask them to consider another
question: What did J. B. Phillips report that C. S. Lewis told him? What
was the fruit of that experience? What did the experience point to? Phillips claims that the experience drew him all the more to Jesus and a
love for God. The fruit of the experience was spiritual fruit—deeper
love, fidelity, and awareness of God's Word and Christ's work in his life.

The Spirit always points to Jesus. We see this time and again in the
biblical tapestry of the Trinity. Each person of the Godhead (Father, Son,
and Spirit) consistently points to the other persons in the Trinity. Jesus
points to the Father. The Spirit points to Jesus. The Father points to the
Spirit. They always point to the other. The persons of the Trinity never
self-glorify, seeking to draw attention to themselves. Rather, they point to
each other. Christian philosopher Cornelius Plantinga brilliantly writes

that this is one of the marks of God's nature: they "exalt each other, commune with each other, and defer to one another. . . . Each divine person harbors the others at the center of his being. In constant movement of overture and acceptance, each person envelops and encircles the others."[13] God's nature is inherently *other*-focused. Conversely, the powers of darkness—the demons, evil, Satan, dark forces of the world—never point to the Father, Son, or Spirit. Instead, they are always pointing to themselves. While the Trinity always points to the other members of the Trinity, evil always points to itself. The irony: the One who *should* be self-centered always points to the other, while the one who should be silenced in the lake of fire won't stop self-referencing. The devil is full of himself. But Jesus is full of the Spirit.

And that's the work—and beauty—of the Spirit. Christopher Holmes perceptively writes, "We see a person who is so secure in himself that he can be entirely given over to the declaration of another. . . . The Spirit has no interest in pointing us to the Spirit's self. . . . The personhood of the Spirit is expressed in the Spirit's binding us to Christ and in him to the Father."[14] The Spirit isn't self-centered. The Spirit points to Jesus. In spiritual formation, this helps us discern: Do these experiences point to the self or to Christ? If the experience puts the self at the center of gravity, we must be wary. Christ is our center. We are not our center. Theologian Gustavo Gutiérrez writes that this is the central mark of conversion: "To be converted is to know and experience the fact that, contrary to the laws of physics, we can stand straight, according to the gospel, only when our center of gravity is outside ourselves."[15]

Rule of Faith

To discern or distinguish the truthfulness of a particular idea, we need something against which it is measured. To name the darkness we must know the light. A measuring stick is necessary. As such, the early church writers spoke of the *regula fidei*—the "rule of faith." This rule was the theological standard against which every human idea was to be measured. Without this rule, how would Christians hold to the saving message of Jesus? Without the *regula fidei*, the church devolves into a sycophant, going along with the world's ways and means.

By God's grace, we have a standard established from the early church and continued over two thousand years of history and tradition: it's called *orthodoxy*, or "right belief." Orthodoxy—what C. S. Lewis called "mere Christianity"—comprises the central and historically rooted Christian beliefs that distinguish true Christianity from the rest. These are the common-ground standards of Christian belief. Orthodoxy represents those core Christian beliefs that transcend time, space, and tradition. This is why the New Testament *does not* emphasize merely "having faith" or "being spiritual" as the Christian goal. Having faith isn't the endgame. The thrust of the entire New Testament is to hold "the faith" in Jesus. We don't have an amorphous faith in some nameless deity in the sky. Rather, we have "the faith" in the person and name of Jesus. We hear this in Paul's writings to a young Timothy: "Keep hold of the deep truths of *the faith* with a clear conscience" (1 Tim. 3:9). He further admonishes in 2 Thessalonians, "So then, brothers and sisters, stand firm and hold to *the teachings* we passed on to you" (2 Thess. 2:15). Paul doesn't command us merely to have faith. He commands us to have *the* faith handed down from generation to generation.

What are these common-ground beliefs? Roger Olson, in *The Story of Christian Theology*, says that different beliefs have different weights. "Valid Christian beliefs—those that are considered true," writes Olson, "are not all on the same level of importance."[16] Olson describes three different kinds of theological belief that carry different levels of importance and weight. First, *dogma* are those core Christian beliefs that have been passed down from the apostles to us today. When we believe in the gospel as freedom from sin, this is a dogma belief. So is belief in the physical resurrection of Jesus, the virgin birth, and the Trinity. Second, Olson writes, there are *doctrines* that remain important but not entirely necessary. These may be views on gifts of the Holy Spirit or practice around communion or how many angels can be on the head of a pin. Finally, there remain what the Reformers called *adiaphora*—theological opinions that are far less important.

Another way to say this is that some beliefs are to die for, others to divide over, and still others to be debated. The tenacity with which we hold to our belief in the resurrected body of Jesus should be different from whether we believe angels are sexual beings or not. Resurrection is much weightier than our nuanced angelology.

Identifying and knowing what is and isn't orthodoxy may actually bring healing to the church. Diversity is a possibility only if there is an agreed upon, unifying set of common beliefs. In jazz, there are the baseline components of a song—chord structure, tempo, and rhythmic movement. When the baseline is played and honored, each instrument is freed up to improvise, or "riff." This duo tandem is what makes jazz incredible, the dance of the structure and the riff coalescing into beauty. Of course, if someone goes off on a solo that goes way outside the boundaries of the baseline—the song fails. That would be two songs being played. In Christian formation, diversity is only possible as long as there is unity in the baseline. We cannot lovingly disagree if we have nothing to agree on.

Things like the resurrection, the virgin birth, the Trinity, the centrality of Scripture—these are beliefs that Christians for two thousand years have literally died for to pass along. This is "the faith" that's been handed down from the apostles. This faith is received in each generation, not to be remade in each generation. Perhaps we've become lost in our language in thinking that having one's own faith means getting to make up one's own faith. But these are two different things. There's a world of difference between having a faith of our own and making up our own faith. The former is living into the story of God that's been ongoing since Abraham, Isaac, Jacob, and Joseph. The latter is a heresy—reinventing the faith for our own desires today. That presents quite the task for the twenty-first-century Christian: to have a deep, rugged, inflexible commitment to historic Christian beliefs with a fluid, flexible posture toward one's method. The church has had a word for those who've chosen their own depiction or theology of Jesus they wanted for themselves: heretics. It's not a mistake—it's from the Greek word *haraomai*, meaning simply "to choose."[17]

Carrying Bones

Even as I write this, I've come across another Instagram deconversion story. But this isn't any old deconversion story. This time it's Joshua Harris, whose book *I Kissed Dating Goodbye* captured my generation in the late 1990s. Harris has undergone a "massive shift" in his faith. He and his wife are divorcing. And he's no longer a Christian.[18]

Harris has his own story to tell—one that likely includes great pain and tribulation that led to his deconversion. If I could sit with Harris, I'd look him in the eyes and apologize. I'd tell him, "Hey, Josh, this isn't all your fault. We played a role. I'm really sorry." This is what happens when we place too much weight on a person. Too much was put on his back. Keep in mind that Harris was twenty-three years old when his book, which sold 1.2 million copies, was first published! He was given so much authority. Too much. Too fast. Scrolling through the comments, it is clear that once again the lost faith of a celebrity shakes the faith of so many others. Why does this liturgy of deconstruction and disavowal of evangelicalism keep repeating itself? What happened?

We need to make a shift and stop propping up Christian celebrities and putting all the pressure on them to hold up our faith. It's sinful human nature to worship celebrities over Jesus. In the book of Acts, Paul and Peter were constantly worshiped as they entered this or that town. But they always rejected it. New Testament Christianity as found in the Bible rejects celebrity. Contemporary Christianity, however, has found a way to be built upon it. And now, whenever our celebrities fall, so does our faith because we placed our faith in them—not in Jesus. We put people on platforms too big for their lives and souls to handle.

We desperately need heroes in the faith. I kind of like how Catholics do their heroes—what they call "saints." To become a saint in the Catholic tradition, you have to have died, performed at least one verifiable miracle, and been a passionate lover of the church. Not many become saints. But the most important part: you're required to be dead. Truthfully, I don't think the living can handle being the hero. When we put people up on stage, buy their books, and tell them they're great, we put too much on them. Our evangelical world has its form of sainthood—mediated not by character or by their tried and tested love of Jesus but by the size of platform, book sales, and church size. We need to return to the old heroes whose lives can handle our attention.

We need to learn to carry the bones.

What does that mean? In the early church, congregants of the church in Smyrna wrote of their former leader: "And so later on we took up [Polycarp's] bones, which are more valuable than precious stones and finer than refined gold."[19] The earliest Christians did something odd in our eyes—they cared for the bones of their heroes, their most beloved leaders. They even saw their bones as holy. Thomas Aquinas went so far as to argue that God chose to do works through the saints even after their death. Touching them brought healing, wholeness, even life. In fact, the catacombs where the earliest Christians were buried were called "dormitories." Christians would gather underground among the dead to take communion during the worst seasons of persecution. Being around the bones was the only safe place to be. They were safe among the dead who were sleeping, awaiting the return of Christ.

All of this may seem odd, if not exotic. But the same practice is actually rooted in Scripture. In the Old Testament, for example, we consistently see Israel carrying around the bones of their fathers who had died. In Exodus 13:19, Moses carries the bones of Joseph toward the promised land. Later, in Joshua 24, Joseph's bones are brought into the promised land. Then there is this enigmatic story in 2 Kings 13:21: As some Israelites were burying a man, the body fell into Elisha's tomb. What happened to the dead man who touched the bones of Elisha? "The man," it reads, "came to life and stood up on his feet."

There *is* life in the bones. We were made by God to carry with us those stories, histories, and traditions of the mothers and fathers and forebears who followed Jesus long before us. We can't move forward into the future without them. This means we maintain relationships with wiser and more seasoned followers of Jesus who have the same old stories to tell over and over again. It means we begin to read the writings of the earliest Christians. Or just dead Christians. C. S. Lewis recommended that for every new book we read, we read three old ones. This is a good starting place. Our vision for diversity should include the Christians who have gone before us and think differently than we do. This is a return to tradition—faithfully caring for the bones of the people who've gone before us.[20]

To move forward, we must remember. We don't jettison the past. We honor it, receive it, listen to it. God's people best move forward into the future by intentionally retrieving the past. We move into life's future by carrying the bones with us. It is like the Chinese philosopher Zhang Guolao who would ride his mule backwards so as not to be distracted by what was ahead and to remember what was behind.

Ten

Embracing the Whole Kingdom

The Big Sort

Cultural fractures are manifesting in our midst. In 2008, Bill Bishop examined our growing divide in American politics in his book *The Big Sort: Why the Clustering of Like-Minded America Is Tearing Us Apart.*[1] Bishop shows how politics is dividing America not only ideologically but increasingly geographically and relationally. A political map of party affiliation some fifty years ago would reveal a landscape of purple, a mix of Democratic blue and Republican red. Everything has changed. Red states get redder. Blue states get bluer. The purple is disappearing. As a result, "political refugees" are physically moving to the states that represent their political values. This has essentially become the death of the swing state. Bishop's work illustrates that a kind of cold civil war has descended on America. In this new war, the new weapons are social media, YouTube, and emotional coercion.

The kingdoms of this world are divided. With this has come a divided vision of God's kingdom. In his book *Kingdom Conspiracy*, New Testament scholar Scot McKnight argues that there have emerged two seemingly competing views of what God's kingdom is in the contemporary church. One side understands God's kingdom as where God's rule is made manifest through the work of prayer, Scripture reading, evangelism, churchgoing, and Christian living—what McKnight calls the "pleated pants Kingdom." Another view of God's kingdom is represented by those who see God's rule through the bearing of justice, mercy, goodness, and a sanctified society that ushers in equality and equity for all peoples— what McKnight calls the "skinny jeans Kingdom."[2] Like our hypertribal political world, these two visions of God's kingdom seem more separated than ever. The kingdom of God *feels* torn. One side of the kingdom believes it has a monopoly on good theology, evangelism, prayer, and the Christian life. The other believes it is changing the world for the better.

For those formed in Christian communities that emphasize personal spirituality, discipline, and conversion, relating their faith to a world of injustice produces a cognitive disconnect. Do we side with the kingdom that teaches us to pray? Or with those fighting to change the broken world system? McKnight strongly contends (and I find myself agreeing) that this division between two visions of God's kingdom is not only illusory but entirely unfounded. The New Testament vision of God's kingdom is *God's* kingdom—not ours. But it puts so many in the position of having to choose between conservatives who live on one side of the kingdom and progressives who live on the other. We all can feel these tensions.

Do we go to progressive churches that stand up for immigrant children at the border? Or do we go to conservative churches that stand up for the unborn?

Do we go to conservative churches that evangelize with the gospel? Or do we go to progressive churches that seem to be living the gospel?

Do we go to conservative churches that hold up a high view of sexual holiness? Or do we go to progressive churches that make space for sexual minorities?

Do we go to conservative churches that tackle the evils of personal sin? Or do we go to progressive churches that fight against systemic evil and injustice?

Do we go to conservative churches that emphasize human economy? Or progressive churches that emphasize climate and ecology?

This theological and emotional disconnect has been eloquently described by Jonathan Wilson-Hartgrove: "I am a man torn in two. . . . And the gospel I inherited is divided."[3]

Our divided vision of God's kingdom didn't just come about. Nor is it the first time God's people have been divided. After the death of Solomon, Rehoboam ascends to power. As he comes to the throne in 1 Kings 12, Israel pleads with him to provide respite from the demands of empire. They aren't cared for. The work is too heavy. They plea that the new regime take a more graceful, just attitude. Rehoboam responds in two ways—first, he goes to the elders of Israel to hear their advice. Then he goes to his peers to consult their advice. The elders tell Rehoboam to extend grace and leniency. But Rehoboam's peers tell him to make the work harder. Rehoboam listens to his peers over the wisdom of his elders. This leads to the divided kingdom. It is notable that the divided kingdom in the Bible comes as the result of a breakdown in intergenerational relationships.

Sociologists point out that much of the Western cultural context in which many of us find ourselves undermines the cultivation of vibrant relationships between the young and the old. Robert Bly's *Sibling Society* argues that one of the major cultural shifts in these societies has been that, in contrast to modern and premodern societies in which the authorities (parents, priests, and presidents) had inherent authority, postmodern people no longer assume those places or functions have inherent authority. The authorities, Bly argues, have been ousted. Bly calls this the "sibling society"—a new world where all are equals and no one is above anyone else.[4] Equality. Everyone on the same level. *The Lonely Crowd* by American sociologist David Riesman further drew attention to our withering views of the old. "Grandparents [have come to] stand as emblems," writes Riesman, "of how little one can learn from one's elders about the things that matter."[5] The sages are gone. There are no authorities anymore. The hierarchies have dissipated. We are now our own authorities.

This fractured vision of God's kingdom cannot be healed apart from a healing of our intergenerational, interracial, and interpersonal relationships. A world without honor and authority is a world of division and strife. Paul even wrote about this among one of the early churches: "Even if you had ten thousand guardians in Christ, you do not have many fathers" (1 Cor. 4:15). The church isn't to be a sibling society. We need mothers and fathers in the faith. We are trading in our role as parents to be our children's best friends—what sociologists call *peerants*. We are turning from the wisdom of the past to cling to anyone who will say what we already want to think. No wonder the kingdoms are divided.

We read the fifth commandment's "Honor your father and your mother" and end there. But the commandment's conclusion matters greatly: "Honor your father and your mother, *so that you may live long in the land the* LORD *your God is giving you*" (Exod. 20:12). God's command of honoring those who have gone before connects directly to peace and justice in the land. We are seeing this play out right now. We have no peace or justice. We also have no one we honor.

Both sides of the kingdom are part of God's work on this planet. Their work is good and important. But they both miss a significant point of the biblical story pertaining to God's kingdom. In his apocalyptic writings, Daniel lists off all the kingdoms of this world. Greece, Rome, Assyria, all of them. Then Daniel stops. In the middle of Daniel 2, he has a vision of another kingdom that will come down from heaven and crush all of these kingdoms. This kingdom was "a rock . . . cut out, but not by human hands. It struck the statue on its feet of iron and clay and smashed them. . . . The rock that struck the statue became a huge mountain and filled the whole earth" (Dan. 2:34–35). Daniel sees all the kingdoms of this world. And in their midst comes God's kingdom, crushing them all.

God's kingdom will "crush" all of our kingdoms. God's kingdom cannot be shaped by human hands. In fact, not once in the New Testament are we invited to "build" God's kingdom. We can't build God's kingdom. Only God can build this kingdom. We *enter* God's kingdom. When we think about this kingdom that is divided, it is critical that we all do our part. Some change history through prayer. Others change history by action. But both will be *crushed* by God's eventual work of establishing his rule and reign forever.

Flaming Swords

The first image we have of God's kingdom is found in the garden of Eden. Eden represented the space where God dwelled—the place where God gave himself and his ideals for human flourishing. It was there that God gave the ideal of the Sabbath, of caring for the garden, and of filling the earth. In Hebrew, the word for "presence" is the same as for "face." God's presence is not simply his generally being around—it is the intimacy of being face-to-face with the Creator of the universe. The man and the woman "walked" with God in the garden. They talked. They pondered sunsets. They were friends.

This intimacy was fractured by humanity's disobedience. Soon they were "banished" from God's presence. Of note, the Hebrew word for "banish" is the same as for "divorce."[6] The first humans lose their face-to-face intimacy with God and their ability to keep his ideals in the Edenic space. To subtly emphasize this, the ancient translators of the Greek Old Testament (known as the Septuagint) use the word *ekballō*. Adam and Eve were "sent into" the desert outside the garden. This same word is used to describe Jesus's temptation in the desert—"the Spirit *sent* him out into the wilderness" (Mark 1:12). Humanity was now divorced from God's intimate presence and ideals.

But the "banishment" from Eden, astonishingly, doesn't mean humanity delves into full-scale moral rot. Quite the opposite. In post-fall human culture, we see God's ideals continuing—just minus God's presence. We see this in the Cain and Abel story. After killing his brother, Cain is protected by God from undue human retribution. "Anyone who kills Cain," the Lord says, "will suffer vengeance seven times over" (Gen. 4:15). God gives limits to justice. However, at the end of Genesis 4, Lamech commits murder. What does Lamech do? He goes to his wives (Adah and Zillah) and confesses his sin. Then he takes justice into his own hands. "If Cain is avenged seven times, then Lamech seventy-seven times" (4:24). Note two things. First, God's ideal of marriage continues to be part of post-Eden human culture. But this ideal becomes perverted. What God dreamed as a covenant relationship between a man and a woman for a lifetime has become a polyamorous relationship of multiple partners. Lamech is doing marriage his way. Second, Lamech enacts justice—*his* version of justice. And, of course, his form of justice goes far beyond God's intention. The human community does something profoundly interesting after the fall—they keep doing God's ideals in their own way. We learn a lesson: God's ideals minus God's presence always become perverted.

God's ideals only make sense in the presence of God. What God tells us to do only works in the context of the one who told us to do it. God's ideals minus God's presence is called *idealism*. Idealism is whenever humanity takes God's ideals into its own hands and "does right in their own eyes," as the book of Judges says. Whenever humans do this, the ideals become twisted. Remember God's word in the creation story? "*Let us* make mankind in our image" (Gen. 1:26). God creates people with an intrinsic stamp of dignity on the deepest part of their being. Then humans are banished from Eden. Where do they go? A place called Babel—a tower that stood as a testimony to human pride and self-accomplishment. We can almost see humanity puffing its chest with pride over its accomplishment. Then they say it—that famous phrase over their own creation: "*Let us* build ourselves a city, with a tower that reaches to the heavens, so that we may make a name for ourselves" (Gen. 11:4). Notice their language is borrowed and twisted. As God had said "*Let us* make humans in our image," the humans say, "*Let us* . . . make a name for ourselves."

We do this all the time. We rob God of his dreams and twist them for ourselves. Listen to Christ's words at the table: "This is my body." Rather than using these words the way God intends, we twist them into a perverse mantra that permits us to take the sacred life of the unborn. Ideals twisted.

We are trying to create a world of justice, goodness, mercy, and love—all without the God who begot them and put them into motion from the beginning. The entire message of the Bible is that our attempts at returning to Eden on our own terms will end in us being cut. Just look at what God put in Eden after our banishment: "flaming swords." We try to get back to Eden on our own, but we are unable to enter. We all experience this. We get so close to Eden on earth—at times feeling as though we are about to ascend to perfection. Then it all falls apart. The sword falls and cuts our plans in half. All of humanity is one large effort at trying to reestablish before God something that humans cannot. Biblical scholar René Padilla writes, "Expelled from Paradise, humanity is increasingly searching for a way back. All of history may be interpreted as a history of unconscious attempts to return to a primeval state characterized by harmony with God, with neighbor, and with nature. The angel of the Lord guards the way to Eden with a flaming sword."[7]

The sin of humanity is not that it runs into evil and disarray. The sin of humanity is that it grabbed the beautiful thing—a piece of fruit that was "pleasing to the eye"—rather than trust what God had said. Our sin is replacing God's word with beauty, goodness, and justice in our own hands. As a result, God puts a flaming sword at the entrance to Eden. Someone else will have to prepare a way to go back. Our idealism won't do.

In her letters, Flannery O'Connor describes a friend (whom she calls "A") who has abandoned her faith and no longer attends her local parish:

> I'll tell you what's with "A." Why all the exhilaration. She just left the church. Those are the signs of release. She's high as a kite and all pure air. . . . She now sees through everything and loves everything and is in a bundle of feelings of empathy for everything. She doesn't believe any longer that Christ is God and so she has found that he is "Beautiful! Beautiful!" I even have restrained myself from telling her that if Christ wasn't God, he was really pathetic not beautiful. And such restraint for me is something! She is now against all intellectualism. She thinks she's at last discovered how to be herself and has at last accepted herself.[8]

This is the response of a post-Christian world. Notice that her friend's faith remains. She has not articulated an outright rejection of Christ. Rather, her faith has reoriented itself to something else—the beauty of this world.[9] Christ is no longer true; Christ has become beautiful.

"Beautiful! Beautiful!" she proclaims in her liberation. Like our post-Christian world, O'Connor's friend has not necessarily rejected religious beauty. There is beauty in all the faiths, she would proclaim. Instead she replaces Christ with beauty. The woman hasn't stopped her pursuit of goodness. She's made her entire pursuit about beauty. The pursuit isn't Jesus anymore.

Dismantling Purity Cultures

Idealism always leads to what we might call "purity culture." One expression of purity culture can be seen in the evangelicalism of the 1990s, when sexual, romantic, and relational purity were emphasized exclusively. In recent years we have seen countless people raised in this culture recount the pain and shame it created. Rigid purity codes can hurt the human soul. The call to dismantle these purity cultures *can* be overstated—but the calls to do so arise out of real pain and suffering. God's ideals can never be fulfilled outside the context of God's radical grace.[10] The human soul is scarred by graceless, burdensome, and unsustainable demands. Any such culture that falsely promises blessing for sexual purity alone—hitching everything to it—entirely overlooks the power of Christ's blood for real human beings in a real world. To say nothing of the fact that so few of the characters in the Bible could have served in churches that honored this kind of culture.

Does this mean we throw away God's ideals? Anything but! God's ideals free and liberate us from the tyranny of sin. But they cannot be followed *outside* the realm of grace. The fundamental flaw with purity cultures is not their invitation to sexual holiness—it is that sexual holiness is portrayed as a means *to* God. Biblical holiness isn't attained or earned. Holiness is ascribed. Purity cultures fail to recognize the core gospel message that Christ's holiness can be found only through *his* righteousness and not our own. Our hope is not in our own sexual purity. Our hope is in Christ's obedience.

Idealism alienates us from God and others. All our efforts at creating perfect and idealized spaces—while based in a desire for the good—end up fragmenting human communities. Utopian dreams of the church as a place free of sin may inspire us, but they will always fail us because the reconciliation of all things cannot arrive prematurely. Idealism creates within us a desire for perfection that can never be attained on earth. It is a false expectation that the perfect church can serve perfect people with perfect leaders who perfectly never hurt anyone. Expectations like this are merely premeditated disappointments. Idealism puts pressure on the church to do what God alone can do—save and reconcile. Idealism causes us to wander. The unrealistic demands of an ideal kingdom are captured by Calvin Miller in his *Once Upon a Tree*:

> Fields of suburbanite Christians migrate from congregation to congregation, propelled by a wanderlust for the greatest Christian show on earth. This ecclesiastical restlessness keeps the holy work of God's saving community at sea. Its saving work cannot prosper while the community wanders in search of something glitzy to fill its shallow heart. Where the reverbs and colored spots meet in only a place of plastic discipleship, where the lost sheep demonstrate how lost they are by begging the shepherd to replace his crook of pastoral care with a vaudeville hat and cane.[11]

Idealism destroys community, causing us to chase human perfection over God's good. Perfection, in this sense, is a mirage. How striking is it that not once in the opening pages of Genesis is Eden described as "perfect"? Not once! Eden is no idyllic perfection. What is it? The garden was "good"—repeated over and over again. The garden was good—not perfect. The sin of idealism is that it demands things to be better than God made them and that we reject anything that falls short.

"Purity cultures" are common among conservative Christians. And progressive Christianity is as guilty. "Safe space" culture, with its dream of utopian places that are free of discord and disagreement, have pervaded so many institutions—often in the churches. The left's sense of "inclusivity" has become so broad and sweeping as to include basically everyone who accepts their same vision of social justice, sexuality, and politics. My friend Richard, a progressive evangelical, angrily shared how he could not get any white liberals to come eat a meal with the homeless in his town at a soup kitchen for the fact that all the food was genetically modified. He was embarrassed. They didn't want to be caught dead complicit in the "injustice" of being with poor people who were being fed food that didn't fit their local, sustainable, GMO-free ethics.

Both sides have built their own purity culture Tower of Babel.

Perhaps this idealism is why so many young Christians raised in conservative churches are opting for more progressive, liturgical expressions. In his book *Against the Tide*, Miroslav Volf discusses the reason he (and many others) are drawn to more liturgical churches that emphasize the Lord's Supper and liturgy over the preacher's personality. Volf grew "disturbed by the failure of many preachers to make the center of the Christian faith the center of their proclamation."[12] Volf's sentiment echoes among many. Being raised in church environments where the authority and personality of the leader is overemphasized, we may yearn for churches where something else—not the pastor—is the center. Hence the move toward liturgical-centered expressions. One friend shared why she transitioned to an Episcopal church from her evangelical upbringing. "It's a safer place to take one of my nonbelieving but seeking friends," she confessed. "Yeah, it's boring, but my friends at least never leave offended." It's understandable why one might hide behind the safety of liturgy—it can protect us from the personality of actual human beings.

Idealism can also be our sly attempt at loving Jesus but not wanting to be found complicit alongside all those *other* dim-witted people who claim obedience to him. Anne Rice, famous for her book *Interview with a Vampire*, returned to her Christian faith later in life. After ten years of being a Catholic, Rice walked away from the church. Her Facebook note dripped with the very idealism that I'm sure pushed her—and pushes so many others—away from Christianity:

> Today, I quit being a Christian. I'm out. I remain as committed to Christ as always but not to being "Christian" or being a part of Christianity. It's simply impossible for me to "belong" to this quarrelsome, hostile, dis-

putatious, and deservedly infamous group. For ten years, I've tried. I've failed. I'm an outsider. My conscience will allow me to do nothing else.[13]

In both its conservative and progressive iterations, idealism ultimately drives us from incarnational life—of following Jesus "in the flesh." In the fourth and fifth centuries, Christians fled to the desert in protest as the church began getting cozy with the Roman Empire. These desert fathers and mothers, as they were called, offered an alternative society that rejected the state/church marriage. One of the fascinating marks of these early Christians was a faithful perseverance with the community where God had placed them. One such father, Anthony, responded to a question about how to please God: "Wherever you go, keep God in mind; whatever you do, follow the example of holy Scripture; wherever you are, stay there and do not move away in a hurry."[14] Benedict's *Rule* offers a word for those who left one monastery in order to find another perfect monastery: he called them *gyrovagues.* These gyrovagues "spend their whole lives tramping from province to province, staying as guests in different monasteries for three or four days at a time. Always on the move, with no stability, they indulge in their own wills, succumb to the allurements of gluttony. . . . Of the miserable conduct of all such, it is better to be silent than to speak."[15] John Climacus puts it this way: "Those who readily go from monastery to monastery are totally unfit since nothing is more conducive to barrenness than impatience."[16]

Idealism tells us there is a better community out there somewhere. There is a group of Christians who are *really* doing the faith right. There is a better way that transcends our brokenness. But the New Testament does not share in this sense of idealism. In one moment, Jesus tells Peter that "on this rock I will build my church" (Matt. 16:18). The next, Jesus says to Peter, "Get behind me, Satan!" (Matt. 16:23). This is in the same chapter! No doubt Luther was right: the church is simultaneously "righteous and sinful." Despite the fact that we want to create pure spaces free of darkness and impurities, that space cannot exist until the redemption of all things. This is important in our time: one of the by-products of the internet age is a front-row view of the sins of the church in real time. With each exposure, our trust in the system erodes a little more. But consider Jesus's own engagement with the broken religious system of his day. Every Saturday Jesus went to the synagogue, where he did ministry and kingdom work. His way of bringing change was to show up. Jesus went to the synagogue. Every week. He went to the temple. He celebrated the festivals. And every time he did, he was choosing to bring holiness into impure spaces in his love for the world.

This brings up Jesus's fascinating posture: Jesus willingly participated in unjust religious systems as a way to heal them. To understand his thinking, we have to hear him tell the parable of the wheat and the tares in Matthew 13:24–30. In this parable, a man goes out to his field to grow wheat. While he sleeps at night, an enemy sneaks in and sows weeds among the wheat. A servant tells the owner that someone has sown weeds in the field and asks, "Do you want us to go and pull them up?" The owner responds to leave the weeds. One might assume that God would want the field purged of all the evil weeds. But he doesn't. The invitation is to leave the weeds. Not only is Jesus showing us a picture of what the world is like—a world where wheat and weeds all grow together—but he is also putting in their place the idealists, the purists, who want to create a world free of impurity. The safe spacers and purity cultists.

In Jesus's time, interestingly, a community of religious purists called the Zealots saw their task as cleansing Judaism of worldly sin and impurity. These were the "purity culture" people of ancient Judaism who wanted a safe space from evil. Some New Testament scholars, including Scot McKnight, suggest that this parable was a direct rebuke of Zealot ideology.[17] The parable invited listeners to see God's kingdom afresh— not as some purity culture free from the marks of broken humanity, nor as some safe space where only the ideologically pure could enter. In God's kingdom, the two exist together. And in God's kingdom, the wheat of God's kingdom grows alongside the weeds of the devil.

The presence of weeds is a bad reason to stop gardening. God allows weeds. Granted, there will come a day when the garden will be cleaned and purified. But until then, the garden is one of coexistence. Weeds and wheat grow together. When we think about how we engage the church today, we are likely to be tempted to abandon her because of the harm she has done. Or to crucify her for being complicit in the problems of the world. Those things are true. The subtle message whispered in our ears is that to be part of her means we are complicit in her sins. But that is just another form of purity culture that pulls apart the body of Christ. We never love a thing by outright abandoning it. We love it by going to it. Serving it. Caring for it. That's the style of Jesus.

Embracing the Whole Kingdom

The task before us is to recapture a vision of God's kingdom that transcends the "big sort" of our theological landscape. We need the *whole* kingdom. We've been good at doing *part* of God's kingdom. Progressives, it's been said, have done the Gospels while the conservatives have done the epistles. But we need the whole New Testament witness. These two ought not to be separated. When we separate the work of God from love and worship of God, our theology goes askew. This is evident in the progressive, secular utopia that is essentially what Mark Sayers calls the "kingdom . . . without the King."[18] We are called to God and God's kingdom. One might sum up this holistic vision of God's kingdom as such: absolutely nothing matters but Jesus Christ and his kingdom—yet when one worships Christ and Christ alone, everything else matters too.[19]

This holistic kingdom places all human ideology and idealism under ultimate critique and judgment by God's gospel. Jesus is King. No one else. We either critique Christ with our weapons of ideology or our ideology will continually be shattered by Christ and his ideals. This will challenge Christianity unendingly. We *shouldn't* fit into the political parties. Christians *shouldn't* fit in the system. Christ's judgment judges all. President Donald Trump will be judged. House Speaker Nancy Pelosi will be judged. Jerry Falwell Jr. will be judged. Father Richard Rohr will be judged. Pastor Mark Driscoll will be judged. So will Rob Bell. My neighbor will be judged. *I will be judged.* Each and every one of us will face Christ's judgment. Our culture may be postmodern, but it's equally prejudgment. Seen in the light of that day of Christ's reconciliation, all principalities and powers await their final judgment. This means we have responsibility.

This changes how I preach. When I preach the *whole* kingdom, both sides of God's kingdom must be proclaimed. I must preach Christ's love for the children at the border and the unborn. I have to preach God's call to sexual holiness and God's eternal love for the sexually broken. I have to preach that ecology and human economy matter to God. When we worship Christ, everything matters. The troubling sign of our times is that I hear little from the mainline progressives that I don't also hear on CNN. And I hear little from conservative evangelical churches that isn't just some retweet of Fox News. In God's kingdom, we aren't disciples of Fox News or CNN—we are disciples of Jesus Christ. No one else. The kingdom confronts all of us and names our sin. We love our ideology more than we love the resurrected Christ. Perhaps the sign that we're starting to understand God's whole kingdom is that *everyone* is offended when they hear it.

This even changes the way we think about diversity. I'm a theologically conservative, charismatic Christian. I believe Jesus is the only way to God. I believe that the Holy Spirit is still alive and still does stuff in real time and in real ways. I believe that people need to have a radical encounter with Jesus Christ. I am wildly conservative and traditional in my theology of sexuality. I think women should and can preach and lead in the church. And while I hold these convictions dearly, it is my vision of God's kingdom that invites me to listen to those with whom I hold great differences. I do listen (and learn) from my friends who think differently about women in the church. I do believe I should constantly learn from my gay, lesbian, and open and affirming friends with whom I differ. I learn about Jesus from them. I do learn about the Bible from my cessationist friends who think that speaking in tongues won't likely happen. I'm a Protestant, and some of the most critical lessons I have learned about Jesus have come from those Catholic saints whose commitment to solitude and silence have led them (and me) deeper into the love of God. God's kingdom frees me. Because Jesus is King, I'm allowed to be unflinching about the centrality of Jesus and entirely openhearted toward those whom Christ graciously puts on my path.

Eleven

Trusting the Right Way

Trust or Convenience

Two trees swayed in Eden's wind: the tree of life and the tree of the knowledge of good and evil. When we read that God commanded that Adam and Eve couldn't eat from the tree of the knowledge of good and evil, little explanation is offered. The command, it seems, is not merely about food choice—the command is an invitation to trust God at his word. Was the forbidden tree *bad*? Not at all. In fact, that tree was "pleasing to the eye" and "good for food." The fruit on that tree would have been profoundly beautiful. Still, they were not to eat it. God said so, plain and simple. The man and the woman were free to eat but within the bounds of trust and covenant.

Along comes a serpent slithering through the garden. He says to the woman, "Did God really say, 'You must not eat from any tree in the garden?' . . . You will not certainly die" (Gen. 3:1, 4). What was the serpent getting at? Certainly, the serpent knew something of human nature—humans were made to be creative, to name animals, to work the garden, to explore. Humans were creative just like God. The serpent uses this to his advantage. In psychology, it's called *reactance*—we want to do something more if we are told *not* to do it. The serpent did his homework. He knew the man and the woman very well.

In sweeping terms, the heart of the serpent's message was that God's word fundamentally couldn't be trusted. *Think for yourself. Become like God. Come on, evolve already.* Not unlike the European Enlightenment in how it cast doubt upon religious claims in the eighteenth century, the undergirding statement of the serpent seems to be *sapere aude*: "dare to think for yourself." The spirit of our age echoes the heart of the serpent—trust in the self, not God.[1] For the Enlightenment fathers, the life of faith and trust in God was best replaced with mind, reason, and sensibility. God called it the tree of the *knowledge* of good and evil for good reason. We choose trust in God or trust in the self.

The echoes of the serpent's words can be heard throughout Western culture's insistent rejection of authority. Question your parents. Question your pastor. Question those with authority. Question every leader. Question the past. Question everything! Trust only in the self. I remember coming home for Thanksgiving in my freshman year of college having just finished my first Western Civilization unit. I had spent the entire semester learning in detail everything that was wrong with America—and there is plenty. And did it ever lead to a big, difficult argument at the dining room table about why we even celebrate our nation in the first place. But the culture of my liberal arts degree was such that everything I'd been taught by my parents, my church, my upbringing, and my earliest educators was probably wrong. Don't trust them! College immersed me in a whole culture that prioritized what my professors knew over what my parents had raised me with. It was a culture that beckoned me to cast aside trust in the authorities I used to cling to—all out of a newfound trust in my professors. Still, with all my new knowledge, I found a way to suffer my way through some turkey that year.

Perhaps part of deconstruction and doubt is learning to desire truth over people-pleasing—something worth applauding. The gospel invites us to trust God above people. The Western tradition's move toward a distrust in authority perhaps has its genesis in the fact that we put too much trust in those people in the past. Michael Specter wryly comments, "We no longer trust authorities, in part because we used to trust them too much."[2] Often we have put far too much trust in the wrong beings and forgotten to trust the One who can hold our trust.

This skepticism about humanity has led us far down the road. It is now required that we reject whatever authorities have handed us. In 1979, sociologist Peter Berger wrote a critical book on this entitled *The Heretical Imperative*.[3] Berger argues that in pre-Enlightenment societies, there were very few "heretics" in the classical sense of the word. Everyone believed—generally speaking—what the authorities told them to believe. The decision of faith was not a personal decision—it was the result of believing what the authorities said. But, Berger argues, in post-Enlightenment societies the authorities *must* be questioned, and we are all "required to be heretics." Berger's critical point had a big impact on the sociology of religion. Before the Enlightenment, belief in authorities was culturally required. After the Enlightenment, critique of authority was culturally required.

This is the framework for all Western learning. When someone undertakes a PhD in the humanities, they are required to write a dissertation. Mine was about 80,000 words. When you write a dissertation in the humanities, you are *required* to articulate a new argument that's never been made. This assumes there is something new under the sun. No longer is differentiation encouraged; it's required as part of being an academic. This dogmatic differentiation demands that we not be or think like anyone else. In this modern academic environment, I'd be fired if I copied someone's material. But if I teach something that might spiritually harm, I am still on track for tenure. Of course, I understand that it would make for a bad dissertation if someone just agreed with someone else. But compulsory differentiation is no better than compulsory agreement. Post-Enlightenment culture prejudices and privileges those who deconstruct belief rather than build it. It is now "liberation" from anything from our parents, our grandparents, or the faith environments we have come from. Trust the self over everyone.

How does this relate to the garden? After Adam and Eve ate from the forbidden tree, they *knew* good and evil. Their eyes were opened. I catch myself doing a double take every time I turn off my phone and it flashes an apple with a bite taken out of it like I'm back in the garden of Eden.

That's our world now. We can eat from whatever tree we wish. And our eyes are "open." All the while we are dying inside.

A mark of self-trust is convenience—we do what is easiest over what is true as defined by God. In his award-winning book *The Omnivore's Dilemma,* Michael Pollan brilliantly explores our modern food system and how utterly broken it has become.[4] He points out that when we go into a modern grocery store, we always find the foods we *shouldn't* be eating in the most convenient spots—in the front, in the middle, and at the checkout counter. If we want to eat right, Pollan points out, we have to go out of our way to the edges of the store to find what's healthy. The vegetables and healthy foods are never located in the middle of the store. Those foods that lead to health, life, and vitality are inconvenient. But the foods that make us sick and overweight are the most convenient.

I'm under no illusion that Pollan knew he was writing a commentary on the early chapters of Genesis. But Pollan helps us understand the Bible. Adam and Eve willingly chose convenience over trust, self-trust over obedience to God's word, self-satisfaction over self-denial. The result? They were banished from God's presence in the garden of Eden. All of this has a fascinating connection to Jesus. In the New Testament, Jesus goes into the temple grounds. There he finds an industry of religious goods available to the masses likely at exorbitant prices. Mark is the only Gospel writer who makes the comment that Jesus "would not allow anyone to carry merchandise *through* the temple" (Mark 11:16). Through where? *Through* the temple space. Instead of walking around this holy space, they are walking "through" it. They have turned God's house into, in the words of Jesus, "a den of robbers." Those temple salesmen repeat Adam and Eve's sin—violating sacred space by doing the convenient thing over the true thing. They are doing the convenient thing. They are violating God's space by walking through the temple courts rather than around, thus creating the image among onlookers that God is into some kind of religious profiteering.

And guess what Jesus does? The same exact thing God does in Eden: he drives everyone from the sacred space. Jesus does the same thing God did in Eden.

A person can relate to God only on the basis of trust and obedience. The sin of modernity is that we choose what works over what God says. Sure, we trust. But in ourselves, not God.

"If . . . Then" Theologies

Following Christ means receiving into ourselves Christ, the story of Scripture, and good teaching *as well as* discerning those patterns of belief that betray our faith. Like building a foundation, our primary concepts about God have a long-term impact on the structure of our faith. They shape us. We trust them. We build our lives on them. The problem becomes when we trust ideas and concepts that God himself never asked us to trust.

As we have discussed, many in my generation were shaped by the purity cultures of the 1990s and early 2000s. In recent years, those raised in a purity culture have begun to talk about the ways it harmed them. For so many, the puritanical vision of romance that it offered was impossible and graceless. An underlying message was received: *if* you do courtship right and save yourself for marriage, *then* God will give you a good husband or a good wife. *If* you don't have sex before marriage, *then* you can be assured of having a fruitful family that loves Jesus. In the idealism of our youth, this seemed like a reasonable exchange. I'll give God my virginity and romantic desires and in exchange I can experience true love.

Whether purity culture intended this to be its message, that was the message received. The harm done to my generation has been enormous. Marriages sometimes fail. People sometimes remain single. Sex isn't as fulfilling as we thought it would be. Whatever it is—the promise that one's faithfulness would lead to fulfillment just didn't always materialize. That whole trust in the "if . . . then" formula let us down.

There is a danger in easy magical formulas. In Acts 8:9–24, we read of a magician named Simon who was making great wealth off people's superstitions. When Simon sees the apostles healing by the laying on of hands, he tries to pay for the same power. He thinks, "If I can get this power . . . then I'll make significant wealth for myself." Simon represents the ultimate "if . . . then" approach to God. Of course, this is entirely unacceptable to God and to the apostles. No power can be bought from heaven. These bargains we strike with God are entirely unacceptable to God. God relates to us only through grace and faith—nothing more. "If I pray, then I won't wrestle with . . ." needs to be retired. "If I go to seminary, then the church will listen to me" needs to be crucified. "If I do enough justice to appease my broken conscience, then I'll be acceptable to God" can be let go as what it is—works theology.

We can easily be tempted to trust false formulas over the words of God. As Jesus is led by the Spirit into the wilderness, he faces the devil's temptations. Each temptation the devil throws at Jesus is formulaic: "If you are the Son of God, tell these stones to become bread"; "If you are the Son of God . . . throw yourself down"; "All this I will give you . . . if you will bow down and worship me" (Matt. 4:3, 6, 9). There we have it— the devil's formula. Do x and y will happen. If . . . then. How did Jesus withstand these temptations? Dietrich Bonhoeffer suggests that the only thing Jesus wanted—and how he perfectly passed the same test that Adam and Eve had so miserably failed—was what God had said. Had Jesus *wanted* more than God's word, he would have failed the test. "If [Jesus] had wanted more than this Word," Bonhoeffer writes, "he would have given place in himself to doubt in God. Faith which demands more than the Word of God becomes a temptation of God. To tempt God is the highest spiritual temptation."[5] The temptation Jesus faced was primarily a temptation to betray his trust in God and to test God. If God really is God, then this thing should happen.

In the heart of the Old Testament are two commands that strongly warn against testing God. In Deuteronomy 6:16, we're told to "not put the LORD your God to the test." And in Exodus 20:7, God commands his people to "not misuse the name of the LORD your God." Both of these commands have many applications. But in our time, the thrust of the command most certainly must be to stop making promises for God where God has not made a promise. To resist the urge to say "ring by spring or your money back" at our Christian universities. To stop promising fulfilling marriages and sex lives if we hold off until "I do." To cease promising prosperity for those who have been faithful to Jesus. In the medical community, the ultimate sin for a doctor is to promise healing. They can't do that. It violates their oath. What they can do is use everything in their realm to help bring about healing and health. But promises can't be made. Using God's name in vain certainly includes those times when we speak up for God when he has not spoken or when we speak for God in places where he has remained silent.

Trusting the Right Way

We all trust in someone or something. To be born into the world and receive food is to trust in the one from whom we receive that food. In using whatever words were given to us as children, we embody implicit trust in the ones who taught those words to us. Trust is universal. Even doubting and deconstructing are acts of trust. Scientist and philosopher Michael Polanyi articulates this principle in his book *Personal Knowledge*. He argues that even an act of skeptical doubt is in itself an act of trusting something else. If we doubt God's goodness, we trust in some alternative message about God *not* being good. Thus, when someone deconstructs their Bible, faith, or ideology—Polanyi's thinking suggests—one is simultaneously putting trust in something else that takes its place.[6] Humans have to place trust in something. Or as Bob Dylan sang, "You gotta serve somebody." In mental health, this principle is called *transference*. Whenever someone loses trust in an authority figure or loved one or religious framework, they must inevitably put their trust in something else. Their trust doesn't simply disappear. Rather, their trust *transfers* to something else. Through this lens, all doubt must actually be understood as a profound act of trust in alternative things. As Søren Kierkegaard says, there are "leaps of faith" in the faith journey.[7] There are leaps of doubt as well. Every doubt, in the end, is a leap.[8]

In his voluminous *Orthodoxy*, G. K. Chesterton discusses a person who's lost all trust in everything. Critiquing those who *only* critique,

Chesterton makes the decisive point that any and all moral judgments one may make against Christianity, the Bible, or the church are judgments taken from some other moral grounding. One can only critique from a place of some faith. Thus, any act of deconstruction is simultaneously an act of constructing some other trust, love, or faith structure. Chesterton writes:

> The new rebel is a skeptic and will not entirely trust anything. He has no loyalty; therefore, he can never be really a revolutionist. And the fact that he doubts everything really gets in his way when he wants to denounce anything. For all denunciation implies a moral doctrine of some kind; and the modern revolutionist doubts not only the institution he denounces, but the doctrine by which he denounces it.[9]

Chesterton scathingly contends that at the moment we cease trusting in the Bible or the church's witness or tradition, we submit ourselves to the oppression of the "oligarchy of those who merely happen to be walking about."[10] When we reject the faith, we end up embracing new faith in the fickle tyranny of what's fashionable at the time. *Vox populi.* The voice of the people becomes the voice of God.

Postmodern philosopher Richard Rorty once famously said that truth is whatever your peers will let you get away with.[11] When we don't trust God, we trust the crowd. Or the peer-review process. Or ourselves. Or love. Or even reason. Whatever it is, everyone trusts something. We have to trust something.

Let's play this out in our vision of love. In the Christian tradition, we're invited to place our trust in God's divine character who is love. The apostle John writes, "God is love" (1 John 4:8). In the ancient world, this New Testament definition of love would have been unique. God was not capricious or drunk with wrath. Nor was love something that God *did*. Love is something God *is*. God's love is ontological—not happenstance or dependent on a good week. The concept of human love as a result of the source of God's love has shaped the Western world in profound ways. Well, what happens when trust is no longer placed in the God who is love? Our trust is laid upon love itself. In the secular, progressive West, love is no longer an attribute of God. God is not love. Love is love. And in almighty love we place our trust. Simon May's *Love: A History*, a breathtaking historical examination of love in the Western mind, makes this point in startling fashion: "I attempt to trace how love came to be the new god. And not any old god—say, one of those self-seeking, lustful, capricious and frankly evil Greek gods—but rather the spitting image of the Christian God. In other words, love—genuine love—has come to be seen as all-good, unconditioned, unchanging, self-less in showing concern for the wellbeing of loved ones, and our chief bulwark against suffering and loss. Today love has arguably become the only truly universal religion in the West—including in the United States." In May's summation, love itself has become a "new god . . . a democracy of salvation open to all."[12]

Why would we trust more in the idea of love than in Love himself? Because trusting God doesn't always get us what we want. Trusting God doesn't always secure us a marriage. Trusting God doesn't get us prosperity. And trusting God doesn't bring us security and wealth and happiness in this marriage. What about stories like Daniel in the Bible where there *are* moments when trust brings prosperity and success? On Daniel there was "no wound . . . because he had trusted in his God" (Dan. 6:23). Daniel's trust in God was beautiful and good! Yes, there are moments when trust leads to this kind of earthly deliverance. But the same could not be said for someone like John the Baptist, who trusted in Jesus, prepared the way for his ministry, and followed him only to lose his head as a result. Likewise, Jesus Christ trusted his Father in heaven with the love that only the Trinity can share, yet he experienced an unjust death on a Roman cross. Did Jesus trust the Father till the end? Did his trust work out for him in the worldly sense? Did his trust lead to a prosperous experience? No—it led to a hole in the ground.

Trusting in God does not always secure redemption this side of death. Yes, Jesus trusted in the Father and was crucified as a result. But his trust was not in temporal alleviation of pain. Jesus had trust that there would be ultimate redemption—even redemption after death. Jesus trusted in

175

resurrection. That trust was not bulletproof security against worldly excruciation. Before the resurrection, Jesus's life meandered through tremendous pain on the way.

In the first chapter, I mentioned the difference between *beliefs* and *faith*. Beliefs are the core convictions we have about ourselves, the world, and God. Beliefs are our theology. Faith, on the other hand, is how those beliefs affect our orientations, affections, and attitudes toward life. For example, I have beliefs about the Trinity. God is three persons in one being. How does that particular belief shape my faith? In many ways: When I worship, I think I do a disservice to the mystery that is God by speaking only to the Father—there are the Spirit and Jesus as well. Similarly, it changes the way I see the church and our inherent need for it. Because I believe in God as a Triune being, it changes *how* I relate to the community of the church. In some small sense, the church becomes a reflection of God's nature—a community of people who are their own persons but are one in Christ.

Faith is a relationship of trust between persons. To have faith is not merely to have an idea about God. It is to have trust in God himself as a person. We have our beliefs about who God is, and our hearts place faith in who we know God to be. The two work together. One problem is when we begin placing faith in our ideas about God over God himself. My marriage of seventeen years has come with its ups and downs— broken dreams, joys, depression, infertility, birth, elation, pain, happiness, disappointment. Through it all, I've learned that I can trust my wife. More than any other person in my life, I can trust that my wife has my greatest good in mind. She will never act in such a way as to violate what is best for me, the person she loves. I trust her more than anyone in the world. At the same time that I trust my wife, I do not trust her to not lose my car keys. It's a little odd saying that, but it's true: I trust my wife, but not with my car keys.

We must embrace covenantal love with God: part of trusting in God is learning to be disappointed by him. That is precisely how we learn to trust in God through the worst of life—we learn to discern the difference between trusting in God and trusting in false beliefs about God that God never promised. That is what leads to so much deconstruction. From our earliest years, we were given false promises of what God would or would not do. When those promises don't pan out, we are left with the bill. We need to keep in mind that it was not God who violated the terms. It was the one who gave us those false promises. Again, the Bible explicitly commands us against making false promises for God: *we are not to take the Lord's name in vain*. Making promises in the name of God that God never makes not only harms human beings at the deepest level but also *requires* them to deconstruct their faith years later. In fact, we would do well to make accurate promises about God to the young. Following God will be entirely painful and disruptive. God will not give you everything you want. God will hurt your feelings. God's greatest goal in your life is not your best life now. God's dream for your life is not simply a good dental plan and a happy family.

There will be times in our Christian journey when elements of our belief structure change. I hope they do! Jesus takes a lifetime to follow. And none of us have arrived yet. I have been following Jesus for twenty-two years. And while the foundation of faith has remained entirely the same, so many of the ways I think about and relate to many issues have changed. On many things, I've just plain changed my mind. That doesn't mean something is wrong. Can a Christian change their mind? Yes, there are times when our beliefs get clarified by Scripture, or in prayer, or in community, or by the writings of other Christians.

Can I invite you to trust in God? And, at the same time, be cautious about equating what that trust is going to get you in this life? I trust God, even more than I do my wife, knowing that God has my ultimate good in mind. God cares for me. God loves me. God will put me through whatever it takes for me to become the child of God he desires me to be. At the same time, I have learned that I cannot trust God to always give me what I want. I have learned that I cannot trust God to always put me through what is most comfortable and beneficial to my emotional state. I have learned that God is not to be trusted to protect me from the pain of sin or the pain of evil in our world. I trust God. But I don't always trust God *for* stuff.

There is a significant difference between trusting in someone and trusting someone *for* something.

At some point, we trusted God to do things he never said he'd do. It's like a trust fall. You know the drill: a person stands in front of another person and falls, to be caught by the trusted person. When done properly, the exercise can help both participants learn to build trust. Imagine a child hearing about this idea of a trust fall and asking if you would catch them. As they stand in front of you, you tell them they can fall. But they fail to recognize how a trust fall works: they fall *forward* rather than backward. They fall and their trust is broken. This happens in a figurative way all the time. We trust in God, but we trust in him the *wrong way*. We trust that God will protect us from harm and difficulty and questions. But God cannot be trusted to keep us from harm, difficulty, and the darkness of life. God didn't prevent that with his own Son in the flesh, and he won't do so for us.

How do we learn to trust God in the right way, falling into him in a way he can be trusted? To begin, we must lean into knowing that his love is for us *in the long run*. Paul puts it in the clearest of language: "He who began a good work in you *will* carry it on to completion" (Phil. 1:6). It often takes an entire lifetime for God to bring about the work in us that he desires to complete. When we fail to take into account the longer vision of God for our lives—and think short-term—then pain and difficulty become the sign that God can no longer be trusted. But we trusted in the wrong thing. There is simply no promise given to us anywhere in the Bible that God protects his dearly loved children from real life.

In the opening chapter of Job, Satan comes before God and asks, "Does Job fear God *for nothing*?" (Job 1:9). Job goes on to walk through immeasurable suffering. He loses everything. Yet he still loves God in the end. Ironically, Job does love God *for nothing*. He does not love God *for* something. He loves God because God is worthy to be loved. Too often, we don't love God. We love God *for* stuff. We don't trust God. We trust God *for* things.[13]

Do we trust God for nothing?

Yet

The Psalms offer us profound hope in our doubts and deconstruction. The Psalms reflect, interestingly, all the stages we have discussed—construction, deconstruction, and reconstruction. Old Testament scholar Walter Brueggemann identifies three rhythms in the Psalms: orientation, disorientation, and reorientation.[14] In the diversity of the Psalter, there are psalms that orient us to God and capture us with deep truths of God's goodness, mercy, and truth. But there are also psalms that confuse us and undo our false sense of certainty. And there are also psalms that bring us back to God all over again. It seems as though the theological journey is weaved into the very structure of the forms of worship of Israel. God wants to move us from secondhand faith to firsthand faith: to move from having faith *through* others to having it ourselves, as in those sacred biblical stories of old.

In Psalm 22, David composes a psalm that navigates the emotional terrain of his experience. We immediately discern a distinct back-and-forth rhythm to David's emotional journey. He first pleas for God's presence—"My God, my God, why have you forsaken me? Why are you so far from saving me?" (v. 1). David has been crying out to God with seemingly no response. Then immediately David stops: "Yet," he writes, "you are enthroned as the Holy One; you are the one Israel praises" (v. 3). Then he goes back to lament: "But I am a worm and not a man" (v. 6). Almost before he can begin his next round of complaints, he returns to praise: "Yet you brought me out of the womb; you made me trust in you" (v. 9). This back-and-forth continues throughout the psalm as David walks his reader through all the emotional extremes that come with life.

This sort of praise is found throughout the psalmist literature. *In the midst* of their pain, the authors of the Psalms will stop seemingly midsentence and offer a refrain or two of praise to Yahweh. The book of Psalms, in fact, is broken into five distinct parts (Pss. 1–41, 42–72, 73–89, 90–106, 107–150), believed to follow the framework of the first five books of the Bible, known as the Torah—Genesis, Exodus, Leviticus, Numbers, and Deuteronomy. Despite the fact that all five books of Psalms reflect the same back-and-forth emotional journey found in Psalm 22, each book notably ends with the same thing: a doxology of praise and blessing to God. Psalm 150, the final psalm in the Psalter, expresses this praise in the most distinctive terms: "Let everything that has breath praise the LORD. Praise the LORD" (Ps. 150:6).

This distinctive mark of the Psalms reveals something greater at work. The authors of the Psalms praise and worship and glorify God, but not just *after* their troubles have passed; rather, they seem to find a way to weave praise and worship *in the middle of* their troubles and tribulation. Old Testament scholars call this "anticipatory praise." This kind of praise, distinctive of the biblical narrative, shows the author praising God *in the middle of* the pain in anticipation of God's eventual breakthrough and redemption. Back to Psalm 22 where we can clearly see the key word in the text: "Yet." In the midst of the emotional turmoil of this life, there is a *yet* for the person following Yahweh. I may not have the spouse I've dreamed up since I was a child, *yet* I know you are God. I may struggle with unwanted desires every single day, *yet* God is my sustainer and my shield. I am not able to walk free of my emotional anxiety and unrest, *yet* you will redeem and restore me in due time as you see fit, God.

The spirit of "yet" praise is found in the songs of African slaves who, by no choice of their own, were ripped away from their homes and forced into enslavement. Their hymns reflect a clear awareness of the emotional torment of their situation and a clear awareness of the power of God to heal and restore and free. Yet they still sang.

This reflects a worldview that is so different from our own—even in the church. Whenever we sing songs that say things like "God will never let us down," I want to take my son out of the room. God *is* going to let us down in the short-term. God *is* going to let us fall. God *is* going to put us through things that hurt greatly. But in the long-term, God will restore.

The marvel of the Psalms is that they simultaneously name the emotional turmoil, unrest, and anxiety of the author *yet* preserve praise for God in the midst of it. The problem happens when we separate one from the other. It is very difficult to watch someone walking through despair and emotional pain without seeing that they have grasped the hope in the midst of that trouble. Experiencing it is even worse. At the same time, it is soul-killing to watch a Christian do the opposite, only talking about hope to the denial of what is really going on. I suspect this is one reason many have deconstructed the faith of their parents in conservative Christianity. Too often, the refrain of "just pray about it" and "we will be praying" becomes a kind of cover to not be honest about the actual pain one is going through. That isn't true prayer though, not in light of the Psalms. Praise or prayer as a synonym for the denial of pain and emotional despair is not praise or prayer—it is religious denialism. The Psalms have no room for this denialism.

In Psalm 22, David experiences what we might call *disillusionment*. He sees clearly what is happening and still praises God in it. Consider that word *disillusionment*: What is the opposite of being disillusioned? It is to be illusioned—to live by mirage, image, illusion. The illusioned life is a life of mirages. A. W. Tozer writes about the importance of disillusionment for the Christian. "Some of us," writes Tozer, "need to be disillusioned so that we might get straightened out. A little boy may run around the house believing he's a Hopalong Cassidy. He may do that up to the age of ten. But if he's eighteen and is still running around with a Hopalong Cassidy hat on, somebody needs to disillusion that boy. He doesn't need consolation—he needs to be disillusioned."[15] Oswald Chambers further writes of the need for Christian disillusionment:

> Disillusionment means that there are no more false judgments in life. . . .
> The disillusionment which comes from God brings us to the place where
> we see men and women as they really are. Many of the cruel things in life
> spring from the fact that we suffer from illusions. We are not true to one
> another as *facts*; we are true only to our *ideas* of one another. Everything
> is either delightful and fine, or mean and dastardly, according to our idea.
> The refusal to be disillusioned is the cause of much of the suffering in
> human life.[16]

Disillusionment is a gift from the Lord of truth who refuses to rock us to sleep with lies and deceit. We should celebrate it—as long as it is in pursuit of truth. A disillusioned faith is worth celebrating. For to pursue "the way, the truth, and the life" is antithetical to *any* illusion. We shouldn't feel bad for the person who is increasingly disillusioned. We should encourage them. As Parker Palmer writes, we do just about everything in our power to avoid coming face-to-face with reality. We don't want to know the truth. The truth hurts. It causes us to change what we do. But in the end, he argues, we should *never* be sad when someone is disillusioned: "Instead of commiserating and offering a shoulder to cry on when a friend says that he or she is disillusioned, we ought to congratulate, celebrate, and ask the friend how we can help the process go deeper still."[17]

The author of Psalm 22 has been disillusioned. The truth is we don't see Psalm 22 as a legitimate emotional journey for the Christian. But it is. The Christian faith is up and down, fickle. Simply look at Paul's language. At one point, he borders on an emotional high: "Thanks be to God for his indescribable gift!" (2 Cor. 9:15). At other points, he is a man seemingly in need of help: "What a wretched man I am! Who will rescue me from this body that is subject to death?" (Rom. 7:24). The same could be said of Jesus, who looked on people with great love and compassion and showed the ability to cry and sweat blood in emotional torment. Were Paul and Jesus doing something wrong? I've often wondered if David, Paul, or even Jesus were to come into our churches or our small groups with this emotional experience in hand whether we'd worry they were bipolar or needed Prozac.

Confession is telling God what's true. There is power in telling God that you want to want him. Confess that you don't want him but that you want to want him. Ask God for the desire to want the desire. It sounds like a trick, but it isn't. It is called confession. God loves it. You can't fake desire. But you can vulnerably ask for it.

To ask is to begin to reconstruct faith.

Postscript

Hope of Reconstruction

After World War II, Germany faced a unique challenge in trying to re-build. Not only did a majority of German able-bodied men lay in fresh graves throughout Europe, 7.5 million Germans were made homeless by the war. In fact, 3.6 million of the 16 million German homes in sixty-two cities were destroyed. The spirit of Germany came down with its buildings and its ideology. Who was to rebuild Germany?[1] In Germany, an unlikely community arose to do the work of rebuilding. Historians point out that it was largely the women who rebuilt Germany after the war. Known as *trümmerfrau*, or "rubble women," a whole generation of daughters, mothers, and grandmothers came together to start to put the nation's architecture back together again.

The work of reconstructing is very different from the work of con-structing or deconstructing—and it's undertaken by unique people. Likewise, the work of theological reconstruction is much different from theological construction or deconstruction. To come back to faith again after having walked through deconstruction is a unique task requir-ing us to approach faith differently. In the professor's words from *The Lion, the Witch and the Wardrobe*, "You won't get to Narnia again by that route."[2] Our goal in this book has been to discern a path forward toward reconstruction for those in deconstruction or deconstruction cultures. Remember the goal: Jesus Christ. Nothing less. We may need to walk through deconstruction. But we mustn't stay there. The danger of remaining in deconstruction too long is the potential for cynicism, resentment, and eventually a loss of faith. We mustn't ignore deconstruction. But we mustn't stay there either.

How do we reconstruct our Christian faith? Do we construct with new beliefs? Or do we return to the old beliefs in a new way? The prophetic words of Isaiah remain instructive: "They will *rebuild* the *ancient ruins* and *restore* the places long devastated; they will renew the ruined cities that have been devastated for generations" (Isa. 61:4). The work of rebuilding is the work of God. But Isaiah says that they are to "rebuild the *ancient ruins.*" Undoubtedly, God's people were accustomed to this kind of rebuilding. Throughout its history, the city of Jerusalem is believed to have been leveled some forty-six times. Time and again, it was captured, destroyed, and rebuilt as a place for worship. For archeologists, it makes it nearly impossible to date certain buildings. Each time Jerusalem was rebuilt, old materials were often used to rebuild the new buildings. To "rebuild the ancient ruins" is not to build in a way that is discontinuous from the old. It is to reconstruct the old. Theological reconstruction, likewise, is not about building something new altogether as much as it is about building the old again in a new way. The goal is not to reconstruct a new Christianity. It is to recapture ancient Christianity in a new, fresh, and prophetic way for our time.

Nor will the work of rebuilding be sanitized of the emotional tumult that comes with the terrain. In Ezra, as the Jews return to Jerusalem to rebuild the temple following their exile, they have a diversity of feelings. Ezra records that "the older priests and Levites and family heads . . . wept aloud" because the new temple was not like the old. But others shouted with joy. Ezra comments that "no one could distinguish the sound of the shouts of joy from the sound of weeping" (3:12–13). Reconstruction is complicated and messy; it is hard and joyful at the same time. It bears the joy of renewed faith, hope, and love, but it also includes painful reminders of the way things used to be. Granted, faith may not look the way it used to. But there is a different kind of joy one gets to experience in returning home.

Few illustrate this return better than theologian Thomas Oden. As a young man, Oden was considered one of the most promising progressive theologians to have studied under the famed H. Richard Niebuhr. In his younger years, Oden was transfixed by the social revolutions of his time—notably, socialism. He considered Ho Chi Minh an agrarian hero to be revered. He cherished the work of Marx, Nietzsche, and Freud, looked up to the Student Christian Movement of the 1950s, and studied theology with Rudolf Bultmann, Hans-Georg Gadamer, and Wolfhart Pannenberg. Oden was moved by the utopian thinking of his youth, remaining with him "like a ghost" into the years after.[3] Those early years of deconstructing the Christian faith led him further and further down the road of liberalism. "Every turn," Oden later reflected, "was a left turn."[4]

Then came a return to historic Christianity—to Jesus. Through a series of events, Oden began questioning the direction of his life. In his subsequent autobiography, Oden began to see that he'd become guilty of using aspects of Christ's teaching to fit his utopian ideology. Rather than following Jesus, he had been using Jesus to fulfill his ideological convictions. In doing so, he'd entirely neglected Christ's incarnation, resurrection, and atonement. This led Oden to begin reading the writings of the earliest Christians. What he found was a community of writers who lived to pass along a set of teachings and beliefs from generation to generation. Many of these fathers and mothers gave their lives to pass on these beliefs—the bodily resurrection of Jesus, the virgin birth, the atonement, and Christ's divinity. This experience put a halt on his move to the theological left.

Oden's attitude toward the Christian faith entirely changed. As a promising liberal theologian, Oden believed that historic Christianity could evolve and improve alongside a progressively evolving society. But he had not taken into account that these beliefs were unlike those of the earliest Christians who had died to pass along a set of traditions about who Jesus was—beliefs that could not be changed. Oden had been trying to *remake* a set of teachings that people had died for him to *receive*. Oden's trajectory changed course, and he eventually made it his life's goal to "never write anything new." Oden's reconstruction meant trading in his progressive ideology and theology for Jesus. He spent the rest of his life studying the Christianity of the early church to meticulously pass along their message. "Once hesitant to trust anyone over thirty," Oden would say, "I now hesitate to trust anyone under three hundred."[5] He once dreamed of having the epitaph on his gravestone read simply, "He made no new contribution to theology."[6]

Oden's journey brought him from the progressive utopianism of his youth to Jesus Christ. Let us be clear as we were at the beginning: the goal of reconstruction is not to get progressives to become conservatives nor to get conservatives to become liberals. The call of Jesus isn't to the right or to the left. Reconstruction is something altogether different. The call of Jesus is to go *deeper* into him. No other route will do. Reconstruction is the process of learning that we are all full of duplicity and need to turn to Jesus entirely. The goal of reconstruction is to crucify our obedience ideology so that we might pursue *all* of Jesus Christ—not just the parts we like. Reconstruction is the church's turn from liberalism and conservativism back to full-fledged obedience to Jesus Christ.

Many have described this journey. French philosopher Paul Ricoeur calls it a "second naiveté."[7] Ricoeur believed that we first encounter God through a primitive set of eyes as children. Yet, at some point, we question those childhood beliefs and enter into a critique of our own faith. Ricoeur believed that this was a central part of the Christian journey. Stephen Seamands comments on this process, "There is a childish, uncritical first naiveté . . . that we need to outgrow." This requires that we question our assumptions, dissecting them to see what's at their core. Seamands draws the connection between Ricoeur's concept of deconstruction and moving on to a state of rebuilding: "The purpose of this deconstruction stage is not to leave us tentative and unsure about everything. Ultimately it should lead to a second naiveté, an understanding arrived at on the far side of complexity, which is truly childlike as opposed to childish." Reconstruction is on the "far side of complexity."[8]

Oden's journey was one back to a second naiveté. In his remarkable autobiography *A Change of Heart*, Oden candidly discusses seeing God's hand in his own deconstruction story and the regret and sadness he felt over the many mistakes he made during that time. He had lost friendships, academic invitations, prestige, and even his career as a result of his turn back toward Jesus. It was a journey of great loss. But it was a journey of profound joy. Richard Neuhaus writes of the power of returning to the Christian faith after enduring seasons of critique and deconstruction: "Having come to recognize that things could theoretically be other than they are, we are brought to the perception that they are as we thought them to be, but on the far side of all of our questioning, we know that in a way we did not know it before."[9]

In the words of C. S. Lewis in *Mere Christianity*, "The longest way round is the shortest way home."[10] T. S. Eliot caught the same vision: "We shall not cease from exploration / And the end of all our exploring / Will be to arrive where we started / And know the place for the first time."[11] Reconstruction is not about building a new faith for ourselves. More often it's about losing ourselves once again in the ancient faith with a whole new set of eyes.

How do we begin this journey toward reconstruction?

We have to begin with honest pursuit. Asking. Seeking. Knocking. When we look at the story of the Bible from the beginning of creation, we find throughout that God is always giving us the *ideal* of what he wants the world to be. In the creation story, God establishes an ideal in which one day a week, every person and all of creation cease from their work and take a full day of Sabbath rest to enjoy life and all the Creator had made.[12] God gives us an ideal picture of rest. As well, God establishes his ideas of human community. As God creates Israel, he gives laws and rules that ensure the poor and disenfranchised are cared for. Throughout Scripture, we see that God establishes a clear picture of what he intends for human sexuality. God did not create sexuality to be abused for purposes of power or coercion. God established sex as a gift to humanity for community, procreation, and enjoyment in the context of fidelity, covenant, and promise.

Yet we see immediately that God's ideals are never fully met by human beings. Interestingly, there are two creation stories in Genesis 1 and 2.

Why two stories? In the first creation story, we find that God establishes the ideal of the Sabbath. But, oddly enough, it is completely omitted from the second creation story. My friend Matthew Sleeth argues that Genesis 1 is God's dream of the world—a world of Sabbath—and the second creation story is the story of what *actually* happened.[13] Clearly, our world has not taken God's ideal into account. And that whole ideal of human community? God's ideal, as beautiful as it is, never actually gets lived out after sin enters the world. The first brother relationship ends in murder as Cain kills Abel. It is the first murder in the Bible. And the first murder in the Bible is religiously motivated.

We might look at so many of the ideals in the Bible and think God is simply a divine rule-bearer and party pooper. But if we actually followed God's ideals, can you imagine how beautiful this world would be? Can you imagine a world where everyone—rich and poor—had a day to rest and be at peace in their world? Or, for that matter, a world where we shared in a rich and beautiful garden with a God of love and a bunch of animals? You can look at the Bible's depiction of sexuality as arcane and stuck in the ancient world. But can you imagine if we actually followed God's ideals? There would be no rape, no abuse, no need for abortion, no parentless children, no nonconsensual anything—all in the context of a loving covenant. One could say that is arcane. I think it sounds like heaven.

We must learn to read the Old Testament alongside the New Testament. When we read the Old Testament, we see so many of God's ideals laid out. The Ten Commandments are God's dream for a world lived rightly. The only problem? We don't have the power to do them. We need someone who can do them, who can show us how to do them in love. The Ten Commandments are God's ideal. Jesus is God's condescension—God coming to our level. God gives us the dream, then comes and lives it in the flesh so we can know how to do as he intended. Jesus was not the end of God's ideal. Jesus was the fulfillment of God's ideal.

Old Testament scholar John Goldingay calls this the biblical theme of "ideal and condescension."[14] God always gives us his ideals. But we can't reach them because only a holy God can live up to the standards. Yet when humans simply try, and honestly seek, to follow God's ways—no matter how hard they are—God always condescends to our level. No matter what. The call of humans is to begin to seek Jesus wherever they are. Today. Now. Here. In this spot.

This immediately brings us back to the problem of the ideological divide in the church. Conservatives often demand the ideal but don't help people do it. We say abortion is wrong but do so little about adoption, such as helping with foster care. We say that sex is for a man and a woman in a committed covenant marriage. But we do little to give homes and options and support to young gay men and lesbian women who seek to live faithfully to God in the bodies in which they find themselves. Conservatives demand the ideal but do little to help. To them, Jesus might say, "You load people down with burdens they can hardly carry, and you yourselves will not lift one finger to help them" (Luke 11:46). On the other hand, progressives tend to offer plenty of help while changing or even abandoning the ideals of God. They evolve on God's vision of sexuality as found in Scripture. And endless support is given to anyone without so much as a call to the holy invitations of a holy God. Jesus might say to the progressives that they have moved the ancient boundary stones. That they give a hand but ignore the ideal. To the progressives, Jesus might say, "You are in error because you do not know the Scriptures or the power of God" (Matt. 22:29).

The ideals don't change. God is to be sought, chased, and pursued. Only in the chasing does the unending, radical, powerful grace of God become evident. As God says in Jeremiah, "You will seek me and find me when you seek me with all your heart" (Jer. 29:13).

The principle throughout Scripture is that God is found by those who actually seek him. This is the lesson of the season of Epiphany—that season in the church calendar when we celebrate the wise men who bear their gifts to Immanuel who was born among us. Epiphany reminds us of the two groups of people who initially came to worship Jesus: shepherds and Middle Eastern stargazers. Neither are those we would expect to first welcome Christ to the world. What's more, during his crucifixion, Jesus is abandoned by his male disciples and attended to at the cross by the women. These are the same women who were willing to go to the tomb to find it empty. So, when Luke writes, "some of our women amazed us" (Luke 24:22), he is not offering a subtle cultural jab at women. Christ's birth, death, and resurrection are always recognized by the lowly, the least, and the less than. It is the people in power—like Herod and Pilate—who *couldn't* see him.

God is seen by those who seek him. That's how we begin the journey of reconstruction—of honestly seeking Jesus right *where* we are *as* we are. We began this book with a young man named Phil. Phil kept seeking. He never gave up. And now he has come back to the faith he tore apart. There are scars. But his faith is living and active. He gives us a reason why we reconstruct. Now he serves others who are walking through the same difficulties he did.

Which brings us back to the harrowing tale of Job, whose life was deconstructed. God blesses Job after he has endured the pain and suffering of losing everything. In the final chapter he gets all his wealth back (and more), and there is his wife and three new daughters. Job names these three daughters, and the author offers some details about the daughters at the end of the book. Jemimah means "dove." Keziah means something like "cinnamon." And Keren-Happuch means "eyeshadow."[15] What beautiful blessings.

But there's one final dynamic that must be attended to—the gift that the one who has walked through doubt can bring to the world. In the final chapter of Matthew's Gospel, Jesus tells his disciples to go into all the world and bear his message. Spread the word—the King has come. We call it the Great Commission. But right before this commission, Matthew comments, "When they saw him, . . . some doubted" (Matt. 28:17). Who was given the invitation to spread the word? The doubters! The ones struggling! The ones with questions! Why? Because a doubter in the hands of Jesus can bear the message too! That's exactly what Job does. He gives his inheritance to all three of his daughters, in addition to his seven sons. In the ancient world, an inheritance was for the boys and the men. Women didn't get an inheritance. But here, Job wildly gives away his inheritance to the daughters to whom he is blessing.

A fitting end to a man who lost it all only to experience the joy of its return.

Why do we walk through doubt and deconstruction to the other side? Because in the story of Job and the last chapter of Matthew, the sufferer and doubter bear the greatest gifts—an inheritance of blessing. The gospel! Deconstruction and doubt are hard. But we endure them because our persistent endurance allows us to arrive on the other side bearing beautiful gifts for those around us.

Is it possible to question our faith without losing it? One might say that's the very goal.

Acknowledgments

"Telling a person to write a poem," opined Carl Sandburg, "is like telling a woman to have a red-haired child. You can't control it. It is God's will."[1] Writing is a miracle—the culmination of sweat, tears, and risk. But mostly it's a work of God. Writing is not the result of some person with a quiet room, a computer, a pen or paper, and some thoughts. Writing is a communal act shaped by a lifetime of stories, experiences, and relationships that give shape to ideas and weight to words.

This book is no different. I'm indebted to a litany of people for what has come of this. None more than my family. My wife, Quinn, persevered once again through long, endless hours as I sat in my study and wrote, edited, screamed, and cried out loud. My loving son Elliot offered unending space and patience to give this project space to develop. Thank you both. My love is yours. And to my parents—Mom, Mike, Popo, and Mimi—thank you.

To Brazos, who has continued to believe in my work through successes and flops—thank you! Bob Hosack has particularly been a friend along the way and offered hands of support and belief.

My friends have equally offered hands of support, companionship, and even a loving lead on a good quote or story along the way that meandered into this book. Thank you, Trevor, John, Andy, Nic, John Mark, Paul, Cam, Brooks, Tyler, Jeff, George, Steve, and Aaron. And no less thanks to my spiritual director for hours of listening to my story—Morris Dirks and the Soul Formation crew.

During the course of the writing of this book, my family endured the most painful transition of our lives from pastoral work of serving the church we established in urban Portland to moving back to our hometown and entering a new life and vocation. So many of the stories in this book have been shaped by the loving community of that church, Theophilus. While the transition was deeply painful and difficult, that decade in Portland shaped our souls in unimaginable ways. Thank you Theophilus. To the staff, elders, leaders, and congregation: we love you and miss you dearly.

Finally, a big thank you to my home teaching institution—Bushnell University. Your support in allowing me to write must not go unnoticed. While I've never missed a committee meeting, faculty assembly, or class as a result of this book, I'm pretty sure I missed a lot of other things that went unseen. For that I'm sorry. I hope this book can serve our students for decades to come.

I love you Jesus.

Notes

Preface

1. Frederick C. Gill, ed., *Selected Letters of John Wesley* (New York: Philosophical Library, 1956), 237.

2. N. T. Wright, *After You Believe: Why Christian Character Matters* (New York: HarperCollins, 2010).

3. Haddon W. Robinson, *Biblical Preaching: The Development and Delivery of Expository Messages*, 3rd ed. (Grand Rapids: Baker Academic, 2014), 135.

Chapter 1: Deconstruction and Doubt

1. Kenneth J. Archer, *A Pentecostal Hermeneutic for the Twenty-First Century: Spirit, Scripture, Community* (New York: T&T Clark, 2004), 7.

2. John D. Caputo, *Deconstruction in a Nutshell: A Conversation with Jacques Derrida* (New York: Fordham University Press, 1997), 77. Stanley Grenz and John Franke point out that many postmodern thinkers reject the deconstructionism emblematic of the French postmodern framers. See Grenz and Franke, *Beyond Foundationalism: Shaping Theology in a Postmodern Context* (Louisville: Westminster John Knox, 2001), 19–20.

3. Millard J. Erickson has outlined four different ways postmodernism and deconstruction have intersected. Erickson, *Evangelical Interpretation: Perspectives on Hermeneutical Issues* (Grand Rapids: Baker, 1993), 102–3. On the diversity of deconstruction, see David Ray Griffin, William A. Beardslee, and Joe Holland, "Introduction: Varieties of Postmodern Theology," in *Varieties of Postmodern Theology* (Albany: State University of New York Press, 1989), 1–7.

4. David Kinnaman, *You Lost Me: Why Young Christians Are Leaving the Church . . . and Rethinking Faith* (Grand Rapids: Baker Books, 2011).

5. Peter Berger, *The Homeless Mind: Modernization and Consciousness* (New York: Penguin, 1981).

6. Byung-Chul Han, *The Burnout Society*, trans. Erik Butler (Stanford, CA: Stanford Briefs, 2015).

7. On Jesus as differentiated being, see the fascinating R. Robert Creech, "Jesus and Differentiation of Self in the New Testament Gospels," Academia.edu, July 2008, https://www.academia.edu/10205885/Jesus_and_Differentiation_of_Self_in_the_New_Testament_Gospels.

8. Yes, Jesus *can* violate boundaries. During the Easter narrative, Jesus walks through walls to surprise the disciples. Sometimes Jesus knocks. Sometimes he doesn't. Karl Barth points out, "It is quite true that a [person] must open the door to Jesus. [Yet] another thing also

remains unreservedly true, that the risen Christ passes through closed doors (John 20:19)." Barth, *Church Dogmatics*, 4 vols. (Edinburgh: T&T Clark, 1956–75), I/1, 283.

9. Raymond Brown, *The Gospel and Epistles of John: A Concise Commentary* (New York: Liturgical Press, 1988), 29.

10. First Kings 19 records Elijah calling Elisha to follow. Notice Elisha's response: He goes home, burns his ploughs, and "kisses his parents." Part of faith even in the Old Testament was to leave all to follow the call of Yahweh. But that call does not dismiss our other call to honor those who brought us up to know Yahweh.

11. Oswald Chambers, quoted in *The Westminster Collection of Christian Quotations*, compiled by Martin H. Manser (Louisville: Westminster John Knox, 2001), 79.

12. Austin Fischer writes that so many of the biblical characters endured these experiences: "When we walk down the long hallway of Christian faith, we find that many of our saints also had an inner skeptic." Fischer, *Faith in the Shadows: Finding Christ in the Midst of Doubt* (Downers Grove, IL: InterVarsity, 2018), 9.

13. G. K. Chesterton, *Orthodoxy* (Chicago: Moody Classics, 2009), 155.

14. Stanley Hauerwas perceptively warns against using the book of Job as an answer to suffering: "To make Job . . . an answer to the problem of evil is to try to make the book answer a question it was not asking." Hauerwas, *God, Medicine, and Suffering* (Grand Rapids: Eerdmans, 1990), 45.

15. Henri Nouwen, *Discernment: Reading the Signs of Daily Life* (New York: HarperOne, 2013), 67.

Chapter 2: The Theological Journey

1. Greg Boyd writes, "Throughout Scripture, the Creator, who gave us our minds, encourages us to *use* them in our relationship with him. . . . The Creator of the mind clearly expects us to *use it*." Boyd, *The Benefit of the Doubt: Breaking the Idol of Certainty* (Grand Rapids: Baker Books, 2013), 36 (emphasis original).

2. Evangelical Carl F. H. Henry writes, "Theology is heretical if it is only creative and unworthy if it is only repetitious." Henry, *God, Revelation and Authority*, vol. 1, *God Who Speaks and Shows, Preliminary Considerations* (Waco: Word, 1976), 9.

3. Madeleine L'Engle, *The Irrational Season* (San Francisco: HarperCollins, 1984).

4. Raymond Brown, *The Gospel and Epistles of John: A Concise Commentary* (New York: Liturgical Press, 1988), 32.

5. As narrated and quoted in Michael L. Lindvall, "Proportionality and Truth," in *Theology in Service of the Church: Essays in Honor of Joseph D. Small 3rd*, ed. Charles A. Wiley et al. (Louisville: Geneva, 2008), 34.

6. Eugene Peterson, *Reversed Thunder: The Revelation of John and the Praying Imagination* (San Francisco: HarperSanFrancisco, 1988), 4.

7. As Francis Schaeffer said, we're allowed substantial truth, not exhaustive truth. See Schaeffer, *He Is There and He Is Not Silent* (Wheaton: Tyndale, 1972), 37–88.

8. C. S. Lewis, *Mere Christianity* (San Francisco: HarperCollins, 2000), 140–41.

9. C. S. Lewis, *Christian Reflections*, ed. Walter Hooper (Grand Rapids: Eerdmans, 1971), 42.

10. James W. Fowler, *Stages of Faith: The Psychology of Human Development and the Quest for Meaning* (New York: HarperCollins, 1995).

11. Eugene Peterson attributes the unpublished work of Dr. Donald G. Miller as the source of this framework. Peterson, *Working the Angles: The Shape of Pastoral Integrity* (Grand Rapids: Eerdmans, 1995), 59–61.

12. E. Randolph Richards and Brandon O'Brien have called this "heart language." See Richards and O'Brien, *Misreading Scripture with Western Eyes: Removing Cultural Blinders to Better Understand the Bible* (Downers Grove, IL: InterVarsity, 2012), 17.

13. Missionary Lesslie Newbigin reflected on how the Indian Christianity he'd encountered was a syncretistic blend of biblical Christianity with Indian culture. But Newbigin admitted that Western Christianity was a blend as well. Everyone's belief is partially syncretistic. Newbigin writes, "My Christianity was syncretistic, but so was theirs. Yet neither of us could discover that without the challenge of the other. Such is the situation in cross-cultural mission." The lesson is critical: no community *perfectly* passes along perfect theological beliefs. Newbigin, *A Word in Season: Perspectives on Christian World Missions* (Grand Rapids: Eerdmans, 1994), 68.

14. This is the impulse of all nihilism, which first thrived post-WWII among those who'd supported the regime of the Third Reich. Sadly, Germany's descent into nihilism after the war's end was (I believe) an emotional means to cope with having been so wrong. This is one of the oddest parts of human sinfulness. When we discover our own sin, we reject truth in total. This is precisely what Paul had in mind when he wrote that the godless "suppress the truth by their wickedness" (Rom. 1:18). For a critique of nihilism, see Helmut Thielicke, *Nihilism: Its Origin and Nature, with a Christian Answer*, trans. John W. Doberstein (London: Routledge & Kegan Paul, 1962).

15. Helmut Thielicke, *A Little Exercise for Young Theologians*, trans. Charles L. Taylor (Grand Rapids: Eerdmans, 1962), 37.

16. Cyd Holsclaw and Geoff Holsclaw, *Does God Really Like Me? Discovering the God Who Wants to Be with Us* (Downers Grove, IL: InterVarsity, 2020), 94.

17. I'm grateful to my friend A. J. Zimmerman for this image.

18. Janet O. Hagberg and Robert A. Guelich, *The Critical Journey: Stages in the Life of Faith*, 2nd ed. (Salem, WI: Sheffield, 2005), chap. 7.

19. Eugene Peterson, *Under the Unpredictable Plant: An Exploration in Vocational Holiness* (Grand Rapids: Eerdmans, 1992), 87.

20. Cited by William Bridges, *Transitions: Making Sense of Life's Changes*, 2nd ed. (Cambridge, MA: Da Capo Press, 2004), 155.

21. Leighton Ford, foreword to *The Emotionally Healthy Church: A Strategy for Discipleship That Actually Changes Lives*, by Pete Scazzero (Grand Rapids: Zondervan, 2010), 173.

22. Patricia Killen, "The Religious Geography of the Pacific Northwest," *Word & World* 24, no. 3 (Summer 2004): 274.

23. George G. Hunter III, *To Spread the Power: Church Growth in the Wesleyan Spirit* (Nashville: Abingdon, 1987), 80.

24. Simone Weil, *The Need for Roots: Prelude to a Declaration of Duties towards Mankind*, trans. Arthur Willis (London: Routledge & Kegan Paul, 1952), 47–48.

25. Flannery O'Connor, *A Prayer Journal*, ed. W. A. Sessions (New York: Farrar, Straus & Giroux, 2013), 49.

26. Fernando Canale identifies Luther's work as positive deconstruction. Canale, "Deconstructing Evangelical Theology?," *Andrews University Seminary Studies* 44, no. 1 (2006): 95–130.

27. James K. A. Smith writes that Jesus continues to deconstruct false forms of the church that "domesticate" Jesus: "The church doesn't need Jacques Derrida in order to be deconstructed, because it's got Jesus! The deconstruction of the church happens from the inside." Smith, introduction to *What Would Jesus Deconstruct? The Good News of Postmodernity for the Church*, by John D. Caputo (Grand Rapids: Baker Academic, 2007), 16.

28. Brian Zahnd tells a story of someone who'd rejected rigid Christian fundamentalism: "As I listened to his story, it quickly became apparent that he had not so much lost his faith in Christianity as he had lost his credulity for fundamentalism. . . . Christianity and fundamentalism were so tightly bound together that he could not make a distinction between them." Zahnd rightly identifies that much contemporary rejection of "Christianity" is really rejection of false and hollow forms of religion—not Jesus. See his foreword to Austin Fischer, *Faith in the Shadows: Finding Christ in the Midst of Doubt* (Downers Grove, IL: InterVarsity, 2018), 1.

Chapter 3: The Problem of "Freedom"

1. Mark C. Taylor—known for applying postmodern deconstruction theory to theology—famously commented that "deconstruction is postmodernism raised to method." So much of our deconstruction age is just embodied postmodernism. Taylor, *Deconstructing Theology* (New York: Crossroad, 1982), xx.

2. I echo Flannery O'Connor's description of the "Christ-haunted South." Discussed in Ralph C. Wood, *Flannery O'Connor and the Christ-Haunted South* (Grand Rapids: Eerdmans, 2004).

3. Adrian Van Kaam, *The Music of Eternity: Everyday Sounds of Fidelity* (Notre Dame, IN: Ave Maria Press, 1990), 57 (emphasis added).

4. Robert Wuthnow, *After Heaven: Spirituality in America since the 1950s* (Berkeley: University of California Press, 1998).

5. Robert N. Bellah et al., *Habits of the Heart: Individualism and Commitment in American Life* (Berkeley: University of California Press, 1985), 228. Timothy Keller speaks extensively of this in his book *The Reason for God: Belief in an Age of Skepticism* (New York: Dutton, 2008).

6. David Brooks, "It's Not about You," *New York Times*, May 30, 2011, https://www.nytimes.com/2011/05/31/opinion/31brooks.html (emphasis original).

7. Walter L. Liefeld, *1 & 2 Timothy, Titus*, NIV Application Commentary (Grand Rapids: Zondervan, 1999), 62.

8. This story is captured in R. C. Sproul, *The Prayer of the Lord* (Orlando, FL: Reformation Trust, 2009), 40–41.

9. Walter Hooper, foreword to *Christian Reflections*, by C. S. Lewis (Grand Rapids: Eerdmans, 1971), ix.

10. For a helpful examination of the history of freedom, see Os Guinness, *Last Call for Liberty: How America's Genius for Freedom Has Become Its Greatest Threat* (Downers Grove, IL: InterVarsity, 2018).

11. Millard Erickson incisively contends that everything hangs on how and why one deconstructs: "If deconstruction succeeds, the gospel will deteriorate into a virtual solipsism. In a sense, the very future of Western culture may depend on the outcome of this struggle." Erickson, *Evangelical Interpretation: Perspectives on Hermeneutical Issues* (Grand Rapids: Baker, 1993), 104.

12. This is a central mark of reading in the postmodern spirit. A "transgressive" reading offers an alternative interpretation other than the traditional interpretation. This is where readings of the biblical text suggest, for instance, that David was gay because he kissed Jonathan or that Jesus married because of his intimacy with women in the Gospels. We must learn to read what the Bible *intends* to say rather than what we *wish* it to say. Jean-Luc Marion writes, "The body of the text does not belong to the text, but to the One who is embodied in it." That is, the meaning of the text is decided not by us but by the Spirit who inspired it. On a brief explanation of "transgressive" reading, see John D. Caputo, *Deconstruction in a Nutshell: A Conversation with Jacques Derrida* (New York: Fordham University Press, 1997), 77–92. Marion's work is found in Jean-Luc Marion, *God without Being* (Chicago: University of Chicago Press, 1991), 1.

13. Augustine, *Contra Faustum* 17.3, in *Essential Sermons*, trans. Edmund Hill (Hyde Park, NY: New City Press, 2007).

14. In one of his last letters, Albert Einstein expressed deep grief that his ideas were formative in making the atomic bomb. Like Einstein, God should not be blamed for our misuse of his book. To reject God because his words were misused is to reject Einsteinian physics because they were misused to create the worst weapon known to humanity.

15. Gil Bailie brilliantly writes, "We didn't stop burning witches because we stopped reading scripture; we stopped burning witches because we *kept* reading scripture." Quoted in Ronald Rolheiser, *Secularity and the Gospel: Being Missionaries to Our Children* (New York: Crossroad, 2006), 29.

16. Walter Hollenweger does point out some complexity regarding this story. Still, Hollenweger aptly writes, "The question behind his story remains: 'How can an African be introduced into a western, critical understanding of the reality of our time without being made useless in his home context?'" Hollenweger, *Pentecostalism: Origins and Developments Worldwide* (Peabody, MA: Hendrickson, 1997), 289–90. Paul Copan similarly points to the philosophy of David Hume, who rejected Scripture for the same reason he saw Africans as inferior—the testimony of miracles chiefly occurs among "ignorant and barbarous people." Hume's philosophy—fraught with racist overtones—blithely rejected the supernatural message of Scripture because it failed to muster up to his "enlightened" worldview. Copan, *When God Goes to Starbucks: A Guide to Everyday Apologetics* (Grand Rapids: Baker Books, 2008), 61.

17. The very fact that we hear the phrase "the church is dying in America" is in and of itself a kind of theological racism. As Soong-Chan Rah has written, "The church is not dying in America; it is alive and well, but it is alive and well among the immigrant and ethnic minority communities and not among the majority white churches in the United States." What we should say is that the church is dying among the people with all the privilege. But for the losers of history, Jesus is doing his very best work. Rah, *The Next Evangelicalism: Freeing the Church from Western Cultural Captivity* (Downers Grove, IL: InterVarsity, 2009), 16.

18. Stanley Hauerwas, "Abundant Life," speech at Trinity Institute, accessed June 3, 2020, https://trinitywallstreet.org/sites/default/files/HauerwasGoodNewsAbundantTranscript.pdf.

19. This is the theme and message of the classic text Francis Schaeffer, *The God Who Is There*, 30th anniv. ed. (Downers Grove, IL: InterVarsity, 2020).

20. Quoted in *The Westminster Collection of Christian Quotations*, compiled by Martin H. Manser (Louisville: Westminster John Knox, 2001), 6.

Chapter 4: Knowing the Whole Self

1. A play on A. W. Tozer's most famous work, *The Knowledge of the Holy* (New York: HarperCollins, 1961).

2. There's little historical doubt that Hitler's childhood experiences shaped his lifetime animus. Manfred Kets de Vries draws a parallel between Hitler's unhealed childhood trauma and the eventual atrocities he'd undertake: "Hitler's perception of authority as unfair and arbitrary, combined with his physical defects, contributed to a violent inner imagery of rage and hatred; unable to assimilate and resolve this imagery within himself, he projected it onto the external world." Kets de Vries, *Leaders, Fools and Impostors: Essays on the Psychology of Leadership* (New York: iUniverse, 2003), 18–19.

3. Steven Pressfield, *The War of Art: Break Through the Blocks and Win Your Inner Creative Battles* (New York: Warner, 2002), xi.

4. Karl Marlantes, *What It Is like to Go to War* (New York: Atlantic Monthly Press, 2011), 32.

5. David Benner says the healing of trauma requires three things: reexperiencing the pain, reinterpreting the hurt, and releasing the anger. Benner, *Healing Emotional Wounds* (Eugene, OR: Wipf & Stock, 2016), 63.

6. C. S. Lewis's theme of "longing"—or *sehnsucht*—played a crucial role in his conversion. He writes, "Our lifelong nostalgia, our longing to be reunited with something in the universe from which we feel cut off is . . . the truest source of our real situation." Lewis, *The Weight of Glory* (Grand Rapids: Eerdmans, 1949), 12.

7. Irenaeus, *Against Heresies* 4.20.7; Thomas à Kempis, *The Imitation of Christ* (Mineola, NY: Dover, 2003), 4.

8. Eberhard Bethge, *Dietrich Bonhoeffer: A Biography*, rev. ed. (Minneapolis: Fortress, 2000), 205. I am grateful to Stanley Hauerwas for pointing this out in *Performing the Faith: Bonhoeffer and the Practice of Nonviolence* (Grand Rapids: Brazos, 2004), 39–40.

9. Thomas Nagel, *The Last Word* (Oxford: Oxford University Press, 1997), 130.

10. John Calvin, *Institutes* 1.1.1, ed. Donald McKim (Louisville: Westminster John Knox, 2001), 1.

11. Augustine, *Confessions*, quoted in Pierre Pourrat, *Christian Spirituality*, vol. 2, *In the Middle Ages* (Westminster, MD: Newman, 1953), 291.

12. Thomas Aquinas, *Summa Theologiae*, art. 3, in *Aquinas on Nature and Grace*, ed. A. M. Fairweather (Louisville: Westminster John Knox, 1954), 39.

13. Thomas Merton, *New Seeds of Contemplation* (Boston: Shambhala, 1961), 38.

14. John Milton, *Paradise Lost*, book 4, lines 453–70.

15. Hans Urs von Balthasar, *Theo-Drama: Theological Drama History*, vol. 5, *The Last Act* (San Francisco: Ignatius, 1998).

16. J. I. Packer, *Knowing God* (Downers Grove, IL: InterVarsity, 2018), 13.

17. Packer, *Knowing God*, 12.

18. Charles Spurgeon, quoted in Timothy Keller, *King's Cross: The Story of the World in the Life of Jesus* (New York: Dutton, 2011), 79–80.

19. Cyprian Smith, *The Way of Paradox: Spiritual Life as Taught by Meister Eckhart* (London: Darton, Longman & Todd, 2004).

20. Campolo's story has been told countless times. But it is written in Alan Hirsch and Debra Hirsch, *Untamed: Reactivating a Missional Form of Discipleship* (Grand Rapids: Baker Books, 2010), 71.

21. Dorothy L. Sayers, *Whose Body?* (New York: Harper & Row, 1923), 9.

22. C. S. Lewis, *A Grief Observed* (New York: HarperCollins, 1996), 69.

23. This point is forcefully made by Simon During, "The Eighteenth-Century Origins of Critique," in *Critique and Postcritique*, ed. Elizabeth S. Anker and Rita Felski (Durham, NC: Duke University Press, 2017), 74–96.

24. Friedrich Nietzsche, *On the Genealogy of Morals*, trans. Walter Kaufmann and R. J. Hollingdale (New York: Vintage, 1967), 160.

25. I'm thankful for Volf and Croasmun's section on critique that informed this material. Miroslav Volf and Matthew Croasmun, *For the Life of the World: Theology That Makes a Difference* (Grand Rapids: Brazos, 2019), 55–57.

Chapter 5: Going to Church

1. A good biography on Kuyper's life is Richard Mouw, *Abraham Kuyper: A Short and Personal Introduction* (Grand Rapids: Eerdmans, 2011).

2. In Acts 9, Jesus "stands" at the Father's side during Stephen's martyrdom—the sole reference in the New Testament to Jesus *standing* in heaven. The imagery suggests Christ's solidarity with the martyr. Augustine later writes that Christ feels pain in his ascended state: "Observe the loving affection of this Head of ours. He is already in heaven, and he is struggling here as long as the Church is struggling here. Christ is hungry here, thirsty here, he's naked, he's a migrant, he's sick, he's in prison. Here, whatever the body suffers here, he said he suffers too." Augustine, *Essential Sermons*, trans. Edmund Hill (Hyde Park, NY: New City Press, 2007), 207.

3. Jürgen Moltmann writes, "The community of Christ is a community in the friendship of Jesus. The person who lives in his friendship also discovers Jesus' friends his brothers and sisters." Moltmann, *A Broad Place: An Autobiography* (Minneapolis: Fortress, 2008), 89.

4. Cynthia Long Westfall's magnificent treatise on Paul's view of gender reveals many other effeminate images in Pauline writings. See Westfall, *Paul and Gender: Reclaiming the Apostle's Vision for Men and Women in Christ* (Grand Rapids: Baker Academic, 2016), chap. 2.

5. Brad J. Kallenberg, *Live to Tell: Evangelism in a Postmodern Age* (Grand Rapids: Brazos, 2002), 77.

6. Quoted in Os Guinness and John Seel, *No God but God: Breaking the Idols of Our Age* (Chicago: Moody, 1992), 199.

7. My friend John Mark Comer told me this.

8. J. D. Vance, *Hillbilly Elegy: A Memoir of a Family and Culture in Crisis* (New York: Harper-Collins, 2016).

9. Terry Gross, "Paul Schrader and Ethan Hawke Test Their Faith in 'First Reformed,'" NPR, June 12, 2018, https://www.npr.org/2018/06/12/619165319/paul-schrader-and-ethan-hawke-test-their-faith-in-first-reformed.

10. Linda Gorman, "Is Religion Good for You?," National Bureau of Economic Research, accessed June 3, 2020, https://www.nber.org/digest/oct05/w11377.html. Greg Sheridan's writing helped shape this section. See Sheridan, "Is God Dead? The West Has Much to Lose in Banishing Christianity," *Australian*, August 26, 2017, https://www.theaustralian.com.au/nation/inquirer/is-god-dead-western-has-much-to-lose-in-banishing-christianity/news-story/b1dcbeabbd5776307debc9ddcb845539.

11. C. S. Lewis, *Mere Christianity* (San Francisco: HarperCollins, 2000).

12. Robert Sherman writes, "Christianity can survive a postdenominational age, but it cannot survive a postecclesial age." Sherman, *Covenant, Community, and the Spirit: A Trinitarian Theology of Church* (Grand Rapids: Baker Academic, 2015), xv.

13. On this, see Tom Shachtman, *Rumspringa: To Be or Not to Be Amish* (New York: North Point Press, 2006).

14. Sebastian Junger, *Tribes: On Homecoming and Belonging* (New York: Hachette, 2016).

15. Robert Kegan, *The Evolving Self: Problem and Process in Human Development* (Cambridge, MA: Harvard University Press, 1982), 127.

16. Kenda Creasy Dean, *Almost Christian: What the Faith of Our Teenagers Is Telling the American Church* (Oxford: Oxford University Press, 2010).

17. Lesslie Newbigin calls the church "the real hermeneutic of the gospel." See Newbigin, "Evangelism in the City," available for download at https://repository.westernsem.edu/pkp/index.php/rr/article/download/1089/1181.

18. David Fitch constructs a Christian vision that's broader than what we're "against." Fitch, *The Church of Us vs. Them: Freedom from a Faith That Feeds on Making Enemies* (Grand Rapids: Brazos, 2019).

19. I take liberties with Pete Scazzero's oft-quoted phrase.

20. Quoted in Dolores Hayden, *Building Suburbia: Green Fields and Urban Growth, 1820–2000* (New York: Vintage Books, 2004), 17.

21. This phrasing borrows from Winston Churchill, who said, "We shape our buildings and afterwards our buildings shape us" in a speech given to the House of Commons on October 28, 1943, available at https://api.parliament.uk/historic-hansard/commons/1943/oct/28/house-of-commons-rebuilding.

22. Eugene Peterson, *Christ Plays in Ten Thousand Places: A Conversation in Spiritual Theology* (Grand Rapids: Eerdmans, 2005), 154.

23. This image comes from Annie Dwyer's poem "Exodus," quoted in Philip Yancey, "A Time to Doubt," PhilipYancey.com, January 12, 2020, https://philipyancey.com/a-time-to-doubt.

24. Thomas Oden, *A Change of Heart: A Personal and Theological Memoir* (Downers Grove, IL: IVP Academic, 2014), 178.

Chapter 6: Feeling Everything

1. C. S. Lewis, *Christian Reflections*, ed. Walter Hooper (Grand Rapids: Eerdmans, 1971), 126.

2. Flannery O'Connor, *The Habit of Being: Letters of Flannery O'Connor*, ed. Sally Fitzgerald (New York: Farrar, Straus & Giroux, 1979), 137.

3. François Fenelon, *Let Go: To Get Peace and Real Joy* (New Kensington, PA: Whitaker House, 1973), 28.

4. For an overview of these three dynamics, see R. Paul Stevens, "Living Theologically: Toward a Theology of Christian Practice," *Themelios* 20, no. 3 (May 1995): 4–8.

5. Eugene Peterson's "badlands" concept is described in this interview: "Walking through Life as 'The Pastor,'" NPR, December 16, 2012, https://www.npr.org/2012/12/16/167399100/walking-through-life-as-a-pastor.

6. Emotions serve as a dashboard indicator light revealing what's going on inside, Larry Crabb writes. Of course, indicator lights can be wrong. Crabb, *Understanding People* (Grand Rapids: Zondervan, 1987), 184–85.

7. Alasdair MacIntyre's description and critique of "emotivism" is found throughout his book *After Virtue: A Study in Moral Theory* (New York: Bloomsbury, 2013).

8. N. T. Wright, *After You Believe: Why Christian Character Matters* (New York: HarperCollins, 2010), 159.

9. Alan Confino, "Why Did the Nazis Burn the Hebrew Bible?," *Journal of Modern History* 84, no. 2 (June 2012): 34.

10. James Kasperkevic, "Poll: 30% of GOP Voters Support Bombing Agrabah, the City from *Aladdin*," *Guardian*, December 18, 2015, https://www.theguardian.com/us-news/2015/dec/18/republican-voters-bomb-agrabah-disney-aladdin-donald-trump.

11. Paul Ricoeur, *The Rule of Metaphor: The Creation of Meaning in Language* (New York: Routledge Classics, 2003), 336.

12. Miroslav Volf and Matthew Croasmun, *For the Life of the World: Theology That Makes a Difference* (Grand Rapids: Brazos, 2019), 54.

13. John Henry Newman brilliantly writes, "There are wounds of the Spirit which never close and are intended in God's mercy to bring us ever nearer to him, and to prevent us from leaving him, by their very perpetuity." Quoted in William A. Beardslee, "Christ in the Postmodern Age: Reflections Inspired by Jean-Francois Lyotard," in *Varieties of Postmodern Theology*, by David Ray Griffin, William A. Beardslee, and Joe Holland (Albany: State University of New York Press, 1989), 78.

14. Charles H. Spurgeon, *Life in Christ*, vol. 3, *Lessons from Our Lord's Miracles and Parables* (Abbotsford, WI: Aneko Press, 2020), 108.

15. James K. A. Smith, *How (Not) to Be Secular: Reading Charles Taylor* (Grand Rapids: Eerdmans, 2014), 49.

16. The best writing on this is Eugene Cho, *Overrated: Are We More in Love with the Idea of Changing the World Than Actually Changing the World?* (Colorado Springs: David C. Cook, 2014).

17. Dan B. Allender and Tremper Longman III, *The Cry of the Soul: How Our Emotions Reveal Our Deepest Questions about God* (Colorado Springs: NavPress, 2015), 25.

18. Larry Crabb, *Finding God* (Grand Rapids: Zondervan, 1993), 18.

Chapter 7: Learning to Tend

1. David Foster Wallace, interview by Charlie Rose, *Charlie Rose*, March 27, 1997, https://charlierose.com/videos/23311. I am grateful to Miroslav Volf and Matthew Croasmun's identification of Wallace's illuminating interview in Volf and Croasmun, *For the Life of the World: Theology That Makes a Difference* (Grand Rapids: Brazos, 2019).

2. Andrew Sullivan, "I Used to Be a Human Being," Intelligencer, September 2016, https://nymag.com/intelligencer/2016/09/andrew-sullivan-my-distraction-sickness-and-yours.html.

3. Volf and Croasmun, *For the Life of the World*, 24.

4. Sullivan, "I Used to Be a Human Being."

5. Cady Lang, "Netflix's CEO Says Entertainment Pills Could Make Movies and TV Obsolete," *Time*, October 25, 2016, https://time.com/4544291/netflix-ceo-pills.

6. Salman Rushdie, *Imaginary Homelands: Essays and Criticism (1981–1991)* (New York: Random House, 2010).

7. Tom Nichols, *The Death of Expertise: The Campaign against Established Knowledge and Why It Matters* (Oxford: Oxford University Press, 2017).

8. Journalist Henry Fairlie defines this as how we deal with others' successes. Rather than celebrate others, we destroy them—rooted in our envious desire for totalitarian, self-centered perfection. See Fairlie, *The Seven Deadly Sins Today* (Notre Dame, IN: Notre Dame Press, 1979), chap. 3.

9. Wolfhart Pannenberg, *Christian Spirituality* (Louisville: Westminster John Knox, 1983), 31 (emphasis added).

10. Dallas Willard, *The Allure of Gentleness: Defending the Faith in the Manner of Jesus* (New York: HarperOne, 2015), xi.

11. How beautiful it is that Reason teaches John in C. S. Lewis's *Pilgrim's Regress* that there is importance in walking the country road with unanswered questions: "For the people who live there have to give an opinion once a week or once a day, or else Mr. Mammon would soon cut off their food. But out here in the country you can walk all day and all the next day with an unanswered question in your head: you need never speak until you have made up your mind." Lewis, *The Pilgrim's Regress: An Allegorical Apology for Christianity, Reason, and Romanticism* (Grand Rapids: Eerdmans, 2014), 69.

12. Willard, *Allure of Gentleness*, 26.

13. This distinction is masterfully articulated in Ronald Rolheiser, *Sacred Fire: A Vision for a Deeper Human and Christian Maturity* (New York: Image, 2014), chap. 5.

14. Quoted by John Buchanan, "Pay Attention" (sermon, Fourth Presbyterian Church, Chicago, IL, June 11, 2006). Flannery O'Connor takes aim at our worship of certainty in her personal letters: "You arrive at enough certainty to be able to make your own way, but it is making it in darkness. Don't expect faith to clear things up for you. It is trust, not certainty." Quoted in Fleming Rutledge, *Help My Unbelief* (Grand Rapids: Eerdmans, 2000), xvi.

15. Alan Kreider's work on the patient church is a masterpiece. Kreider, *The Patient Ferment of the Early Church: The Impossible Rise of Christianity in the Roman Empire* (Grand Rapids: Baker Academic, 2016).

16. N. T. Wright has written on this: "This isn't to say there aren't hard bits in the Bible. . . . Avoid the easy solutions to these: that these bits weren't 'inspired,' or that the whole Bible is wicked nonsense, or that Jesus simply abolished the bits we disapprove of. Live with the tensions. Let the troubling words jangle against one another. Take the opportunity to practice some patience and humility. In fact, humility is one of the key lessons which comes through reading the Bible over many years; there are some bits we find easy and other bits we find hard, but not everybody agrees as to which is which." Wright, *After You Believe: Why Christian Character Matters* (New York: HarperCollins, 2010), 262.

17. Francis Bacon, "Of Truth," in *Bacon's Essays*, ed. Franklin Fiske Heard (New York: Lee, Shepard, and Dillingham, 1875), 1.

18. Benedicta Ward, *The Desert Fathers: Sayings of the Early Christian Monks* (New York: Penguin, 2003), 6.

19. "Tend" is a combination of the Latin *ad* and *tendere*—to "stretch toward." See the *Oxford English Dictionary*, vol. 1 (Oxford: Clarendon, 1989), 765.

20. In Genesis 22, God instructs Abraham to sacrifice Isaac on Mount Moriah. Abraham listens and begins to obey. But, of course, God stops Abraham at the last moment from finishing the task. Abraham *kept* listening—and thank God. Had he listened momentarily, the Messiah's line would have ended at the crest of Mount Moriah. Listening isn't a one-time activity. Biblical listening is a posture.

21. B. Alan Wallace, introduction to *The Attention Revolution: Unlocking the Power of the Focused Mind* (Boston: Wisdom, 2006).

22. Nicholas Carr, "Is Google Making Us Stupid?," *Atlantic*, July/August 2008, https://www
.theatlantic.com/magazine/archive/2008/07/is-google-making-us-stupid/306868.

23. Augustine, *Essential Sermons*, trans. Edmund Hill (Hyde Park, NY: New City Press,
2007), 119.

24. "We must be open to the possibility of God's addressing us in whatever way he chooses,"
Dallas Willard writes, "or else we may walk right past a burning bush instead of saying, as
Moses did, 'I must turn aside and look at this great sight and see why the bush is not burned
up.'" Willard, *Hearing God: Developing a Conversational Relationship with God* (Downers Grove,
IL: InterVarsity, 1999), 120.

25. Alan Fadling, *An Unhurried Life: Following Jesus' Rhythms of Work and Rest* (Downers
Grove, IL: InterVarsity, 2013), 150–51.

26. Dietrich Bonhoeffer, *Life Together*, trans. Jon W. Doberstein (New York: Harper, 1954), 98.

27. Evelyn Underhill, *Modern Guide to the Ancient Quest for the Holy* (New York: State
University of New York Press, 1988), 75.

Chapter 8: Practicing Being Wrong

1. "Suddenly" is used sparingly yet intentionally throughout Acts—including, of course,
at Pentecost in Acts 2.

2. Jan Ransom, "Weinstein Appealed to Bezos and Bloomberg for Help, Documents Show,"
New York Times, March 10, 2020, https://www.nytimes.com/2020/03/10/nyregion/harvey
-weinstein-bezos-bloomberg-aniston.html (emphasis added).

3. A wordplay borrowed from Ryan Burge, "The Age of Nones May Favor Churches That
Welcome Doubters," Religion News Service, January 14, 2020, https://religionnews.com/2020
/01/14/the-age-of-nones-may-favor-churches-who-welcome-doubters.

4. William Placher, *Narratives of a Vulnerable God: Christ, Theology, and Scripture* (Louisville: Westminster John Knox, 1994), 138.

5. See the research of David Kinnaman and Gabe Lyons, *UnChristian: What a New Generation Really Thinks about Christianity . . . and Why It Matters* (Grand Rapids: Baker Books,
2007).

6. A. W. Tozer, *Man: The Dwelling Place of God* (Chicago: Moody, 1997), chap. 37 (emphasis
added).

7. Chuck Klosterman, *But What if We're Wrong? Thinking about the Present as if It Were the
Past* (New York: Red Rider Press, 2016).

8. Klosterman, *But What if We're Wrong?*, 136.

9. Kathryn Schulz, *Being Wrong: Adventures in the Margin of Error* (New York: HarperCollins, 2010).

10. See Leah Libresco, "Didn't You Ever Break on the Floor?," *Unequally Yoked* (blog), August 12, 2012, https://www.patheos.com/blogs/unequallyyoked/2012/08/didnt-you-ever-break
-on-the-floor.html.

11. As narrated in Michael Specter, *Denialism: How Irrational Thinking Hinders Scientific
Progress, Harms the Planet, and Threatens Our Lives* (New York: Penguin, 2009).

12. C. S. Lewis, *A Grief Observed* (New York: HarperCollins, 2001), 65–66 (emphasis added).

13. Cited by Will Willimon, "A Peculiarly Christian Account of Sin," *Theology Today* 50
(1993): 228.

14. Christopher Derrick, "Trimming the Ark," *First Things*, December 26, 2017, https://
www.firstthings.com/web-exclusives/2017/12/trimming-the-ark (emphasis original).

15. This story about Chesterton is suspected to be true, but no documentary evidence has
been found. See "What's Wrong with the World?," Society of Gilbert Keith Chesterton, April
29, 2012, https://www.chesterton.org/wrong-with-world.

16. Thomas Merton, *The School of Charity: The Letters of Thomas Merton on Religious Renewal and Spiritual Direction*, ed. Patrick Hart (New York: HarperCollins, 1990), 137–38 (emphasis original).

17. Eugene Peterson, *Practice Resurrection: A Conversation on Growing Up in Christ* (Grand Rapids: Eerdmans, 2010), 29.

Chapter 9: Discerning the Truth

1. Ignatius, *To the Trallians* 6, in Michael W. Holmes, trans. and ed., *The Apostolic Fathers in English*, 3rd ed. (Grand Rapids: Baker Academic, 2006), 109.

2. Parker Palmer, *A Hidden Wholeness: The Journey toward an Undivided Life* (San Francisco: Jossey-Bass, 2004), 26.

3. Sinclair Ferguson, "Discernment: Thinking God's Thoughts after Him," Alliance, accessed June 3, 2020, http://www.alliancenet.org/eternitymagazine/discernment-thinking -gods-thoughts-after-him. Evan B. Howard defines discernment as "a process of coming to 'know' that which is from God." *Affirming the Touch of God: A Psychological and Philosophical Exploration of Christian Discernment* (Lanham, MD: University Press of America, 2000), 265.

4. Stanley Hauerwas, "Abortion: Theologically Understood (1991)," in *The Hauerwas Reader*, ed. John Berkman and Michael G. Cartwright (Durham, NC: Duke University Press, 2001), 611.

5. Neil Postman, *Amusing Ourselves to Death: Public Discourse in an Age of Show Business* (New York: Penguin, 1985), vii–viii, brilliantly unpacked and quoted in D. A. Carson, *The Gagging of God: Christianity Confronts Pluralism* (Grand Rapids: Zondervan, 1996), 463–64.

6. Quoted in Gregg Easterbrook, "A Hundred Years of Thinking of God: A Philosopher Soon to Be Rediscovered," *US News and World Report*, February 23, 1998.

7. Charles Taylor, *A Secular Age* (Cambridge, MA: Harvard University Press, 2007).

8. Gordon Fee, *God's Empowering Presence* (Peabody, MA: Hendrickson, 1994), 28–32.

9. John Stott, *The Letters of John*, Tyndale New Testament Commentaries (Downers Grove, IL: InterVarsity, 1988), 153.

10. Victor A. Shepherd, *Interpreting Martin Luther: An Introduction to His Life and Thought* (Vancouver: Regent College Publishing, 2008), 121.

11. Sandra L. Richter, "What Do I Know of Holy? On the Person and Work of the Holy Spirit in Scripture," in *Spirit of God: Christian Renewal in the Community of Faith*, ed. Jeffrey W. Barbeau and Beth Felker Jones (Downers Grove, IL: InterVarsity, 2015), 30.

12. J. B. Phillips, *Ring of Truth: A Translator's Testimony* (Wheaton: Harold Shaw, 1977), 116–19.

13. Cornelius Plantinga, *Engaging God's World: A Christian Vision of Faith, Learning, and Living* (Grand Rapids: Eerdmans, 2002), 20–23.

14. Christopher R. J. Holmes, *The Holy Spirit*, New Studies in Dogmatics (Grand Rapids: Zondervan, 2015), 23–24.

15. Gustavo Gutiérrez, *A Theology of Liberation* (Maryknoll, NY: Orbis Books, 1973), 205.

16. Roger Olson outlines these different levels of belief in *The Story of Christian Theology: Twenty Centuries of Tradition and Reform* (Downers Grove, IL: InterVarsity, 1999), 17–19.

17. "Heresy" comes from the Greek word *haeresis*, meaning "the act of choosing," referring to those "holding perverse dogma, [who] draw apart from the Church of their own free will." G. R. Evans, *A Brief History of Heresy* (Malden, MA: Blackwell, 2003), xii.

18. Joshua Bote, "He Wrote the Christian Case against Dating. Now He's Splitting from His Wife and Faith," *USA Today*, July 29, 2019, https://amp.usatoday.com/amp/1857934001.

19. *The Martyrdom of Polycarp* 18.2, in Michael W. Holmes, trans. and ed., *The Apostolic Fathers in English*, 3rd ed. (Grand Rapids: Baker Academic, 2006), 154.

20. Even tradition must be held to the fires of Scripture. Alister McGrath wisely writes that we should "be on guard and understand why we believe certain things rather than just accepting

them passively from those we recognize as masters and teachers. Tradition is something that is to be actively and selectively appropriated, not passively and unthinkingly received." McGrath, "Engaging the Great Tradition: Evangelical Theology and the Role of Tradition," in *Evangelical Futures: A Conversation on Theological Method*, ed. John G. Stackhouse (Grand Rapids: Baker Books, 2000), 149.

Chapter 10: Embracing the Whole Kingdom

1. Bill Bishop, *The Big Sort: Why the Clustering of Like-Minded America Is Tearing Us Apart* (New York: Mariner Books, 2009).

2. Scot McKnight juxtaposes these in his *The Kingdom Conspiracy: Returning to the Radical Mission of the Local Church* (Grand Rapids: Brazos, 2014).

3. Jonathan Wilson-Hartgrove, *Reconstructing the Gospel: Finding Freedom from Slaveholder Religion* (Downers Grove, IL: InterVarsity, 2018), 16–17.

4. Robert Bly, *The Sibling Society: An Impassioned Call for the Rediscovery of Adulthood* (New York: Vintage Books, 1996).

5. David Riesman, *The Lonely Crowd* (New Haven: Yale University Press, 2000), 57.

6. Sandra L. Richter, *The Epic of Eden: A Christian Entry into the Old Testament* (Downers Grove, IL: InterVarsity, 2008), 112.

7. René Padilla, "God's Words and Man's Myths," *Themelios* 3, no. 1 (September 1977): 8.

8. Flannery O'Connor, *The Habit of Being: Letters of Flannery O'Connor*, ed. Sally Fitzgerald (New York: Farrar, Straus & Giroux, 1979), 460–61.

9. I hear this echoing Paul's reference of a "fellow worker" named Demas with whom he'd been in prison (Philem. 1:24; Col. 4:14). Later, Paul grieves Demas's faith abandonment because he loved the present world more than he loved Jesus (2 Tim. 4:10). Demas continued to have deep love in his heart—just not a deep love for Jesus.

10. Francis Schaeffer points out in his *No Little People* that God's law was carried around in the ark of the covenant. Inside were the Ten Commandments. But on top was the mercy seat—representing the mercy of God upon which the blood of sacrifice would be placed. Schaeffer points out that someone coming to the law would have to go through the mercy seat to get there. The imagery is profound. No one gets to the mercy of God by going through the law of God. Rather, one must come to God's law by going through God's mercy. Schaeffer, *No Little People* (Wheaton: Crossway, 2003), chap. 7.

11. Calvin Miller, *Once Upon a Tree: Answering the Ten Crucial Questions of Life* (West Monroe, LA: Howard, 2002), 77.

12. Miroslav Volf, *Against the Tide: Love in a Time of Petty Dreams and Persisting Enmities* (Grand Rapids: Eerdmans, 2010), 89–91.

13. Jessie Kunhardt, "Anne Rice: 'I Quit Being a Christian,'" *Huffington Post*, July 29, 2010 (updated December 6, 2017), www.huffingtonpost.com/2010/07/29/anne-rice-i-quit-a_n_663915 .html.

14. Benedicta Ward, *The Desert Fathers: Sayings of the Early Christian Monks* (New York: Penguin, 2003), 1.

15. Quoted in *Readings in Medieval History*, ed. Patrick J. Geary (Toronto: University of Toronto Press, 2010), 161.

16. John Climacus, *The Ladder of Divine Ascent*, trans. Colm Luibheid and Norman Russell (Mahwah, NJ: Paulist Press, n.d.), 112.

17. Suggested by Scot McKnight, "The Parable of the Wheat and the Weeds," in *Kingdom Roots* (podcast), accessed June 3, 2020, https://soundcloud.com/user-212639123/the-parable-of -the-wheat-and-the-weeds-kr-63.

18. Mark Sayers, *Reappearing Church: The Hope for Renewal in the Rise of Our Post-Christian Culture* (Chicago: Moody, 2019), chap. 1.

19. Borrowed from Puritan Henry Zylstra's articulation: "Nothing matters but the Kingdom of Jesus Christ; but because of the kingdom, everything else matters." Quoted in Rick Ostrander, "The Distinctive of a Christian College," in *The Soul of a Christian University: A Field Guide for Educators*, ed. Stephen T. Beers (Abilene, TX: Abilene Christian University Press, 2008), 39.

Chapter 11: Trusting the Right Way

1. Lesslie Newbigin argues that the serpent's words were the spirit of the Enlightenment. Newbigin, *The Gospel in a Pluralist Society* (Grand Rapids: Eerdmans, 1989), 39.

2. Michael Specter, "Denialism," *New York Times*, November 4, 2009, https://www.nytimes.com/2009/11/05/books/excerpt-michael-specter.html.

3. Peter Berger, *The Heretical Imperative: Contemporary Possibilities of Religious Affirmation* (Garden City, NY: Doubleday, 1979).

4. Michael Pollan, *The Omnivore's Dilemma: A Natural History of Four Meals*, 10th anniv. ed. (New York: Penguin, 2016).

5. Dietrich Bonhoeffer, *Creation and Fall Temptation: Two Biblical Studies* (New York: Touchstone, 1997), 119–20.

6. Michael Polanyi, *Personal Knowledge: Towards a Post-Critical Philosophy* (London: Routledge, 2005), 272–75.

7. For two texts dealing directly with this "leap of faith" concept, see Søren Kierkegaard, *Training in Christianity*, trans. W. Lowrie (Princeton: Princeton University Press, 1941); and Kierkegaard, *Concluding Unscientific Postscript*, trans. W. Lowrie (Princeton: Princeton University Press, 1968).

8. Timothy Keller suggests, "All doubts, however skeptical and cynical they may seem, are really a set of alternate beliefs. You cannot doubt Belief A except from a position of faith in Belief B. . . . Every doubt, therefore, is based on a leap of faith." Keller, *The Reason for God: Belief in an Age of Skepticism* (New York: Dutton, 2008), xvii.

9. G. K. Chesterton, *Orthodoxy* (New York: John Lane, 1908), 73–74.

10. Chesterton, *Orthodoxy*, 85.

11. Quoted by Cynthia Haven, "Richard Rorty: 'Truth Is What Your Contemporaries Let You Get Away with Saying,'" *Book Haven* (blog), November 15, 2017, https://bookhaven.stanford.edu/2017/11/richard-rorty-truth-is-what-your-contemporaries-let-you-get-away-with-saying.

12. See Simon May, "Author Article by Simon May: Rethinking Our Fascination with Love," *YaleBooks* (blog), April 27, 2011, https://yalebooksblog.co.uk/2011/04/27/author-article-by-simon-may-rethinking-our-fascination-with-love. I'm particularly grateful to Patrick Mitchel for his summation of May's thought: Mitchel, "The Idolisation of Love," *FaithinIreland* (blog), October 28, 2016, https://faithinireland.wordpress.com/2016/10/28/the-idolisation-of-love.

13. To hear more, listen to Miroslav Volf's beautiful sermon given on February 26, 2012, at Eugene Faith Center, available at http://eugenefaithcenter.org/worship-services/watch-listen/miroslav-volf.

14. Walter Brueggemann, *Spirituality of the Psalms* (Minneapolis: Fortress, 2001).

15. A. W. Tozer, *Tozer on Worship and Entertainment*, ed. James L. Snyder (Camp Hill, PA: Wing Spread, 1997), chap. 1.

16. Oswald Chambers, *My Utmost for His Highest*, ed. James Reimann (Grand Rapids: Our Daily Bread, 1992), July 30.

17. Parker Palmer, *The Active Life: A Spirituality of Work, Creativity, and Caring* (New York: HarperCollins, 1990), 26–27.

Postscript

1. C. N. Trueman, "Bombing and World War Two," History Learning Site, May 19, 2015, https://www.historylearningsite.co.uk/world-war-two/the-bombing-campaign-of-world-war-two/bombing-and-world-war-two.

2. C. S. Lewis, *The Lion, the Witch and the Wardrobe* (New York: HarperCollins, 2000), 188 (emphasis added).

3. Thomas Oden, *A Change of Heart: A Personal and Theological Memoir* (Downers Grove, IL: IVP Academic, 2014), 42.

4. Oden, *Change of Heart*, 46.

5. Quoted in Terry W. Glaspey, *Great Books of the Christian Tradition* (Eugene, OR: Harvest House, 1996), 22–23.

6. Christopher A. Hall, "He Made No New Contribution to Theology," *Christian History* 129 (2019), available at https://christianhistoryinstitute.org/magazine/article/he-made-no-new-contribution-to-theology.

7. Paul Ricoeur, *The Symbolism of Evil* (New York: Harper & Row, 1967), 351.

8. Stephen Seamands, *Ministry in the Image of God: The Trinitarian Shape of Christian Service* (Downers Grove, IL: InterVarsity, 2005), 115–16.

9. Richard John Neuhaus, *Death on a Friday Afternoon* (New York: Basic Books, 2000), 134.

10. C. S. Lewis, *Mere Christianity* (New York: Harper, 2001), 87.

11. T. S. Eliot, "Little Gidding," available at http://www.columbia.edu/itc/history/winter/w3206/edit/tseliotlittlegidding.html.

12. I wrote a book about this very ideal: *Subversive Sabbath: The Surprising Power of Rest in a Nonstop World* (Grand Rapids: Brazos, 2018).

13. Matthew Sleeth, personal conversation with the author.

14. John Goldingay, *Approaches to Old Testament Interpretation* (Toronto: Clements, 2002), 61–65.

15. For more on the significance of these names, see the helpful Tina Pippin, "Job 42:1–6, 10–17," *Interpretation* 53, no. 3 (July 1999): 301–3.

Acknowledgments

1. Anthony Coniaris, *Preaching the Word of God* (Brookline, MA: Holy Cross Orthodox Press, 1983), 8.